OKLAHOMA

ARKANSAS

LOUISIANA

Wilbarger
Wichita
Clay
Montague
Cooke
Grayson
Fannin
Lamar
Red

Baylor
Archer
Jack
Wise
Denton
Collin
Hunt
Delta
Hopkins
Franklin
Titus
Camp

Throck-
morton
Young

Shackel-
ford
Stephens
Palo Pinto
Parker
Tarrant
Dallas
Rock-
wall
Rains
Wood
Upshur
Harrison

Kaufman
Van
Zandt
Smith
Gregg
Panola

Callahan
Eastland
Erath
Hood
Somer-
vell
Johnson
Ellis
Henderson
Cherokee
Rusk
Shelby

Coleman
Brown
Comanche
Hamilton
Bosque
Hill
Navarro
Freestone
Anderson
Nacog-
doches
San
Augus-
tine
Sabine

McCulloch
Mills
Coryell
McLennan
Limestone
Houston
Angelina
Newton

San Saba
Lampasas
Falls
Leon
Trinity

Mason
Llano
Burnet
Bell
Robertson
Madison
Polk
Tyler
Jasper

Milam
Brazos
Grimes
Walker
San
Jacinto
Hardin

Gillespie
Blanco
Travis
Williamson
Burleson
Lee
Washing-
ton
Montgomery
Liberty
Orange

Kerr
Kendall
Comal
Hays
Bastrop
Austin
Waller
Harris
Jefferson

Bandera
Guadalupe
Caldwell
Fayette
Colorado
Fort Bend
Chambers

Medina
Bexar
Wilson
Gonzales
Lavaca
Wharton
Brazoria
Galveston

Frio
Atascosa
Karnes
DeWitt
Jackson
Matagorda

Goliad
Victoria
Calhoun

La Salle
McMullen
Live Oak
Bee
Refugio
Aransas

San Patricio

Webb
Duval
Jim
Wells
Nueces

Kleberg

Zapata
Jim Hogg
Brooks
Kenedy

Starr
Hidalgo
Willacy

Cameron

GULF OF MEXICO

TAMAULIPAS

Field Guide to the Wild Orchids of Texas

UNIVERSITY PRESS OF FLORIDA

Florida A&M University, Tallahassee
Florida Atlantic University, Boca Raton
Florida Gulf Coast University, Ft. Myers
Florida International University, Miami
Florida State University, Tallahassee
New College of Florida, Sarasota
University of Central Florida, Orlando
University of Florida, Gainesville
University of North Florida, Jacksonville
University of South Florida, Tampa
University of West Florida, Pensacola

University Press of Florida

Gainesville

Tallahassee

Tampa

Boca Raton

Pensacola

Orlando

Miami

Jacksonville

Ft. Myers

Sarasota

Field Guide to the
Wild Orchids of Texas

Paul Martin Brown,

with original artwork by Stan Folsom

Foreword by Carl R. Slaughter, M.D.

13 12 11 10 09 08   6 5 4 3 2 1

Library of Congress Cataloging-in-Publication Data
Brown, Paul Martin.
Field guide to the wild orchids of Texas/Paul Martin Brown,
with original artwork by Stan Folsom; foreword by Carl R. Slaughter.
p. cm.
Includes bibliographical references and index.
ISBN 978-0-8130-3159-0 (alk. paper)
1. Orchids—Texas—Identification. 2. Orchids—Texas—Pictorial works. I. Title.
QK495.O64B7382 2008
584.'409764—dc22   2007031353

The University Press of Florida is the scholarly publishing agency for the
State University System of Florida, comprising Florida A&M University,
Florida Atlantic University, Florida Gulf Coast University, Florida International
University, Florida State University, New College of Florida, University of Central
Florida, University of Florida, University of North Florida, University of South
Florida, and University of West Florida.

University Press of Florida
15 Northwest 15th Street
Gainesville, FL 32611-2079
http://www.upf.com

To Joe Liggio and Ann Orto Liggio, in thanks for their many years of work to bring the wild orchids of Texas to the orchid-loving public

University Press of Florida gratefully acknowledges

The McAllen International Orchid Society

est. 2000
www.miosjournal.org

and

the Native Plant Society of Texas–Houston Chapter

for their support of this project.

A Reminder

Our wild orchids are a precious resource. For that reason they should never be collected from their native habitats, either for ornament or for home gardens. All orchids grow in association with specific fungi and these fungi are rarely present except in the orchids' original habitat. Seeking and finding these choice botanical treasures is one of the greatest pleasures of professional and amateur botanists alike. Please leave them for others to enjoy.

Contents

Foreword

People with a deep passion for one plant group can seem strange to people who
lack that intense feeling. The most passionate, therefore the strangest, group of plant
people are the orchid people. A psychoanalyst would probably classify their fervor
as a severe obsessive-compulsive disorder, but to orchid people it is simply called
orchid fever.

—*Gerald Klingaman*

Paul Martin Brown has had this passion since childhood and it has bloomed into
copious productivity. Paul and his partner, Stan Folsom, have published a number of orchid books: *Wild Orchids of the Northeastern United States* (1997), *Wild
Orchids of Florida* (2002), *The Wild Orchids of North America, North of Mexico*
(2003), Wild Orchids of the Southeastern United States (2004), *Wild Orchids of the
Canadian Maritimes and Northern Great Lakes Region* (2005), *Wild Orchids of the
Pacific Northwest and Canadian Rockies* (2006), and *Wild Orchids of the Prairies
and Great Plains Region of North America* (2006). Stan is the gifted artist who
provided the artwork and drawings for the books while Paul did the photography
and composition.

Paul has provided numerous articles for botanical journals. He was founder of
the *North American Native Orchid Alliance* and editor of its journal. He has led
orchid safaris from Newfoundland to Alaska, from the West Coast and Mexico
to Florida, and to Europe and the Pacific. He knows the location of more orchids
than any individual I have ever met. He has taught courses at several universities
and is a research associate at the University of Florida and at the Botanical Research Institute of Texas. Obviously he has the knowledge and the experience to
author this book.

Field Guide to the Wild Orchids of Texas is a handsome book, from its cover to
the photographs of individual orchids, but its beauty is not the most important
aspect of this worthy book. *Field Guide to the Wild Orchids of Texas* has the usual
Latin and common names, locations, and descriptions. It also offers a number of
tables that give blooming times and other pertinent data.

In his series of books, Brown documents the presence of wild orchids in specific regions of North America. To facilitate locating and identifying wild orchids
in Texas, he uses the various geophysical areas into which Texas is frequently
divided. Thus he is able to provide more accurate blooming times for each species
in the botanical ecoregions.

Ongoing research frequently results in changes in plant identifications. This can cause frustrations among nonbotanical enthusiasts. It seems that every month there is a correction or change in orchid nomenclature. A book is written—and by the time it reaches the public, orchid names have been changed or new orchids have been found. This makes it very confusing for the reader. Brown has included an overview of many of the changes and explains the reasons for each change. This is very helpful, even if it is irritating for those who wish that the world would stand still for just a while.

Not everyone who purchases this book will have a deep passion for orchids. A large number will acquire it for its display of photographs of beautiful flowers. Those readers who do have orchid fever will find within its covers enough to satisfy and deepen those passions.

Carl R. Slaughter, M.D.
Author, *Wild Orchids of Arkansas*

Preface

Texas presents some of the most varied opportunities for the native orchid enthusiast to search and discover more than fifty species and varieties of orchids growing in the wild. The primary goal of this work is not only to assemble all the known information on the orchids in this region but also to pique the interest and curiosity of the user enough to go to just one more roadside or mountain to find even more wild orchids.

A Note about Field Guides

The primary purpose of a field guide is to assist the user in identifying, in this case, the wild orchids of Texas. It is meant to be neither an exhaustive treatise on these species, nor the ultimate reference for the particular area. It is designed to be used primarily in the field, for locating information easily while one foot is in the proverbial bog. The photographs have been taken in the field and are intended to illustrate the species as the user will see them. They are neither studio shots nor great works of art—just good, diagnostic photos that portray the plants in their habitats. The line drawings also have the same goal, of assisting the user in identifying the orchids. Many times line drawings can communicate different aspects of the plants that photographs cannot. The user is always encouraged to consult additional references for more detailed descriptions and regional accounts of individual species. It is always possible to write more on any subject and more certainly could be said for each species, but, first and foremost, this is a field guide. By combining the resources of the keys, descriptions, photographs, and line drawings, the user should be able, with relative simplicity, to identify all the orchids within the range of this book.

Acknowledgments

This work, with such a large and varied geographic scope, has involved the advice and counsel of many people. Those who facilitated the research and made major contributions to the information gathered in this book include Norris Williams, keeper, and Kent Perkins, manager, of the University of Florida Herbarium, Florida Museum of Natural History, Gainesville; Gustavo Romero, Orchid Herbarium of Oakes Ames, and Judith Warnement, Botany Libraries, Harvard University

Herbaria; Betty Alex and Allison Leavitt, Big Bend National Park; and Chuck Sheviak, Paul Catling, Scott Stewart, Joe Liggio, Margaret Brown-Waite, Tom Wendt, Ron Coleman, Bill Jennings, Cliff Pelchat, Dick Pike, Fred Armstrong, Mike Powell, Bill Carr, Dick Worthington, Mark Larocque, Dick and Geraldine Pike, Bob Ferry, and Ann Malmquist.

Special thanks must be given to Barney Lipscomb and Helen Jeude, Botanical Research Institute of Texas, for their many hours of patience, advice, and encouragement.

The staff at University Press of Florida has continued its usual support, in particular John Byram and Gillian Hillis, without whose much-appreciated editorial assistance this book would never have been completed. And, again, my partner, Stan Folsom, whose paintings and drawings grace the pages of this book, has been a source of support and inspiration through the entire project. For that I am most grateful.

Abbreviations and Symbols

AOS = American Orchid Society
BBNP = Big Bend National Park
BRIT = Botanical Research Institute of Texas
ca. = about or approximate, in reference to measurements
cm = centimeter
f. = *filius*; son of, or the younger
m = meter
mm = millimeter
subsp. = subspecies
var. = variety
× multiplication sign between or preceding a name denotes a hybrid or hybrid
   combination
* = naturalized
≠ = misapplied name

Publications

FNA = *Flora of North America North of Mexico*, vol. 26.
IPNI = *International Plant Names Index*
NANOJ = *North American Native Orchid Journal*

Acronyms for Herbaria

AMES = Orchid Herbarium of Oakes Ames
BRIT = Botanical Research Institute of Texas, Ft. Worth
HUH = Harvard University Herbaria
LL = Lundell Herbarium, University of Texas, Austin
NY = New York Botanical Garden
SMU = Southern Methodist University, at BRIT
SRSC = Sul Ross State College, Alpine
TAMU = Texas A&M, College Station
US = National Herbarium, Washington, D.C.
UTEP = University of Texas, El Paso

Part 1

Orchids and Texas

Stan Folsom

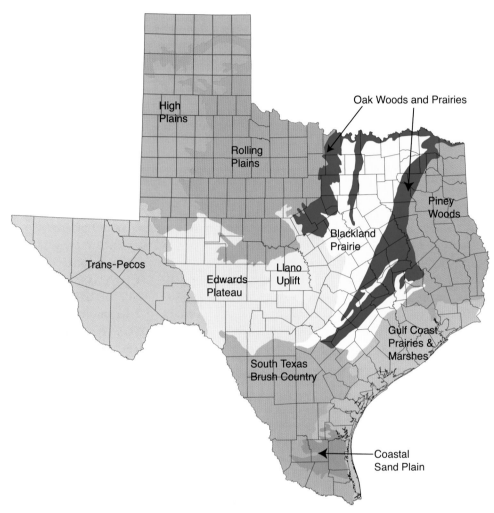

Map 1.1. Botanical ecoregions of Texas

Orchids and Texas

The earliest collections of wild orchids in the region were made while the Republic of Texas was still an autonomous political entity. Collections by Drummond, Wright, and Lindheimer were all likely were made between 1836 and 1846, though some information is missing. By the mid-twentieth century such names as Palmer, Tharp, Steyermark, Lundell, and, eventually, Correll became associated with the orchids of Texas.

Several publications have included the orchids growing in Texas as part of a continental work, in a state treatment, or as portions of a regional work. The first statewide list was that of Cory and Parks (1937), and the first comprehensive treatment was that of Correll in 1944 as a contribution to the *Flora of Texas* (Lundell, 1944). Only three years later Correll followed with "Additions to the Orchids of Texas" in *Wrightiana*. Both Correll (1950) and Luer (1975) treated all of the Texas species, but from a continental standpoint. It was not until 1999, when the Liggios published *Wild Orchids of Texas*, that a contemporary statewide treatment of the family was available. A detailed natural history account of the orchids rather than a taxonomic one, their text provided distribution maps and color photographs of most of the species known to grow in Texas at that time. With the publication of volume 26 of *Flora of North America North of Mexico* (hereafter *Flora of North America* or *FNA*) in 2002, even more information and full taxonomic details were available for Texas species. *The Atlas of Vascular Plants of Texas* (Turner et al., 2003) provided maps and several more county records than were previously reported. The *Flora of North Central Texas* (Diggs et al., 1999) listed those species found in that part of the state as did the *Flora of East Texas* (Diggs et al., 2006). Brown and Folsom (2003, 2004, 2006) provided more information, from both a continental standpoint in *Wild Orchids of North America, North of Mexico* and a regional view in *Wild Orchids of the Southeastern United States*, for eastern Texas, and *Wild Orchids of the Prairies and Great Plains Region of North America* for the northern portions of the state. Each of these publications contained material not found in one or more of the previous publications and all contributed to our growing knowledge of the orchids of Texas. Five newly described species— *Calopogon oklahomensis*, *Malaxis wendtii*, *Schiedeella arizonica*, *Spiranthes eatonii*, and *Spiranthes sylvatica*—proved to be present in the state, although known under older names in the past or as part of well-known species complexes. One species, *Deiregyne confusa*, was rediscovered in 2004 (USGS, 2004; Ambs, 2006, Coleman et al., 2006) after not having been seen since its original collection by Steyermark in 1935!

Our understanding of generic and species concepts has advanced greatly since Correll did his first Texas work. For this reason it can be confusing to consult Correll, Luer, Diggs, and Turner, and to a much lesser extent, Liggio and Liggio, as they often are discussing the same plant but under different names and concepts. To facilitate understanding of many of these synonyms, a chart that specifically cross-references those Texas publications is provided in Part Three.

Although easily defined as a state, Texas is often divided into several geophysical areas or, perhaps more appropriately, botanical ecoregions. For the purpose of this field guide, rather than frequent lists of many of the 252 counties in Texas, these botanical ecoregions are used to indicate distribution. Although the terms may be slightly different in various resources and one reference may define eight regions and another ten, they are all very well defined by the various habitats. Map 1.1 includes the Llano Uplands, which is part of the Edwards Plateau, and the Sand Coastal Plain, part of the South Texas Scrub. These regions are not specified in Liggio and Liggio but are included within other regions.

Pineywoods: uplands dominated by longleaf pines and rich hardwood forests line the bottomlands; thrifty in many orchid species that are more commonly found in the Southeast from Louisiana to South Carolina and reach the western limit of their range in eastern Texas.

Gulf Prairies and Marshes: extending for much of the Texas Gulf Coast with boundary ranges of 15–150 km inland, with a complex of marshes and upland grassland and rare forested islands; cypress-tupelo to hackberry-ash-elm to water oak-willow oak communities make up the bottomland hardwood forests that drain the Coastal Prairies.

Post Oak Savannah; Oak Woods and Prairies: prairielike grasslands with occasional wetlands and freshwater marshes often found within the Oaks and Prairies area, associated primarily with the peripheral areas of streams, rivers, and reservoirs.

Blackland Prairies: divided into four narrow, north-south areas—from west to east—the Eagle Ford Prairie, the White Rock Cuesta, the Taylor Black Prairie, and the Eastern Marginal Prairie (Montgomery, 1993). With the area's rich soils and riparian woodlands, many of the more northerly prairie species are at their southern limits. The Blackland Prairies include the orchid-rich areas west of Dallas.

Cross Timbers and Prairies: characterized by rolling, wooded savannahs that extend north beyond the Texas-Oklahoma border, and prairie intermixed with scrubby cedar-mesquite woodland that reaches into north central Texas. This region is the southernmost of the tallgrass prairie physiographic areas.

South Texas Plains; South Texas Brush Country (including Coastal Sand Plain):

part of the Tamaulipan biotic province that extends into adjacent northern Mexico. The area is dominated by chaparral, or brushland habitat, and recent agricultural fields; also includes extensive grasslands, oak forests, and some tall riparian forests.

Edwards Plateau (including the Llano uplift): a hilly area clearly demarcated by the Balcones Fault escarpment to the east and south, and passes into the Chihuahuan Desert to the west and the Great Plains to the north. The plateau comprises four subregions: the central and western portions characterized by broad, relatively level uplands moderately dissected by gently sloping stream divides; the deeply dissected portion adjacent to the escarpment, the Balcones Canyonlands, popularly known as the Texas Hill Country, with fast-moving streams through steep-sided canyons; the northeast plateau, the Lampasas Cut Plains, characterized by broad valleys; and the Central Mineral Valley, or Llano Uplift, with its granitic substrate that clearly differentiates this area from surrounding habitats.

Rolling Plains: extending north from the Edwards Plateau, with flat to rolling plains and natural vegetation consisting of mixed grass plains, shortgrass high plains, shinnery oak grasslands, and mesquite grasslands.

High Plains: occupying the western panhandle, high and dry plains covered with a shortgrass prairie dominated by grama and buffalo grasses; hot in summer and cold in winter.

Trans-Pecos: the region west of the Pecos River, bounded by the Rio Grande on the south and west, and on the north by New Mexico; physically different from the rest of Texas with dramatic Basin and Range topography; included here are the Big Bend, and the Glass, Chisos, and Guadalupe mountains with their broad basins and valleys. The Rio Grande and Pecos rivers in this arid region provide riparian corridors with critical habitats for many orchids; and the mountains are charcterized by uphill landforms of oak-juniper woodlands and occasional coniferous forests in the highest elevations.

The identification and distribution of all genera found in Texas have been greatly clarified in recent work reported in volume 26 of *Flora of North America* (2002). The generic treatments in the *Flora* were authored by individuals and teams considered authorities on these genera. Although there were some variations in the treatments, specific guidelines were followed by the authors. With respect to distribution, authors verified each state record with an herbarium specimen or otherwise substantiated record. The orchids were treated at the species, subspecies, and varietal levels; in general, forma were not discussed. Some authors also treated hybrids. The present compendium brings together information that has been fragmented, at best, for many years, which necessitated the completion of many species treatments that had been in progress. Each author or team of authors set its own parameters for delimitation of species based upon their research; several new species were described and new, or possibly older, names were used in the *Flora*.

An Introduction to Orchids

Orchids hold a special fascination for many people, perhaps because of their perceived extreme beauty, rarity, and mystery. In actuality, orchids are the largest family of flowering plants on earth, with well over 30,000 species. Although many are exceedingly beautiful, many more are small and dull colored, often barely 2 or 3 mm across! There is hardly any place on this planet, other than Antarctica, that does not have some species of orchid growing within its native flora. Even the oases within the great deserts of the world harbor a few species. In the more northerly climes orchids can be found well above the Arctic Circle. Orchids grow at elevations greater than 15,000 feet as well as within highly developed urban areas of the globe.

Texas, occupying nearly one quarter of the south central part of the United States, may at first glance appear not to have a great deal of orchid-friendly habitat, but many excellent orchid regions are to be found, especially in the eastern and coastal areas and far west of the Trans-Pecos. Some of the rarest species globally are found here. The considerable distances longitudinally and extremes in elevation accommodate species of both colder northern and warmer Gulf habitats.

Because of the sheer number of orchids in the world a considerable degree of morphological diversity occurs among them. Although all orchids possess certain qualifying characters, their general morphology can be as variable as the imagination. However, viewed closely under a lens, even the tiniest of orchids has those distinctive characteristics that make it an orchid!

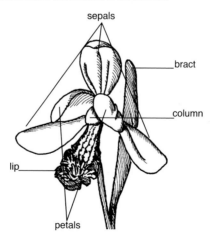

Characteristics of the orchid family, the Orchidaceae, are quite simple, despite their diversity. First, they are monocots (monocotyledons)—a major class of the plant kingdom that emerges with a single leaflike structure when the seed germinates (as opposed to dicots—dicotyledons—that emerge with two leaflike structures). Bromeliads, grasses, lilies, and palms are also monocots. Second, orchids have three sepals, two petals, and a third petal that is modified into a lip. This prominent structure is actually a guide for an insect pollinator—sort of a landing platform that directs the agent of pollination toward the nectary. Third, the stamens and pistil are united into a column, a structure unique to the orchids that effects fertilization when the agent of pollination passes by on its way to the nectary. Again, because of the size of the family, there are many pollinators, not just insects. Orchids are documented to be pollinated by the usual bees, butterflies, wasps, and flies, as well as by hummingbirds, and a few are even rain-assisted in their pollination. Many orchids emit a fragrance at a certain time of day, or at night, to attract their specific pollinator. Beyond that there are those species that, by various means, are self-pollinating.

Because of the great number of genera and species, occasionally there are what appear to be exceptions. A few genera have monoecious or dioecious flowers—male and female flowers on separate inflorescences or separate plants. In others, the petals and/or lip may be so modified that they are barely recognizable; in yet others, the flowers never open: they are cleistogamous and self-fertilized in the bud. But all of these exceptions aside, the vast majority of orchid flowers look like orchids!

Within the varied habitats of Texas all of the orchids currently found are terrestrial. (If *Epidendrum magnoliae* is eventually discovered here, that would change.) These terrestrials grow with their roots within the ground and take in water and nutrients through root hairs and/or swollen stems that are tuber-, bulb-, or corm-like.

In nature, all orchids consume fungi as a food (carbon) source. Each wild orchid has this unique relationship with naturally occurring fungi. While nearly impossible to see with the naked eye, these fungi are essential to the growth and development of any wild orchid. In this relationship, a fungus infects the orchid roots and the fungus is then consumed as a food source, initially prompting seed germination and then sustaining seedling development. As mature plants, the orchids are capable of producing food via both photosynthesis and the consumption of their root-inhabiting fungus. A number of different fungi may contribute nutrients, growth regulators, vitamins, and moisture at various levels and at different times throughout the orchid's life cycle. It is this special relationship between orchid and fungus that makes native orchids extremely difficult to transplant. In some cases, native orchids that are moved from their natural location die within a few years as a result of this disruption of the orchid-fungal association, while in the genus *Cypripedium* damage to the root tips often causes death.

The leaves of orchids are nearly as diverse as the flowers. As is characteristic of all monocots, they have parallel primary veins. They may be long and slender, or grasslike, or round and fat, or hard and leathery, or soft and hairy—just about any configuration. If you are a novice, take a few moments to look through the photographs and drawings and see the typical floral parts before trying to use the book. Try to get a better feeling for what an orchid is and then go out and find some!

Which Orchid Is It?

A key is a written means for identifying an unknown species. The principles used in keying are very simple. A series of questions is asked in the form of couplets, or paired questions; the user needs to determine a positive or negative response to each half of the pairs. Be sure to read both halves of the couplet before deciding on your answer. The half of the couplet that matches your observation of the orchid directs you to the next set of couplets, which leads to the next, and so on, with the last choice ending at the genus and/or species name. As you progress through the key, the illustrations may help you in making your determinations.

Choose the specimen you wish to identify carefully. Look for a typical, average plant—neither the largest nor the smallest. This key is designed so you should be able to use it without picking any orchids. Only in the case of a few similar species will detailed examinations be necessary. The use of measurements has been kept to a minimum, as has the use of color. Be aware that white-flowered forms exist in many of the species and they usually occur along with the typical color form.

Before you start to use the key, you should always mentally note the following:

1. placement and quantity of leaves; i.e., basal vs. cauline; opposite vs. alternate; 1, 2, or more
2. placement and quantity of flowers, i.e., terminal vs. axillary; single vs. multiple
3. geographic location and habitat; i.e., where you are and what you are standing in!

Three vocabulary words that will help in your understanding of the key:

pseudobulb—the swollen storage organ at the base of the leaves, primarily on epiphytes (which do not grow in this region), occasionally on terrestrials (*Malaxis*)
bract—a small, reduced leaf that is usually found on the flowering stem and/or within the inflorescence
spur/mentum—a projection at the base of the lip; it may be variously shaped, from slender and pointed (spur) to short and rounded (mentum)

Other terms are illustrated in the key or can be found in the glossary on page 291.

Using the Key

If you are using the key for the first time, start with a species with which you are familiar—perhaps the beautiful **rose pogonia**, *Pogonia*.

Starting with couplet 1:

1a   leaves lacking [absent or just emerging or withering] at flowering time . . . 2

1b   leaves present at flowering . . . 8

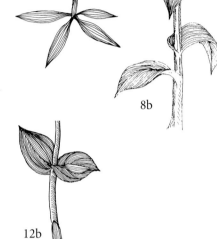

which takes us to couplet 8

8a   leaves basal . . . 9

8b   leaves cauline . . . 12

which takes us to couplet 12

12a   leaves opposite or whorled . . . 13

12b   leaves singular or alternate . . . 14

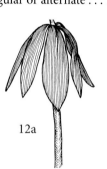

which takes us to couplet 14

14a   leaves one; a leaflike bract subtending the flower . . . 15

14b   leaves alternate . . . 16

which takes us to couplet 15

15a   lip with a fringe and beard; petals and lip distinct . . . . . *Pogonia*, p. 121

15b   lip otherwise; petals and lip somewhat forming a tube . . . . . *Cleistes*, p. 25

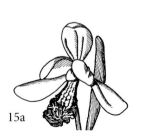

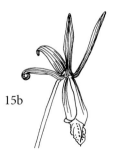

which then takes us to the generic treatment of *Pogonia* on page 121. If there are more than one species in the genus, follow the same procedure with the key to the species.

This key is constructed for use in the field or with live specimens and is based on characters that are readily seen. It is not a technical key in the strictest sense, but intended simply to aid in field identification.

Keys are not difficult if you take your time, learn the vocabulary, and hone your observational skills. Like any skill, the more you use it, the easier it becomes.

Key to the Genera

1a   leaves lacking (absent or just emerging or withering) at flowering time . . . 2

1b   leaves (fully developed) present at flowering . . . 8

2a   plants lacking chlorophyll (or appearing so) . . . 3

2b   green stems or bracts evident . . . 5

3a   flowers whitish with a distinctive red spot on the lip underside . . . . . *Schiedeella*, p. 129

3b   flowers otherwise . . . 4

4a   lip spotted or striped; never with ridges; technically, flowers with a mentum (a very small spur that is difficult to see) at the base of the lip . . . . . *Corallorhiza*, p. 29

4b   lip with a series of distinctive ridges or crests; flowers lacking a mentum . . . . . *Hexalectris*, p. 73

4a

4b

5a   flowers small, white or whitish, numerous, in a slender twisted spike . . . . . *Spiranthes*, p. 132

5b   flowers otherwise . . . 6

5a

6a   flower with a long distinctive spur; flowers brown, purple, and green, asymmetrical . . . . . *Tipularia*, p. 167

6b   flower without a spur; flowers variously colored, all plants of Big Bend, Trans-Pecos Region . . . 7

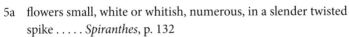

6a

7   petals and sepals including the lip nearly the same in appearance, all with green stripes . . . . . *Dichromanthus* (*michuancanus*), p. 49

7   petals and sepals and lip distinctively different; often twisted . . . . . *Deiregyne*, p. 45

8a

8b

LEAVES PRESENT AT FLOWERING

8a   leaves basal . . . 9
8b   leaves cauline . . . 12

9a   leaves one or two, inflorescence a spike or raceme of small, crowded flowers . . . . . *Malaxis*, p. 95
9b   leaves three or more in a distinct basal rosette or nearly so . . . 10

10a flowers cinnabar red . . . . . *Dichromanthus* (*cinnabarinus*), p. 49
10b flowers otherwise . . . 11

11a flowers numerous (10–20+), small, white in a twisted spike . . . . . *Spiranthes*, p. 132
11b flower fewer, white with green stripes (5–10+) . . . . . *Ponthieva*, p. 125

12a leaves opposite or whorled . . . 13
12b leaves singular or alternate . . . 14

13a leaves two—opposite, flowers small on a slender spike . . . . . *Listera*, p. 91
13b leaves 5 or 6 in a whorl, flowers usually 1 or rarely 2 . . . . . *Isotria*, p. 87

12a

12b

14a leaves one; a leaf-like bract subtending the flower . . . 15
14b leaves alternate . . . 16

15a lip with a fringe and beard; petals and lip distinct
. . . . . *Pogonia*, p. 121
15b lip otherwise; petals and lip somewhat
forming a tube . . . . . *Cleistes*, p. 25

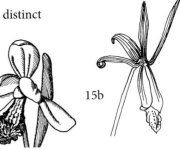

15b

15a

16a lip of flower distinctly pouch-like . . . 17
16b lip otherwise . . . 18

16a

17a petals slender and twisted . . . . . *Cypripedium*,
p. 39
17b petals broadened and similar to sepals
. . . . . *Epipactis*, p. 54

18a flowers with a distinct spur . . . 19
18b flowers lacking a spur . . . 22

19a lip toothed or merely erose . . . 20
19b lip divided, lacerate or fringed . . . 21

20a margin of lip entire, lip with a prominent
tubercle . . . . . *Platanthera* [*flava*] p. 103
20b margin of lip 3-toothed or erose . . . . .
Gymnadeniopsis, p. 58

20a

21a petals (as well as lip) deeply divided . . . . .
Habenaria, p. 67
21b petals crested or shallowly fringed or entire
. . . . . *Platanthera*, p. 103

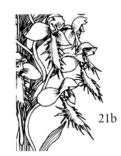

21b

22a leaves green . . . 23
22b leave coppery bronze; flowers with a yellow lip . . . . . *Zeuxine*, p. 176

23a flowers small, less than 1 cm, numerous in a slender twisted spike . . . . .
Spiranthes, p. 132
23b flowers larger, showy . . . 24

24a lip uppermost, flowers usually bright shades of pink or magenta
   arranged in a spike . . . . . *Calopogon*, p. 19

24b lip lowermost, flowers few—1–5(-10), in an open cluster, white or
   flushed with pink; lip with distinct green ridges . . . . . *Triphora*, p. 171

Some Important Notes About . . .

PLANT NAMES

Example: *Platanthera ciliaris* (Linnaeus) Lindley

The Latin name used for a plant consists of two parts and together they constitute the name of a species. The first word indicates the genus and the second is the specific epithet. The genus is the broader group to which the plant belongs and the specific epithet (usually, but erroneously, referred to as the species name) is the specific plant being treated. The specific epithet is an adjective or descriptive noun in the genitive that tries to impart information about the species.

After the two Latin names (genus and specific epithet), the name or names of the people who first described the plant are given. The example given above illustrates two different author citations. Linnaeus originally described the species as *Orchis ciliaris* in 1753; therefore his name appears immediately after the genus and specific epithet. Subsequently Lindley transferred it to the genus *Platanthera* in 1835. Therefore, Lindley's name appears after Linnaeus', which has been placed in parentheses to indicate that Linnaeus was the original describer. Two other synonyms occur for this species but they always retain Linnaeus' name in parentheses: *Habenaria ciliaris* (Linnaeus) R. Brown 1813 and *Blephariglottis ciliaris* (Linnaeus) Rydberg 1901. In the latter two cases different generic concepts were used. Current nomenclature embraces the concept of *Platanthera*. In 1837 Rafinesque described *Blephariglottis flaviflora* but that plant was identical to the previously described *Orchis ciliaris* and therefore is a synonym.

Other ranks may occur, such as subspecies, variety, and forma. Subspecies and variety usually designate a variation that has a distinctive morphological difference from the species and a definite geographic range apart from the nominate variety. Although the two varieties may overlap, they maintain their differences, as in *Platanthera flava* var. *herbiola*, hence it is a variety. Varieties and subspecies should always breed true—bearing a marked resemblance to the parent. There can always be a bit of disagreement over the rank of variety versus subspecies and which term is better used. Color variations, which occur throughout the range of the species, are best treated as forma, as in the white-flowered form of the *Calopogon oklahomensis*—forma *albiflorus*. These forms can, and do, occur randomly and rarely breed true. All forma that have received names for the species occurring within Texas are listed, although several have yet to be documented for this region. Orchid enthusiasts and botanists alike will note several new forms as well as a number of 'old' forms that have been resurrected. The new combinations were necessary to recognize certain taxa at the forma level. Recent research has uncovered a number of forms previously published many years ago that, although plants corresponding to these forms are easily found, have been abandoned.

COMMON NAMES

Common names are never as consistent throughout the range of the plants as we would like. The most frequently used common names are used in this book, as well as some regional names. Texas appears to have a wealth of common names in the orchid literature. A cross-reference to those common names is provided in Part Three.

Orchid or Orchis? For common names either orchid or orchis may be used, but traditionally orchis has been used for certain genera and the practice has been maintained here.

SIZE

Average height of the plants, width and height of flowers, and number of flowers are given, with extremes in parentheses. The relative scale of each line drawing is for an average plant and is based upon the flower size.

COLOR

The color given is that of the flowers as they normally occur. Remember to check to see if color variants such as white- flowered forms occur. In some genera the overall color of the petals and sepals, the perianth, is given and is followed by the color of the lip.

FORMS AND HYBRIDS

The diversity within a given species may vary from virtually nonexistent to plants with a wide range of color and growth forms. When the natural range of color grades from light to dark or even within such hues as purple to red to pink, that variation is considered the norm. However, variations with distinctive color or growth forms occur randomly, such as white-flowered forms (often incorrectly called albinos) or ecological dwarfs, and these variations and hybrids are what can take hunting for native orchids to another level. After mastering the identity of many of the species, one can become challenged to search for all the variations. It would be unrealistic to think that all of these forms occur within the range of this work, but many of them do. To better understand these forms, note that each is annotated with the original publication and the geographic type locality of the taxon, the geographic location from where the form was originally described. Those that have been documented from Texas are often noted within the text and it is expected that several of the other forms will also be found.

Hybrids present a very different situation. Whereas forms are the result of genetic diversity within a species, hybrids rely on an outside element, the pollinator, to create the resulting hybrid as a cross between two species. In certain parental combinations hybrids are very predictable, but in other situations they are very rare. Most are obviously intermediates between the putative parents, and when both parental species are present the hybrids should be carefully sought. Few hybrids occur within Texas and those are found in the genus *Spiranthes*.

FLOWERING PERIODS

Flowering periods are affected by latitude, exposure, elevation, and, perhaps more critically, by rainfall. In drought years flowering may be greatly delayed or even omitted, whereas in an El Nino year, with excessive rainfall, flowering may commence earlier. Typically plants flower earlier in the spring in the more temperate areas and later in the mountains, whereas autumn-flowering species tend to flower earlier in higher elevations and later southward or along the Coastal Plain.

RANGE MAPS

Both the continental range and the local physiographic range are given for each species. The range maps are intended to illustrate the general range of a given species and are based on verifiable specimens in herbarium records, normally housed in herbaria at any number of colleges and universities. Upon rare occasion a photograph from a reliable source, documented with date and place as a verifiable report, would be allowed. Literature reports are noted in the text and are just that: a report in any one of a number of publications that cannot be backed up by either a specimen or verifiable record. The range maps do not attempt to differentiate between extant and extirpated populations, nor do they convey how many populations are known from a given area or the size of those populations. Green dots represent widespread populations and red dots local populations; red dots bordered by black indicate documented historical populations; black circles indicate reports. If the range of a species or variety extends beyond the boundaries of Texas, an arrow is used to indicate such.

Part 2

The Wild Orchids of Texas

Calopogon

The genus *Calopogon* is a New World genus comprising five species, only one of which also occurs outside of the United States and Canada. Two of these species are found in Texas. The non-resupinate (uppermost) lip is distinctive and easily identifies the genus.

Key to the grass-pinks, *Calopogon*

1a flowers opening nearly simultaneously, central portion of the lip narrower than long; spring flowering plants of prairie habitats . . . . . **Oklahoma grass-pink**, *Calopogon oklahomensis*, p. 20

1b flowers opening sequentially over a period of time, central portion of the lip wider than long; early summer flowering plants of various wetlands . . . . . **common grass-pink**, *Calopogon tuberosus*, p. 22

Calopogon oklahomensis D.H. Goldman

Oklahoma grass-pink

forma *albiflorus* P.M. Brown—white-flowered form
North America Native Orchid Journal 9: 33–34. 2003, type: Arkansas

Range: southern Minnesota east to western Indiana, south to southern Georgia and central South Carolina, and west to eastern Texas

Texas: Pineywoods, Gulf Prairies and Marshes, Post Oak Savannah—local in remnant prairies

Plant: terrestrial, 15–36 cm tall

Leaves: 1 or 2; lanceolate, slender, 0.5–1.5 cm wide × 7.0–35.0 cm long

Flowers: 3–7(13), non-resupinate, with most open simultaneously; color is highly variable from lilac-blue to bright magenta-pink or, in the forma *albiflorus*, white, all with a golden crest on the lip; individual flower size 2.5–4.0 cm

Habitat: prairies, pine savannahs, open flatwoods, and frequently mowed damp meadows

Flowering period: late April into May

The **Oklahoma grass-pink**, *Calopogon oklahomensis*, is the most recent species of grass-pink to be described from the United States. It was originally thought to be restricted to the prairies of the south central states, but herbarium specimens indicate that it is much more widespread, although currently considered extirpated from much of the original range. This is one of the most variable species in coloration, from pale lilac to deep magenta and the occasional white-flowered form, forma *albiflorus*. In Texas, plants previously identified as **bearded grass-pink**, *Calopogon barbatus* (a species now known to be confined to the Deep South) are all **Oklahoma grass-pink**. Watch for small plants with a relatively broad leaf nestled within the grasses, unlike the later-flowering **common grass-pink** of wetter areas that usually holds itself well above the surrounding vegetation. Goldman (2000, Goldman et al., 2004) suggests that this species may have risen from ancient hybridization of *C. barbatus* and *C. tuberosus*. For more details concerning *C. barbatus*, see *Wild Orchids of the Southeastern United States* (Brown and Folsom, 2004).

Hatch et al. (1990) noted *Calopogon barbatus* (read *C. oklahomensis*) for the High Plains region but there has never been a voucher for that area. That region was omitted from the 2001 revision.

forma *albiflorus*

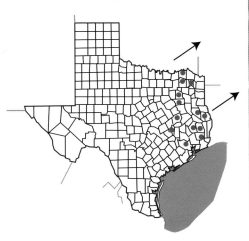

Calopogon tuberosus (Linnaeus) Britton, Sterns, & Poggenberg var. *tuberosus*

common grass-pink

forma *albiflorus* Britton—white-flowered form
Bulletin of the Torrey Botanical Club 17: 125. 1890, type: New Jersey

Range: Minnesota east to Newfoundland, south to Florida and west to Texas
Texas: Pineywoods, Gulf Prairies and Marshes, Post Oak Savannah—occasional to frequent
Plant: terrestrial, 25–80 cm tall
Leaves: 1(–3); slender, ribbed, up to 0.3–4.0 cm wide × 3–45 cm long and less than the height of the plant
Flowers: 3–17, non-resupinate, opening in slow succession; deep to pale pink or, in the forma *albiflorus*, white; with a golden crest on the lip; individual flower size 2.5–3.5 cm
Habitat: wet meadows, pine flatwoods, seeps, and sphagnous roadsides
Flowering period: June to July

Reaching the southeastern limit for its range in Texas the **common grass-pink**, *Calopogon tuberosus*, one of the orchids most frequently found in the eastern and central United States and Canada, is a brilliant, showy plant that prefers open, wet, sandy roadsides, sphagnum bogs, and seeps. Plants flower over a very long period of time, with only a few flowers open at once. It is not unusual to find local stands of several hundred plants. Like all grass-pinks, the flowers have the lip uppermost, non-resupinate, and this feature easily separates the genus from any other with a similar morphology. Plants may be found in a variety of habitats including open fens, roadside seeps, bogs, and damp flatwoods. The var. *simpsonii* is found in rocky marls of the southernmost counties of Florida.

Hatch et al. (1990) also noted *Calopogon tuberosus* for the Blackland Prairies but it has never been vouchered from that region.

forma *albiflorus*

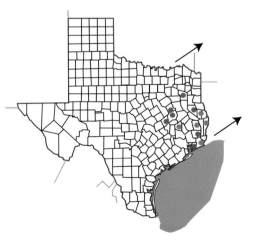

Cleistes

The genus *Cleistes* comprises about 25 species in the Western Hemisphere, many of which grow in wet savannahs in northern South America. Most of the species were, at one time, classified as *Pogonia*, a very closely related genus, and some current authors still treat them as such. Based on recent DNA analyses, the two species in the United States may properly belong in a new genus.

Cleistes bifaria (Fernald) Catling & Gregg

upland spreading pogonia

Range: West Virginia south to Florida, west to eastern Louisiana, eastern Texas

Texas: Pineywoods—extirpated in Texas

Plant: terrestrial, 20–50 cm tall

Leaf: 1; broadly lanceolate, glaucous, 3 cm wide × 15 cm long; a smaller floral bract, 1.5 cm wide × 6.5 cm long, resembling a leaf, subtends the flower

Flowers: 1, rarely 2; sepals bronzy green, petals pale pink to blush; lip whitish veined in darker pink with a yellow crest; lip to 21–33 mm long and appearing with a broadened apex; individual flower size 5 × 5 cm

Habitat: open pine flatwoods, shaded prairies, and seepy meadows

Flowering period: May

While the **upland spreading pogonia**, *Cleistes bifaria*, is not as dramatic and showy as its cousin *C. divaricata*, it is somewhat of an enigma in Texas. Donovan Correll (1944) reported having seen a specimen from Texas collected by Palmer, but was never able to relocate that specimen, so precise information is not available. Catling and Gregg (1992) searched for the specimen without success, and the Liggios included *C. bifaria* based upon all of this information. It is found to the east in Louisiana so the veracity of the Correll report of the Palmer plant is to be seriously considered. Abundant similar habitat to that in Louisiana exists within the Pineywoods region.

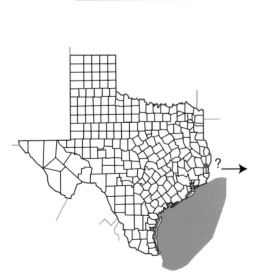

Corallorhiza

The genus *Corallorhiza* comprises 13 species found throughout North America and Hispaniola. One species, *C. trifida,* is widespread across Eurasia. The plants are entirely mycotrophic and some are thought to be saprophytes. They arise from a coralloid rhizome, hence the name. The entire genus is easily recognizable from its leafless stems, which may be variously colored, and by their small flowers. *Corallorhiza* is easily separated from *Hexalectris,* the other mycotrophic genus in Texas, by the lack of ridges (crests) on the lip and the presence of a mentum or small spur, although the mentum may be minute in some cases. Four species are found within Texas.

Key to the coralroots, *Corallorhiza*

1a   flowers cleistogamous, flower very small, less than 3 mm, autumn flowering; northern Pineywoods . . . . . **autumn coralroot**, *Corallorhiza odontorhiza* var. *odontorhiza*, p. 32

1b   flowers chasmogamous . . . 2

2a   lip white; plain or more often with dark spots . . . 3

2b   lip red or tan, solid or faintly striped, flowers red to orange, tepals striped; late spring flowering, Trans-Pecos . . . . . **striped coralroot**, *Corallorhiza striata* var. *striata*, p. 34

3a   lip unlobed, spade-shaped, spotted; late winter into early spring flowering, widely distributed . . . . . **Wister's coralroot**, *Corallorhiza wisteriana*, p. 36

3ba   sides of lip broadened, flowers open wide, late spring flowering; Trans-Pecos . . . . . **western spotted coralroot**, *Corallorhiza maculata* var. *occidentalis*, p. 30

Corallorhiza maculata (Rafinesque) Rafinesque var. *occidentalis* (Lindley) Ames

western spotted coralroot

forma *aurea* P.M. Brown—golden yellow/spotted form
North American Native Orchid Journal 1: 195. 1995, type: Washington

forma *immaculata* (Peck) Howell—yellow spotless form
Marin Flora, ed. 2: 363. 1970 as *Corallorhiza maculata* Rafinesque var. *immaculata* M.E. Peck, type: California

forma *intermedia* Farwell—brown-stemmed form
Report (Annual) of the Michigan Academy of Sciences 19: 247. 1917 as *Corallorhiza maculata* (Rafinesque) Rafinesque var. *intermedia* Farwell, type: Michigan

forma *punicea* (Bartholomew) Weatherby & Adams—red-stemmed form
Rhodora 24: 147. 1922 as *Corallorrhiza maculata* (Rafinesque) Rafinesque var. *punicea* Bartholomew, type: Michigan

Range: British Columbia east to Newfoundland, south to California, Arizona, New Mexico, Minnesota, New England, and Virginia

Texas: Trans-Pecos—rare and scattered

Plant: terrestrial, mycotrophic, 20–50 cm tall; stems bronzy tan or, in the formae *immaculata* and *aurea*, yellow or, in the forma *intermedia*, brown or, in the forma *punicea*, strikingly deep red

Leaves: lacking

Flowers: 5–20+; tepals typically colored bronzy tan as the stems or, in the forma *intermedia*, the stems brown or, in the forma *punicea*, the stems strikingly deep red with the lip spotted in purple or dark red or, in the forma *aurea*, the lip spotted or, in the forma *immaculata*, the stems and flowers yellow to white, the lip lacking all spotting; lip 3-lobed with the middle lobe expanded, the sides obviously broadened; individual flowers 5.0–7.5 mm, the floral parts wide-spreading, mentum obscure

Habitat: rich mesic and mixed forests

Flowering period: late May through July

The common name **western spotted coralroot** for *Corallorhiza maculata* var. *occidentalis* is somewhat misleading as this variety extends eastward to Newfoundland. Plants found in Texas are disjunct from the southern Rocky Mountains, where the variety extends south into northern Mexico. The broad, full, crisp spotted lip on colorful leafless stems easily identifies this plant. It may grow singly or in clumps and will vary from year to year in its thriftiness. The indication from Travis County is based upon a report from the 1930s and has been perpetuated in several other publications (Hatch et al., 1990, 2000) although omitted from Liggio and Liggio (1999). Without a specimen or photograph it is impossible to determine the variety that may have been noted in central Texas. *Corallorhiza* *maculata* var. *maculata*, with the sides of the lip parallel, is more widespread in eastern North America and the variety *mexicana*, with spots coalesced and/or on the margin of the lip, is found sparingly in southern Arizona and well into Mexico.

forma *aurea*

var. *maculata*   forma *immaculata*

Corallorhiza odontorhiza (Willdenow) Nuttall var. *odontorhiza*

autumn coralroot

forma *flavida* Wherry—yellow-stemmed form
Journal of the Washington Academy of Science 17: 36. 1927, type:
Washington, D.C.

Range: South Dakota east to Maine, south to Texas and northern
Florida
Texas: Pineywoods, Post Oak Savannah—this plant is both rare
and easily overlooked
Plant: terrestrial, mycotrophic, 5–10 cm tall; stems bronzy green
or, in the forma *flavida*, yellow
Leaves: lacking
Flowers: 5–12; cleistogamous; sepals green suffused with purple,
covering the petals; lip, rarely evident in this variety, white spot-
ted with purple or, in the forma *flavida*, unspotted; individual
flower size 3–4 mm
Habitat: rich, calcareous woodlands
Flowering period: September through October

The fact that this inconspicuous little orchid is rarely found may
be attributed more to its size and habit than necessarily to its
rarity. The **autumn coralroot**, *Corallorhiza odontorhiza* var. *odontorhiza*, appears to be never common anywhere and is often
found by accident. The short stems often flower among the fallen
leaves in the autumn months and the coloration, *sans* chlorophyll, makes them even harder to see. Plants favor damp, often
calcareous woodlands and are best seen in the deciduous forests
that border streams. Early reports for *C. odontorhiza* in Texas
by Coulter and Small are actually *C. wisteriana*, a curious error
considering the opposing flowering times. Ajilvsgi discovered
Corallorhiza odontorhiza in Texas for the first time in 1979, and subsequently
Magrath found an additional site in 1981 although the Liggios were unable to
locate plants in 1991 (Liggio and Liggio, 1999). Excluding segregate species from
known populations (*Cypripedium kentuckiense* from *C. parviflorum* var. *pubescens*; *Calopogon oklahomensis* from *C. barbatus*, etc.), this is the most recent new
species to be found for Texas.

Corallorhiza striata Lindley var. *striata*

striped coralroot

forma *eburnea* P.M. Brown—yellow/white form
North American Native Orchid Journal 1(1): 9. 1995, type: New
  Mexico
forma *fulva* Fernald—tan-colored form
Rhodora 48: 197. 1946, type: Quebec

Range: British Columbia east to Newfoundland, south to California, Texas, and New York
Texas: Trans-Pecos—rare and local
Plant: terrestrial, mycotrophic, 20–50 cm tall; stems golden
pink with reddish purple lines or, in the forma *eburnea*, the
stems yellow or, in the forma *fulva*, dull tan
Leaves: lacking
Flowers: 8–35; tepals yellowish pink with reddish purple lines;
lip white but striped purple-red with confluent lines and appearing solid or, in the forma *eburnea*, flowers yellow to white
or, in the forma *fulva*, the flowers dusky tan in color, the petals
and sepals not as wide spreading, and the flower proportions
smaller; individual flowers ca. 0.75–1.5 cm
Habitat: rich mesic and mixed forests
Flowering period: late May through July

The **striped coralroot,** *Corallorhiza striata* var. *striata*, is the
largest and certainly the showiest of all the coralroots in North
America. A common orchid of the western states and upper
Great Lakes area, this striking species has been found in Texas only in the Trans-
Pecos. Fernald described the forma *fulva* in 1946, from Percé in eastern Quebec,
as a plant with smaller, duller tan-colored flowers—a description that is similar to
Vreeland's striped coralroot, *Corallorhiza striata* var. *vreelandii*, of the western
states.

Hatch et al. (1990) also noted *Corallorhiza striata* for the Edwards Plateau region but it has never been vouchered from that area.

forma *eburnea*

Corallorhiza wisteriana Conrad

Wister's coralroot

forma *albolabia* P.M. Brown—white-lipped form
North American Native Orchid Journal 1(1): 9–10. 1995, type: Florida

forma *cooperi* P.M. Brown—cranberry-pink form
North American Native Orchid Journal 10: 22. 2004, type: Florida

forma *rubra* P.M. Brown—red-stemmed form
North American Native Orchid Journal 1(1): 62. 2000, type: Florida

Range: Washington east to New Jersey, south to Arizona and Florida; Mexico

Texas: Pineywoods, Gulf Prairies and Marshes, Post Oak Savannah, Blackland Prairies, Edwards Plateau—widespread and local

Plant: terrestrial, mycotrophic, 5–30 cm tall; stem brownish yellow or, in the forma *albolabia*, yellow or, in the forma *cooperi*, cranberry-pink or, in the forma *rubra,* red

Leaves: lacking

Flowers: 5–25; sepals green, petals yellow suffused and mottled with purple; lip white spotted with purple or, in the forma *albolabia*, yellow-stemmed, sepals and petals yellow with a pure white lip or, in the forma *cooperi*, the stems, petals, and sepals cranberry-pink, the lip white with dark pink markings or, in the forma *rubra*, red-stemmed, sepals and petals red, with flowers marked red; individual flower size 5–7 mm

Habitat: rich, often calcareous woodlands, pine flatwoods, occasionally in lawns and foundation plantings

Flowering period: late March through May

Wister's coralroot, *Corallorhiza wisteriana*, with its pale brown stems and small spotted white flowers, can often be seen early in the spring growing in a variety of locations in open woods and even homesites. It is one of the few orchids in Texas that is reasonably widespread throughout the eastern and central counties. Although it often is found as an individual, sites with several hundred plants in large clustered colonies are not uncommon. The three color forms are exceedingly rare and known from very few sites.

Hatch et al. (1990, 2000) also noted *Corallorhiza wisteriana* for the South Texas Plains region but it has never been vouchered from that area.

forma *rubra*

forma *cooperi*

forma *albolabia*

Cypripedium

Cypripedium is a distinctive genus of about 45 species with 12 occurring in North America north of Mexico. Although the leaf arrangement is variable, the lip, an unmistakable pouch-shaped slipper, is always diagnostic. This is often the genus that is first recognized by orchid enthusiasts. There are two species found within Texas.

Key to the lady's-slippers, *Cypripedium*

1a   lip orbicular, dorsal sepal arching forward; flowers very large; white, ivory, or yellow; large plants of East Texas . . . . . **ivory-lipped lady's-slipper**, *Cypripedium kentuckiense*, p. 40

1b   lip oval to oblong, dorsal sepal more or less erect; plants of the western panhandle (formerly) . . . . . **large yellow lady's-slipper**, *Cypripedium parviflorum* var. *pubescens*, p. 42

Cypripedium kentuckiense C.F. Reed

ivory-lipped lady's-slipper

forma *pricei* P.M. Brown—white-flowered
form
North American Native Orchid Journal 4: 45, 1998;
type: Arkansas
forma *summersii* P.M. Brown—concolorous
yellow-flowered form
North American Native Orchid Journal 7: 30–31;
type: Arkansas

Range: northeastern Virginia; Kentucky west
to Arkansas and south to eastern Texas and
Georgia
Texas: Pineywoods, Post Oak Savannah—rare
and local in most areas
Plant: terrestrial, 35–98 cm tall
Leaves: 3–6; alternate, evenly spaced along the
stem, broadly ovate to ovate-elliptic, 5–13 cm wide × 10–24 cm long
Flowers: 1–2(3); sepals and petals green to yellowish green prominently striped
or spotted with dark reddish brown or, in the forma *pricei*, pale green or, in the
forma *summersii*, yellow, the lateral sepals united; petals undulate and spiraled to
15 cm long; lip ivory or pale to deep yellow with delicate green spotting within
or, in the forma *pricei*, white or, in the forma *summersii*, yellow and unspotted;
individual flower size ca. 20 × 15 cm; lip 5.0–6.5 cm, the opening ovate at the
base of the lip, with the overall lip compressed laterally, unlike any other of our
lady's-slippers
Habitat: deciduous wooded seeps, alluvial forests, bases of slopes; occasionally
in adjacent floodplains
Flowering period: late spring; mid April–early May

Cypripedium kentuckiense, the **ivory-lipped or Kentucky lady's-slipper**, is the
largest flowered of all of the lady's-slippers to be found in the United States and
certainly one of the showiest. The enormous flowers may be nearly twice the overall size of any of the other yellow-flowered lady's-slippers. The largest colonies
are found in Arkansas, and in many of the other areas the plants are few and
scattered. Texas populations are few and widespread but well established in the
eastern counties, primarily in the Pineywoods region. Because these plants are
so showy, they have long been removed from the wild for cultivation. Both of
the distinctive color forms were found by eagle-eyed searchers: Jack Price, from
northern Louisiana and Bill Summers, author of *Orchids of Missouri*.

forma *summersii*

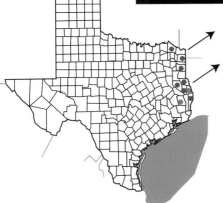

forma *pricei*

Cypripedium parviflorum Salisbury var. pubescens (Willdenow) Knight

large yellow lady's-slipper

Range: Alaska east to Newfoundland, south to Arizona and Georgia
Texas: High Plains; extirpated
Plant: terrestrial, 15–60 cm tall
Leaves: 3–5; alternate, somewhat evenly spaced along the stem, spreading; ovate to ovate-elliptic to lance-elliptic, 2.5–12.0 cm wide × 8.0–20.0 cm long; the outer surface of the lowermost sheathing bract densely pubescent with short, silvery hairs when young
Flowers: 1–3(4); sepals and petals spotted, splotched, or marked with brown, chestnut, or reddish brown spots, rarely appearing as a uniform color; lateral sepals united; petals undulate and spiraled to 10 cm long; lip slipper-shaped, from pale to deep rich yellow, less often with scarlet markings within the lip; individual flower size ca. 4.5 × 12.0 cm; lip 2.5–5.4 cm, the opening ovate-oblong at the base of the lip; scent moderately to faintly reminiscent of old roses
Habitat: a wide variety of mesic to calcareous, wet to dry woodlands, streamsides, bogs, and fens
Flowering period: late May into early June

The **large yellow lady's-slipper,** *Cypripedium parviflorum* var. *pubescens,* is the classic yellow lady's-slipper so familiar to so many wildflower lovers and gardeners. A single record exists for Texas, in Bailey County near the New Mexico border. Tharp collected it in June 1929 and no other specimens or reports have been found since then. Typically it may be seen in rich forests and swamps throughout much of the mesic and calcareous woodlands of nearby eastern Oklahoma and Arkansas and should be sought in northeastern Texas.

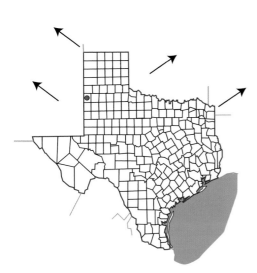

Deiregyne

Deiregyne is a small Spiranthoid genus of about fourteen species, with only one found in the United States and the others in Mexico and Central America. The species within this genus have often been treated as *Spiranthes*. Leaves are usually absent at flowering time.

Deiregyne confusa Garay

rimrock ladies'-tresses

Range: Texas; northern Mexico
Texas: Trans-Pecos—Big Bend area, very rare
Plant: 25–50 cm tall; stems with 6–9 bladeless cauline sheaths
Leaves: 2–3, mostly basal; linear-lanceolate, 2.0–3.5 cm wide ×
15.0–30.0 cm long
Flowers: Inflorescence with up to 15 deflexed flowers, secund
or loosely spiraled, glandular-pubescent; floral bracts ovate-
lanceolate, striate-veined, 1.0–2.5 cm long. Flowers pink or dull
brown to purplish with green veins; sepals recurved, dorsal sepal concave, slightly constricted to form a sac 1.2–1.9 × 0.42–
0.52 cm; lateral sepals linear-lanceolate, glandular-pubescent
on the outer surface; lip whitish pink with green veins, strongly
pandurate, basal portion orbiculate, pubescent, margins crenulate or erose; flowers 6 × 18 cm
Flowering Period: May to July
Habitat: open grassy slopes in rimrock at about 2,000 m elevation

Deiregyne confusa, the **rimrock ladies'-tresses**, is known in the United States only
from the original collections made in 1931 in the Chisos Mountains of Brewster
County, Texas. The species remained undetected until it was rediscovered in 2004
(USGS, 2004). Searches made in the interim failed to find any more plants (Luer,
1975; Liggio and Liggio, 1999).

In 2005 Ambs, Pelchat, Coleman, and others (Ambs, 2006; Coleman et al.,
2006) observed *Deiregyne confusa* at scattered locations in Big Bend. One plant
found in flower had robust healthy leaves present and several plants found with
fruit had robust healthy leaves present. It might be interesting to note that the
basal rosette of leaves bears a striking resemblance to *Dichromanthus cinnabarinus* and can be found persisting into early September when *D. cinnabarinus*
is flowering. The difference is that those of *Deiregyne* form a smaller rosette and
appear to be young plants of *Dichromanthus cinnabarinus*. Pelchat (pers. comm.)
observed plants of *Deiregyne confusa* in September 2000 growing within several
hundred feet of *Dichromanthus cinnabarinus* (which was flowering at that time)
and overlooked them, not recognizing them as *Deiregyne confusa*. It is suspected,
based on observations of plants found flowering, that *Deiregyne confusa* needs
optimal conditions to flower, and that because of this and its remote accessibility
it has been overlooked.

The Texas plants were originally identified as *Spiranthes durangensis* Ames &
C. Schweinfurth (Correll, 1950). They were subsequently placed in *Deiregyne* and

described as *D. confusa* Garay. L. A. Garay (1980[1982]) stated that *D. durangensis* does not occur in the United States. The illustrations in Luer (1975) and Brown (2003) are of *D. durangensis* photographed in Mexico.

Dichromanthus Garay

A small Spiranthoid genus with distinctive foliaceous sheaths on the stems and showy tubular flowers; leaves may be present at flowering time in some species. Traditional *Dichromanthus* was treated as a monotypic genus (Brown in *FNA*, 2002). Salazar et al. (2002) presented an excellent argument for three species in this genus, including what was formerly treated as *Stenorrhynchos michuacanum*. Ron Coleman, who has worked extensively in the field with both of the species found in Texas, supports this conclusion (pers. comm.)

Key to the species of *Dichromanthus*

   1a   flower brilliant orange . . . . . **cinnabar ladies-tresses**, *Dichromanthus cinnabarinus*, p. 50

   1b   flowers white to grey . . . . . **Michoacan ladies'-tresses**, *Dichromanthus michuacanus*, p. 52

Dichromanthus cinnabarinus (La Llave & Lexarza) Garay

cinnabar ladies'-tresses

forma *aureus* P.M. Brown—golden-yellow flowering form
McAllen International Orchid Society Journal 7(12): 4–5, type: Texas

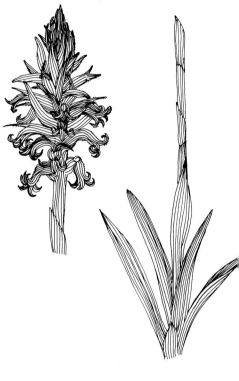

Range: Texas; Mexico, Central America
Texas: Trans-Pecos—Big Bend region
Plant: 50–90 cm tall; stems with 6–9 bladeless cauline sheaths.
Leaves: 3–4, ascending stem, dark green, linear-oblanceolate, present at flowering time, 1.5–3.0 cm wide × 10.0–20.0 cm long, passing into orange bracts with green stripes or, in the forma *aureus*, yellow
Flowers: 30–40 in a congested spike, 4–17 cm tall; floral bracts red, lanceolate, 3.5–8.0 mm long; flowers yellow-orange to scarlet, tubular; apices strongly recurved; ovaries red, stout, 10 × 4 mm, pubescent; dorsal sepal recurved, vermilion, lanceolate, 15–20 × 3–4 mm; lateral sepals linear-lanceolate, 15.0–22.0 × 2.0–3.5 mm, apex acute; petals yellow with vermilion apex, linear, falcate, 15.0–20.0 × 2.0–2.5 mm; lip yellow-orange with vermilion apex, lanceolate, or, in the forma *aureus*, the petals, sepals, and bracts golden yellow; flowers ca. 2–3 cm long
Flowering period: (late July) September into early October, usually after the summer rains
Habitat: rocky mountain slopes, grassy hills, and canyon meadows, often in limestone at ca. 1,800 m in elevation

Dichromanthus cinnabarinus, the **cinnabar ladies'-tresses** is without question the most striking of the spiranthoid segregate species owing to the brilliant cinnabar to orange-colored flowers held well above the foliage on similar colored stems and with the floral bracts of the same color. The overall impression is that of a fiery torch! Plants are found in moist pockets at moderate to high elevations in several mountain ranges in Brewster County.

forma *aureus*

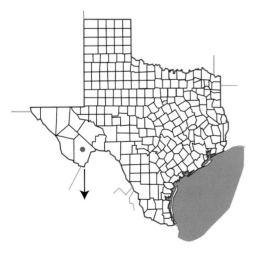

Dicromanthus michuacanus (La Llave & Lexarza) Salazar & Soto-Arenas

Michoacan ladies'-tresses

Range: Arizona, Texas; Mexico
Texas: Trans-Pecos—local and scattered
Plant: 13–80 cm tall; sheaths 3–6, bladeless, striate, scarious, glabrous with floral bract green basally, becoming reddish brown apically and the basal portions of bracts, stem, and outer surfaces of sepals densely hairy with tapered, tortuous hairs
Leaves: 2–5, mostly basal; lanceolate, 1–3 cm wide × 10–50 cm long; elliptic, apex acute or acuminate.
Flowers: cream or white with 1 or more longitudinal green stripes or markings; sepals, petals (including the lip) similar; overall flower size ca. 1.0–1.5 cm
Habitat: open grassy slopes, sandy pine-oak woodlands, especially in zones of periodic seepage at elevations of 1,900–2,200 m
Flowering Period: September into November

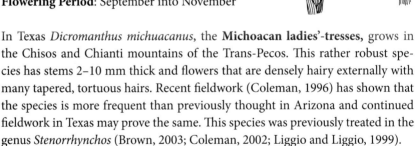

In Texas *Dicromanthus michuacanus*, the **Michoacan ladies'-tresses,** grows in the Chisos and Chianti mountains of the Trans-Pecos. This rather robust species has stems 2–10 mm thick and flowers that are densely hairy externally with many tapered, tortuous hairs. Recent fieldwork (Coleman, 1996) has shown that the species is more frequent than previously thought in Arizona and continued fieldwork in Texas may prove the same. This species was previously treated in the genus *Stenorrhynchos* (Brown, 2003; Coleman, 2002; Liggio and Liggio, 1999).

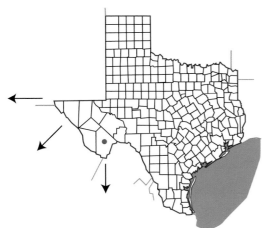

Epipactis

Epipactis is a cosmopolitan genus of about 25 species, only one of which, *E. gigantea*, is native to North America, and found primarily in western North America. Two Eurasian species can also be found in North America, including the widespread *E. helleborine*.

Epipactis gigantea Douglas *ex* Hooker

stream orchid, chatterbox

> forma *citrina* P.M. Brown—yellow-flowered form
> *North American Native Orchid Journal* 7(4): 257. 2001, type:
>   California
> forma *rubrifolia* P.M. Brown—red-leaved form
> *North American Native Orchid Journal* 1(4): 287. 1995, type:
>   California

Range: southern British Columbia east to Montana, south to California and Arizona, New Mexico, South Dakota, and Texas; Mexico

Texas: Blackland Prairies, Cross Timbers and Prairies, Edwards Plateau, Rolling Plains, Trans-Pecos—widely distributed and with a preference for lakeshores and seeps; increasingly rare at the eastern limit of its range

Plant: terrestrial, 30–100 cm tall

Leaves: 4–12; alternate, oval-lanceolate, 2.5–7.0 cm wide × 5.5–20.0 cm long, passing into slender floral bracts, light green or, in the forma *rubrifolia*, dark red

Flowers: 5–25; sepals and petals similar, ovate-lanceolate, green to yellow striped with purple veins, the dorsal sepal and petals thrust forward, forming an arched hood over the lip, the lateral sepals wide-spreading; lip divided into two portions, the upper portion with two broad lobes and, below the constriction, the lower portion spade-shaped; yellow with purple and orange markings or, in the forma *citrina*, the flower entirely yellow or, in the forma *rubrifolia*, the flowers suffused with dark red; individual flowers 1–3 cm across

Habitat: lakeshores, streamsides, and seeps

Flowering period: late June well into August

One of the most colorful members of the genus, the **stream orchid**, *Epipactis gigantea*, is the only native helleborine in North America. The slender stems hold numerous green, yellow, purple, and orange flowers throughout much of the summer months. Although somewhat widespread in Texas, **stream orchid** is still rare and local at the eastern limit of its range. Colonies may often have several hundred stems and the only real problem in viewing these striking flowers is that you usually have to stand in the water to look back at the plants on the shoreline! Both of the interesting color forms were originally found in California by Ron Coleman (1995). The yellow-flowered forma *citrina* might occur almost anywhere the species is present. The red-leaved forma *rubrifolia* was found in a serpentine area and is therefore unlikely in Texas. It has been propagated commercially and is often available at western native plant nurseries.

forma *citrina*

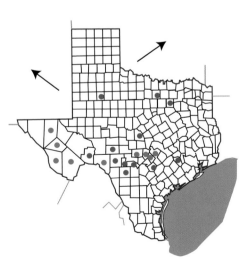

Gymnadeniopsis

Gymnadeniopsis was formerly placed within the genera *Habenaria* and *Platanthera* (Rydberg, 1901). The three species that Rydberg used to created the genus *Gymnadeniopsis* have recently been reassessed (Sheviak in *FNA*, 2002; Brown, 2003). Several differences are present that render them distinctive, including the presence of tubers on the roots as well as small tubercles on the column. The three species in this genus have occasionally been known as the frog orchids, and all three are found in Texas.

Key to the frog orchids, *Gymnadeniopsis*

1a flowers white; non-resupinate (lip uppermost) . . . . . **snowy orchis**, *Gymnadeniopsis nivea*, p. 64

1b flower yellow or green (rarely pale greenish white); flowers resupinate (lip lowermost) . . . 2

2a flowers yellow; lip acute, merely erose . . . . . **yellow fringeless orchis**, *Gymnadeniopsis integra*, p. 62

2b flowers green to straw colored to nearly white; lip three-toothed; spur swollen at the tip . . . . . **little club-spur orchis**, *Gymnadeniopsis clavellata*, p. 60

Gymnadeniopsis clavellata (Michaux) Rydberg var. *clavellata*

little club-spur orchis

forma *slaughteri* (P.M. Brown) P.M. Brown—white-flowered form
North American Native Orchid Journal 1(3): 200. 1995, as *Platanthera clavellata* var. *clavellata* forma *slaughteri* P.M. Brown, type: Arkansas
forma *wrightii* (Olive) P.M. Brown—spurless form
Bulletin of the Torrey Botanical Club 78(4): 289–291. 1951, as *Habenaria clavellata* var. *wrightii* Olive, type: North Carolina

Range: Wisconsin east to Maine, south to Texas and Georgia
Texas: Pineywoods: rare to occasional
Plant: terrestrial, 15–35 cm tall
Leaves: 2; cauline, ovate-lanceolate, 1–2 cm wide × 5–15 cm long, passing upward into bracts
Flowers: 5–15; arranged in a loose terminal raceme, flowers usually twisted to one side; sepals ovate, petals linear, enclosed within the sepals and forming a hood; lip oblong, the apex obscurely 3-lobed; perianth yellow-green or, in the forma *slaughteri*, white; individual flower size 0.5 cm, not including the 1 cm spur or the small swollen (clavate) tip; or, in the forma *wrightii*, the spur absent
Habitat: damp woods, streamsides, open, wet ditches
Flowering period: June through August

The **little club-spur orchis,** *Gymnadeniopsis clavellata,* is primarily a northeastern North American species that becomes increasingly rare as its range progresses southward and westward. The small, pale greenish flowers of the **little club-spur orchis** are very different from any other orchid we have, and they hold themselves at curious angles on the stem. The distinctive spur, with its swollen tip, is what gives this plant its common name. Plants of the nominate variety are found primarily in wooded swamps and occasionally in open fens and mesic prairies. *Gymnadeniopsis clavellata* var. *ophioglossoides* is found primarily in the northern and higher elevation areas of northeastern North America.

forma *slaughteri*   forma *wrightii*

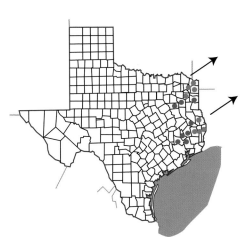

Gymnadeniopsis integra (Nuttall) Rydberg

yellow fringeless orchis

Range: New Jersey south to Florida, west to Texas
Texas: Pineywoods—rare to local
Globally Threatened
Plant: terrestrial, to 60 cm tall
Leaves: 1–2(3); cauline, lanceolate, keeled, conduplicate, 1–3 cm wide × 5–20 cm long, rapidly reduced to bracts within the inflorescence
Flowers: 30–65; arranged in a densely flowered terminal raceme; sepals ovate, petals oblong-ovate, enclosed within the dorsal sepal forming a hood; lip ovate, the margin erose; perianth bright yellow-orange; individual flower size 5–6 mm, not including the 6 mm spur
Habitat: open wet meadows, seeps, damp pine flatwoods
Flowering period: late July–September

Although the **yellow fringeless orchis,** *Gymnadeniopsis integra*, ranges from southern New Jersey to Texas, it is rapidly becoming one of the rarer orchids in North America. Habitat destruction, specifically the draining of wetlands for agriculture and business, is the primary cause of the decline. Sites throughout the range are very local and do not flower reliably each year. The plants of *G. integra* are not difficult to distinguish from the similarly colored fringed orchises (*Platanthera* spp.), as they are considerably smaller, with a slender, more compact, conical raceme of flowers, and lack the distinctive fringe on the margin of the lip. The **yellow fringeless orchis** in Texas has an interesting history as a specimen collected by Drummond prior to 1840 and labeled *Habenaria integra* actually proved to be *G. nivea* (Holmes, 1983). Conversely a specimen collected in 1950 in Hardin County originally labeled *H. integra* and subsequently annotated as *H. nivea* proved to be *G. integra*. Discoveries of the latter error and, subsequently, of the **yellow fringeless orchis** in Texas were made by Bridges and Orzell (1989).

Gymnadeniopsis nivea (Nuttall) Rydberg

snowy orchis

Range: southern New Jersey south to Florida, and west to Texas
Texas: Pineywoods, Gulf Prairies and Marshes, Blackland Prairies—
locally common in damp flatwoods
Plant: terrestrial, 20–60 cm tall
Leaves: 2–3; cauline, lanceolate, keeled, conduplicate, 1–3 cm wide
× 5–25 cm long
Flowers: 20–50; non-resupinate, arranged in a densely flowered ter-
minal raceme; sepals and petals oblong-ovate; lip uppermost, linear-
elliptic and bent backward midway; perianth stark, icy white; indi-
vidual flower size 8–10 mm, not including the slender 1.5 cm spur
Habitat: open wet meadows, prairies, seeps, damp pine flatwoods
Flowering period: late May–July

The **snowy orchis,** *Gymnadeniopsis nivea,* is a typical southeastern species and occurs in scattered locales throughout much of the
Gulf Coastal Plain element, often in prairie-like habitats and savannahs. Recently burned pine flatwoods are also an excellent habitat
in which to search for this orchid. The flower has the added feature
of being deliciously fragrant. The uppermost lip is unique among
the species of *Gymnadeniopsis, Habenaria,* and *Platanthera* found in
Texas and the Southeast. Hatch et al. (1990) also noted *G. nivea* (as
Platanthera nivea) for the High Plains region but it has never been
vouchered from that area and suitable habitat does not exist for this
species there. That region was omitted from the 2001 revision.

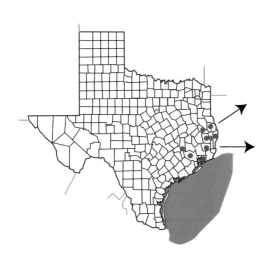

Habenaria

The genus *Habenaria* is pantropical and subtropical and consists of about 600 species. It reaches the northern limit of its range in North America in the southeastern United States. In its broadest sense, it has often included those species that are currently found in *Platanthera*, *Coeloglossum*, *Gymnadeniopsis*, and *Pseudorchis*. As treated here, in the narrow sense, the genus contains five species, three of which are found within the southeastern United States and the other two confined to central and southern Florida. Two of the North American species have been found in Texas, although only one is extant.

Key to the rein orchids, *Habenaria*

1a flowers white and green; lateral segments of the lip and petals deeply divided; plants of pine flatwoods . . . . . **Michaux's orchid**, *Habenaria quinqueseta*, p. 68

1b flower greenish yellow; segments deeply divided; plants of wet to aquatic habitats . . . . . **water-spider orchid**, *Habenaria repens*, p. 70

Habenaria quinqueseta (Michaux) Eaton

Michaux's orchid

Range: South Carolina south to Florida, and west to Texas; Mexico, West Indies, Central America
Texas: Pineywoods?—presumed extirpated
Plant: terrestrial, up to 30(50) cm tall
Leaves: 3–7; glossy bright green, elliptic, to 4–6 cm wide × 20 cm long; gradually reduced in size and passing to bracts within the inflorescence
Flowers: 15–25; in a loose raceme; sepals light green with dark green stripes, ovate to oblong; petals white with 2 linear divisions; lip white with 3 divisions; spur 5–8 cm long, but local clones may have longer spurs; individual flower size ca. 4 × 4 cm, not including the spur
Habitat: rich moist hardwood hammocks, pine flatwoods
Flowering period: August–September

Although widespread and locally common throughout much of northern Florida, **Michaux's orchid,** *Habenaria quinqueseta,* is one of the rarest orchids elsewhere within its range. A single collection from Texas was made by Charles Wright between 1837 and 1844 and is presumed to be from what is now known as the Big Thicket although Hatch (1991) indicates that it was from the Gulf Prairies and Marshes region. Abundant habitat abounds here for this species. *Habenaria quinqueseta* is a plant primarily of damp pinelands and hedgerows. The greenish white flowers are produced on a spike to 30+ cm tall and with up to 14 flowers, but more often with only 6–8 flowers. The spur typically is shorter than 5 cm. Colonies of non-flowering plants are often encountered, and easily overlooked, especially in open pine flatwoods. The flowers of *H. quinqueseta* have a very "square" aspect to them whereas those of the more southern, and closely allied, *H. macroceratitis* have a very "rectangular" aspect to them (Brown, 2002, 2004, 2005).

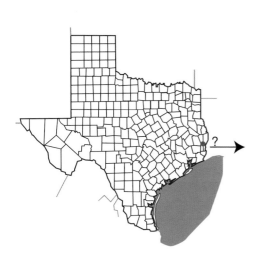

Habenaria repens Nuttall

water-spider orchid

Range: North Carolina south to Florida, west to southeastern Arkansas and Texas; Mexico, West Indies, Central America

Texas: Pineywoods, Gulf Prairies and Marshes, Post Oak Savannah, Blackland Prairies, South Texas Plains—widespread and often locally abundant

Plant: terrestrial or aquatic, up to 50 cm tall

Leaves: 3–8; yellow-green, linear-lanceolate, 1.0–2.5 cm wide × 3.0–20.0 cm long; rapidly reduced in size and passing to bracts within the inflorescence

Flowers: 10–50; in a densely flowered terminal raceme; sepals light green, ovate to oblong; petals greenish white, with 2 divisions; lip with 3 divisions, the central being shorter than the lateral divisions; spur slender, ca. 1.3 cm long; individual flower size ca. 2 × 2 cm, not including the spur

Habitat: open shorelines, seasonally wet grasslands, stagnant pools

Flowering period: January in the south, more typically May through October elsewhere

The **water-spider orchid,** *Habenaria repens*, is one of the few truly aquatic orchids in North America. Masses of several hundred floating plants can often be found and they also frequently colonize wet roadside ditches and canals. It is the most wide-ranging of the *Habenaria* species in the United States and is widespread throughout the Southeast, reaching the western limit of its range in central Texas.

Hexalectris

A genus of seven species that is found primarily in the southern United States and Mexico, *Hexalectris* is similar in appearance to another mycotrophic genus, *Corallorhiza*. Although not that closely related, each has a leafless stem lacking all chlorophyll that terminates in colorful flowers. The crested flowers on *Hexalectris* are much larger than those of *Corallorhiza*, and intricately more beautiful. All known species in the United States are found in Texas. Two species regularly produce cleistogamous flowers, i.e., closed or nearly closed. Catling (2004) provides the most complete treatment to date.

Key to the crested coralroots, *Hexalectris*

1a flowers chasmogamous (fully opened) . . . 2
1b flowers cleistogamous (closed and never opening) . . . 6

2a sepals, petals pink, color uniform without patterning or striping; lip pink with central portion white; ridges or crests white . . . . . **Greenman's crested coralroot**, *Hexalectris grandiflora*, p. 74
2b sepals, petals, and lip variously colored and patterned but never as above . . . 3

3a lip shallowly lobed . . . 4
3b lip deeply lobed . . . 5

4a sepals less than 12 mm long, faintly marked or striped if at all . . . . . **shining crested coralroot**, *Hexalectris nitida*, p. 76
4b sepals greater than 12 mm, prominently marked or striped . . . . . **crested coralroot**, *Hexalectris spicata* var. *spicata*, p. 80

5a petals and sepals strongly recurved . . . . . **recurved crested coralroot**, *Hexalectris revoluta* var. *revoluta*, p. 78
5b petals and sepals not recurved . . . . . **Texas purple-spike**, *Hexalectris warnockii*, p. 84

6a sepals less than 10(12) mm long, faintly marked or striped if at all . . . . . **shining crested coralroot**, *Hexalectris nitida*, p. 76
6b sepals greater than 10(12) mm long, marked or striped . . . . . **Arizona crested coralroot**, *Hexalectris spicata* var. *arizonica*, p. 82

Hexalectris grandiflora (A. Richard & Galeotti) L.O. Williams

Greenman's crested coralroot, giant coralroot, Greenman's cock's-comb

forma *luteoalba* P.M. Brown—whitish-yellow flowering form

McAllen International Orchid Society Journal 7(12): 6–7, type: Texas

Range: Texas; Mexico

Texas: Trans-Pecos Texas, Blackland Prairies—very rare and local

Plant: Stems pink, pink-red, or red-purple or, in the forma *luteoalba*, whitish yellow; 10–60 cm; sheathing bracts 3–5

Leaves: lacking

Flowers: 5–20; pink, magenta to crimson or, in the forma *luteoalba*, whitish yellow; sepals and petals slightly recurved, oblanceolate to elliptic, falcate; lip ovate to obovate, deeply 3-lobed, middle lobe cuneate, rounded; crests 5, white; flower size ca. 2.5 cm

Habitat: Moist canyons in pine-oak-juniper woodlands in leaf litter and humus at elevations of 700–2,500 m in west Texas and 200 m in central Texas

Flowering Time: late June through early September, depending on rainfall

Perhaps the showiest and most beautiful of the crested coralroots, *Hexalectris grandiflora*, **Greenman's crested coralroot,** has the largest individual flowers in the genus. The brilliant pink coloring makes the species unmistakable. Until recently the species was thought to be restricted to a few sites in the Trans-Pecos in the Davis and Chisos mountains. In 2005 it was discovered near Dallas in an area that is rich in *Hexalectris* species (Brown-Marsden, 2006). The documentation of **Greenman's crested coralroot** in an area more than 800 km from the known populations leaves many unanswered questions regarding distribution and the possibility of discovery in the Edward Plateau region that also hosts several other species of *Hexalectris*.

forma *luteoalba*

Dallas County

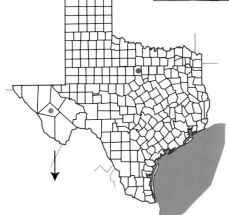

Hexalectris nitida L.O. Williams

shining crested coralroot, shining cock's-comb

Range: New Mexico, Texas; Mexico
Texas: Blackland Prairies, Cross Timbers and Prairies, Edwards Plateau, Trans-Pecos: rare and local
Plant: Stems pinkish, pale red, or brown-purple or, in a rare form, whitish-yellow, 10–32 cm tall with 3–5 sheathing bracts
Leaves: lacking
Flowers: 6–24, pink to purple or, in a rare form, whitish-yellow, with the sepals and petals spreading to recurved; most plants are chasmogamous with fully opened flowers but cleistogamous plants with essentially closed flowers are often found, especially in the Edwards Plateau region; lip shallowly 3-lobed with the middle lobe nearly rounded; crest 5–7, minimally raised, flower size ca. 1.5 cm
Habitat: Moist canyons in oak-juniper-pinyon pine woodlands growing in humus, often in decaying juniper needle litter
Flowering Time: June through much of August

Hexalectris nitida, the **shining crested coralroot**, occurs in all three of the *Hexalectris* "hot spots" in Texas—the Chisos and Glass mountains, on the Edwards Plateau, and in the Dallas area. Plants from the Edwards Plateau frequently have cleistogamous flowers, and open flowers are seen only occasionally, whereas both forms may be easily found in the Dallas area populations. Late spring rains often trigger flowering.

whitish-yellow form

Hexalectris revoluta Correll var. *revoluta*

recurved crested coralroot, Correll's cock's-comb

Range: Arizona, Texas; Mexico
Texas: Trans-Pecos—rare and local
Plant: Stems tan to pale pink to pale brown-purple, 30–50 cm tall with 3–5 sheathing bracts
Leaves: lacking
Flowers: 5–15(20); sepals and petals strongly recurved, tan to pinkish brown; lip broadly elliptic with a truncated apex, deeply 3-lobed, middle lobe white with purple and pale yellow near the base; with 3, 5, or 7 obscure white to yellow crests; flowers ca. 2 cm
Habitat: Oak-juniper-pinyon pine woodlands in leaf litter and humus, occasionally in rocky, open terrain at 1,000–1,600 m elevation
Flower Time: May through August; often rain dependent

Restricted in Texas to the Guadalupe and Chisos mountains of the Trans-Pecos, the **recurved crested coralroot**, *Hexalectris revoluta*, has a less densely flowered raceme than the more widespread *H. nitida*, and the petals and sepals are markedly more recurved, with the lip somewhat more deeply lobed. This is the most locally distributed species of *Hexalectris* in Texas, and the recently described var. *colemanii* (Catling, 2004) that is known only from Arizona and New Mexico decreases the range of the nominate variety even more.

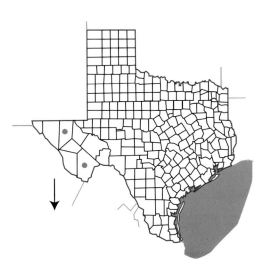

Hexalectris spicata (Walter) Barnhardt var. *spicata*

crested coralroot

> forma *albolabia* P.M. Brown—white-lipped form
> *North American Native Orchid Journal* 1(1): 10. 1995, type: Florida
> forma *lutea* P.M. Brown—yellow-flowered form
> *North American Native Orchid Journal* 10: 23. 2004, type: Florida
> forma *wilderi* P.M. Brown, albino form
> *North American Native Orchid Journal* 10: 23. 2004, type, Florida

Range: Arizona, Missouri; southern Illinois east to Maryland, south to Florida, west to Texas; Mexico

Texas: Pineywoods, Gulf Prairies and Marshes, Post Oak Savannah, Blackland Prairies, Cross Timbers and Prairies, Edwards Plateau, Trans-Pecos—widespread, although never common

Plant: terrestrial, mycotrophic, 10–80 cm tall; stems yellow-brown to deep purple or, in the forma *wilderi*, the stems white or, in the forma *lutea*, yellow

Leaves: lacking

Flowers: 5–25; sepals and petals brown-yellow with purple striations; lip pale yellow with purple stripes (crests), 3-lobed, the lateral lobes incurved or, in the forma *albolabia,* the lip pure white with pale yellow striations and the petals and sepals mahogany or, in the forma *wilderi*, the flowers white or, in the forma *lutea*, the flowers yellow; individual flower size 2.5–4.0 cm

Habitat: dry, open hardwood forest, especially under live oak

Flowering period: late April through August depending on rainfall and habitat

The **crested coralroot,** *Hexalectris spicata*, is by far the handsomest of all the mycotrophic orchids (crested coralroots and coralroots), and one of the most beautiful of the orchids in Texas. One of several species of entirely mycotrophic orchids in North America, the plants lack all traces of chlorophyll and therefore often blend in with their surroundings. From a distance they may appear to be just dead sticks, but upon close examination the striking and colorful flowers reveal an intricate pattern of crests upon the lips. Plants have a preference for live oak woodlands and the number of plants, depending on the rainfall in a given season, may vary greatly from year to year. *Hexalectris spicata* var. *arizonica* occurs from central Texas westward.

forma *wilderi*

forma *lutea*

Hexalectris spicata (Walter) Barnhardt var. *arizonica* (S. Watson) Catling & Engel

Arizona crested coralroot

Range: Arizona, New Mexico, Texas; Mexico

Texas: Pineywoods, Blackland Prairies, Cross Timbers and Prairies, Edwards Plateau, Trans-Pecos—rare and local

Plant: Stems pinkish red, pale pink-yellow, or pink-white, 15–70 cm with 3–5 sheathing bracts

Leaves: lacking

Flowers: 5–20, yellow-tan, pinkish, red-brown, or purple-brown with dull magenta, faint pink-brown to purple-brown veins; usually cleistogamous or rarely chasmogamous; sepals and petals usually not recurved on open flowers, lip white or creamy white with darkly colored veins and paler margin; crests pale; overall flower size on closed flowers ca. 1 cm, open flowers 2 cm

Habitat: organic mesic to dry soil over limestone or sandstone, in juniper, pine, and oak woodlands at elevations of 100–600 m

Flowering Time: early May to early August

This autogamous and florally reduced segregate of *Hexalectris spicata* has been thought to be of hybrid origin, derived either from *H. spicata* var. *spicata* and *H. nitida*, or less likely from the former taxon and *H. revoluta* (Catling and Engel, 1993). In Texas this plant tends to begin flowering later than the typical variety, and may be seen in June and July.

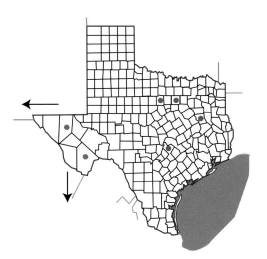

Hexalectris warnockii Ames & Correll

Texas purple-spike

forma *lutea* Catling
Native Orchid Conference Journal 1(2): 5–25. 2004. type: Arizona

Range: Arizona, Texas; Mexico
Texas: Blackland Prairies, Edwards Plateau, Trans-Pecos—widespread and local
Plant: Stems dark red-purple, 15–40 cm; sheathing bracts 2–4; floral bracts lanceolate to ovate
Leaves: lacking
Flowers: 3–10; sepals and petals spreading, dark purple to maroon or, in the forma *lutea*, yellow; lip ovate, deeply 3-lobed with the margins maroon, and centrally white with purple or maroon veins or, in the forma *lutea*, yellow, middle lobe white, the margins strongly undulate, crests 5, yellow-margined and very prominent
Habitat: Shaded slopes and dry, rocky creek beds in canyons, in leaf mold in oak-juniper-pinyon pine woodlands
Flowering Period: June through September

Although fewer flowered than many of the other species of *Hexalectris,* the **Texas purple-spike**, *Hexalectris warnockii*, has individual flowers that are some of the most beautiful of the genus. With their striking dark purple petals and sepals and contrasting white lip with its prominent yellow crests, it is unmistakable in the field. Again, like several other species in the genus, plants grow in the Davis and Chisos mountains of the Trans-Pecos region, the Edwards Plateau, and the Dallas area. *Hexalectris warnockii* was first collected by Mueller in 1932 and served as the type for the species named by Ames and Correll in 1943 based upon a specimen collected by Barton Warnock in 1937 and named in his honor.

forma *lutea*

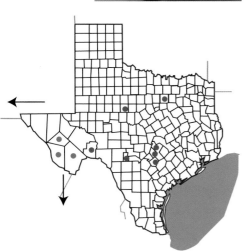

Isotria

The genus *Isotria* consists of only two species, both found in the eastern half of the United States and adjacent Canada. They are related to the genera *Pogonia* and, more distantly, *Triphora*, and early in their history were placed in the genus *Pogonia*. Only one species, *I. verticillata*, occurs in Texas.

Isotria verticillata (Willdenow) Rafinesque

large whorled pogonia

Range: Michigan east to Maine, south to Texas and Florida

Texas: Pineywoods, Gulf Prairies and Marshes, Post Oak Savannah, Blackland Prairies—rare and local

Plant: terrestrial; to 20 cm tall in flower, mature plants expanded, up to 40 cm tall

Leaves: 5 or 6; in a whorl at the top of the stem, up to 3 cm wide × 9 cm long

Flowers: 1, rarely 2; sepals purplish, wide-spreading, slender and spidery; petals pale yellow, ovate, arched over the column; lip white, edged in purple with a fleshy, yellow central ridge; individual flowers ca. 10 cm across

Habitat: deciduous forests

Flowering period: late April through much of May, usually before the trees fully leaf out

The **large whorled pogonia,** *Isotria verticillata,* will often form colonies of considerable numbers of stems because the plants produce stolons. Seed set from the flowers is minimal and few fruits are usually found in these large colonies. The fanciful flowers of *I. verticillata* are unmistakable and the plants have the unusual habit of nearly doubling in both leaf surface and height after flowering.

Listera

The genus *Listera* comprises twenty-five species that occur in the cooler climes of both the northern and southern hemispheres. Eight species in the genus grow in the United States and Canada, one of which, *Listera ovata*, is a very common species in Europe that has become naturalized in southern Ontario. We have only one species in Texas. Recent trends in Europe are to nest species in *Listera* with the genus *Neottia* (Pridgeon et al., 2005). That position has not been taken by most North American orchidists.

Listera australis Lindley

southern twayblade

> forma *scottii* P.M. Brown—many-leaved form
> *North American Native Orchid Journal* 6(1): 63–64. 2000, type:
> Florida
>
> forma *trifolia* P.M. Brown—3-leaved form
> *North American Native Orchid Journal* 1(1): 11. 1995, type: Vermont
>
> forma *viridis* P.M. Brown—green-flowered form
> *North American Native Orchid Journal* 6(1): 63–64. 2000, type:
> Florida

Range: Quebec to Nova Scotia, and south to Florida and Texas

Texas: Pineywoods—rare to local

Plant: terrestrial in damp soils, up to 35 cm tall

Leaves: 2; opposite, midway on the stem, green, usually flushed with red, ovate 2.0 cm wide × 3.5 cm long or, in the forma *scottii*, leaves several scattered along the stem or, in the forma *trifolia*, leaves 3 in a whorl

Flowers: 5–40; in a terminal raceme; sepals purple, ovate; petals purple, narrowly spatulate, recurved; lip purple, linear, split into 2 slender filaments or, in the forma *viridis*, flowers entirely lime-green; individual flower size 6–10 mm

Habitat: rich, damp woodlands, often in sphagnum moss

Flowering period: late winter into early spring: February into early April

A spring ephemeral, the **southern twayblade**, *Listera australis*, appears quickly in March and early April. Plants have a preference for damp, often seasonally flooded, deciduous woodlands. In many sites, it prefers the presence of sphagnum moss. Although most populations consist of fewer than a dozen plants, occasional sites may have several hundred individuals and contain an amazing degree of variation with all described forma present. The plants at many of these larger sites tend to be more robust than elsewhere, and flower over a very long period of time, forming dense, lush clumps. The species sets seed and senesces very quickly so that a month after flowering there usually is no sign of the plants until next season.

forma *viridis*

forma *scottii*

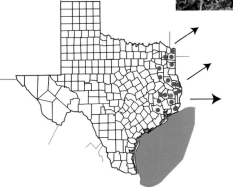

Malaxis

The genus *Malaxis* is a cosmopolitan one of about 300 species. Eleven species are found in Canada and the United States, and three occur in Texas. Three additional species are found in nearby Arizona and New Mexico and two Mexican species near the Texas border. See page 184 for more details. All species have a pseudobulbous stem that is more evident in the subtropical and tropical species. In the temperate species it appears more cormlike. The genus possesses some of the smallest flowers in the Orchidaceae, many not more than a few millimeters in any dimension.

Key to the adder's-mouths, *Malaxis*

1a   flower cranberry-red to purple . . . . . **Wendt's adder's-mouth**, *Malaxis wendtii*, p. 100

1b   flowers green . . . 2

2a   inflorescence a dense cylindrical spike . . . . . **rat-tailed adder's-mouth**, *Malaxis soulei*, p. 96

2b   inflorescence an open, flat-topped raceme . . . . . **green adder's-mouth**, *Malaxis unifolia*, p. 98

Malaxis soulei L.O. Williams

rat-tailed adder's-mouth; mountain malaxis

Range: Arizona, New Mexico, Texas; Mexico, Central America.

Texas: Trans-Pecos—rare and local

Plant: 11–60 cm tall, the stem swollen at the base into a (pseudo)bulb

Leaf: 1, at middle or lower third of stem, (1)2–5.4(6) cm wide × 2.4–15.0 cm long, ovate-elliptic or oblanceolate, with a prominent keel on the lower side

Flowers: 40–160, green to yellowish green in a dense cylindrical spike, non-resupinate; lip ovate with auricles at the base, apex usually 3-toothed

Habitat: moist, wooded canyons and ravines, rocky open slopes at moderate to high elevations (2,000–3,000 m)

Flowering Period: July into September

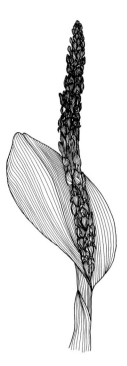

Malaxis soulei, **rat-tailed adder's-mouth**, known only in Texas from the Davis Mountains in the Trans-Pecos, is unmistakable in a genus that may often have similar species.

The slender green spike with numerous tightly packed flowers remains on the plant until the fruiting capsules are fully ripened. Unlike most other species of *Malaxis* the sessile flowers are distinctive. The name *Malaxis macrostachya* has been applied to *M. soulei* (Luer, 1975; Liggio and Liggio, 1999). The nomenclatural history surrounding the epithet *macrostachya* is unclear, and therefore it is a *nomen confusum* and should not be applied to this species (Williams, 1965).

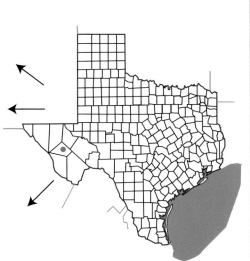

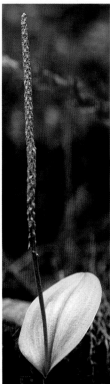

Malaxis unifolia Michaux

green adder's-mouth

forma *bifolia* Mousley—2-leaved form
Orchid Review 35: 163. 1927, type: Quebec
forma *variegata* Mousley—variegated-leaf form
Orchid Review 35: 164. 1927, type: Quebec

Range: Manitoba east to Newfoundland south to Texas and Florida; Mexico

Texas: Pineywoods—local to occasional, but often overlooked

Plant: terrestrial; 8–25+ cm tall, stem swollen at the base into a (pseudo)bulb

Leaves: 1 or, in the forma *bifolia*, 2; ovate, keeled, to 6 cm wide × 9 cm long, midway on the stem; green or, in the forma *variegata*, with white markings

Flowers: 5–80+; arranged in a compact raceme, elongating as flowering progresses; sepals oblanceolate, green; petals linear and positioned behind the flower; lip green, broadly ovate to cordate, with extended auricles at the base and bidentate at the summit; individual flower size 2–4 mm

Habitat: damp woodlands, moist open barrens, mossy glades, fens, and sphagnum bogs

Flowering period: late April through much of June

Often considered one of the most widespread and common orchids in eastern North America, the **green adder's-mouth**, *Malaxis unifolia*, may be a real challenge to find. Plants vary greatly in size and their natural camouflage blends in with much of the surrounding vegetation. Only when growing in open mossy barrens do they really stand out. The **green adder's-mouth** is widely scattered within the Pineywoods region and easily overlooked. Large plants are not uncommon and they, like most members of the genus, bear up to 100 flowers and present them over a long period of time—up to two months. Hatch et al. (1990) also noted *M. unifolia* for the High Plains region but it has never been vouchered from that area. That region was omitted from the 2001 revision and Gulf Plains and Marshes was added.

forma *bifolia*

forma *variegata*

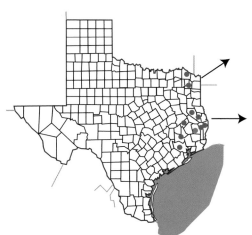

Malaxis wendtii Salazar

Wendt's adder's-mouth

Range: Texas; Mexico
Texas: Trans-Pecos—very rare
Plant: 16–45 cm, stem swollen at the base into a (pseudo)bulb **Leaf**: 1, within the lower third of stem; ovate or ovate-lanceolate, up to 2.0–4.5 cm wide × 4.1–8.5(10) cm long
Flowers: 14–141 in a loose raceme; deep maroon or greenish maroon; sepals papillose, not glabrous; petals strongly recurved, linear to filiform; lip linear to linear-lanceolate, base with auricles broad and diverging, apex narrowly acuminate; overall flower size 2–3 mm
Habitat: Open coniferous and mixed forests on dry slopes; 2,000 m
Flowering Period: July–September

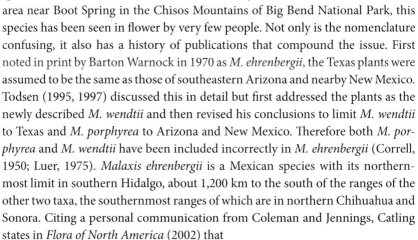

Malaxis wendtii, **Wendt's adder's-mouth**, must vie with a few Florida species for the title of rarest orchid species in the United States. Confined to a very local area near Boot Spring in the Chisos Mountains of Big Bend National Park, this species has been seen in flower by very few people. Not only is the nomenclature confusing, it also has a history of publications that compound the issue. First noted in print by Barton Warnock in 1970 as *M. ehrenbergii*, the Texas plants were assumed to be the same as those of southeastern Arizona and nearby New Mexico. Todsen (1995, 1997) discussed this in detail but first addressed the plants as the newly described *M. wendtii* and then revised his conclusions to limit *M. wendtii* to Texas and *M. porphyrea* to Arizona and New Mexico. Therefore both *M. porphyrea* and *M. wendtii* have been included incorrectly in *M. ehrenbergii* (Correll, 1950; Luer, 1975). *Malaxis ehrenbergii* is a Mexican species with its northernmost limit in southern Hidalgo, about 1,200 km to the south of the ranges of the other two taxa, the southernmost ranges of which are in northern Chihuahua and Sonora. Citing a personal communication from Coleman and Jennings, Catling states in *Flora of North America* (2002) that

> The following criteria are used to separate *Malaxis wendtii* from *M. porphyrea*: the sepals of *M. wendtii* are papillose while the sepals of *M. porphyrea* are essentially glabrous, although they have prominent cell structures that may appear to be very small papillae; the lip of *M. wendtii* is linear to linear-lanceolate with a narrowly acuminate apex, and the auricles at the base of the lip are broad and diverging, while the lip of *M. porphyrea* is nearly

triangular to triangular-lanceolate with a broadly acuminate apex, and the auricles at the base of the lip are narrow and nearly parallel. Also, *M. wendtii* has a denser inflorescence and the flowers are not quite as intensely colored as in *M. porphyrea*.

Tamayo and Szlachetko (1998) have recently split the genus *Malaxis* into several additional genera and has included *M. wendtii* in the new genus *Tamayorkis*. This position has not been universally embraced at this time. *Malaxis wendtii* was named in honor of Tom Wendt of the University of Texas, who collected the type specimens in northern Mexico.

Platanthera

The genus *Platanthera* comprises about forty North American and Eurasian species, primarily of temperate climes, and is one of the major segregate genera traditionally placed by many botanists within *Habenaria*. It is the largest genus of orchids in the United States and Canada but with only six species found in Texas. The plants are distinguished from *Habenaria* by their lack of both basal rosettes and tubers or tuberoid roots. Many of the species have large, colorful, showy flowers in tall spikes or racemes. There are several sections to the genus but the most prominent is the section Blephariglottis, the fringed orchises. There are two groups within this section: those species with an entire, or unlobed, lip, and those with a three-parted lip.

Note: nearly all species of *Platanthera* can be found in both full sun and deeply shaded habitats. Plants in the sun tend to be shorter and have more densely flowered inflorescences, with the leaves more upright, whereas those growing in shaded areas tend to be taller and have elongated, loosely flowered inflorescences with spreading leaves. The individual flower size remains the same, but the overall appearance of the plants can be markedly different—to the point that some observers initially think they have two different species!

Key to the fringed and rein orchises, *Platanthera*

1a lip with a distinct tubercle . . . 2

1b lip lacking a tubercle . . . 3

2a lip ovate; bracts generally equal to or shorter than the flowers . . . . . **southern tubercled rein orchis**, *Platanthera flava* var. *flava*, p. 112

2b lip oblong; bracts generally longer than the flowers . . . . . **northern tubercled rein orchis**, *Platanthera flava* var. *herbiola*, p. 114

3a margin of lip fringed, flowers orange or yellow . . . 4

3b flowers green or white . . . 6

4a spur distinctly longer than the lip . . . . . **orange fringed orchis**, *Platanthera ciliaris*, p. 106

4b spur equal to or distinctly shorter than the lip . . . 5

5a spur equal to the lip in length, orifice keyhole-shaped . . . . . **Chapman's fringed orchis**, *Platanthera chapmanii*, p. 104

5b spur distinctly shorter than the length of the lip; orifice rounded . . . . . **orange crested orchis**, *Platanthera cristata*, p. 110

6a flowers green to greenish white to greenish yellow; lip three-parted . . . . . **green fringed orchis, ragged orchis**, *Platanthera lacera*, p. 116

6b flowers white, lip undivided . . . . . **southern white fringed orchis**, *Platanthera conspicua*, p. 108

Platanthera chapmanii (Small) Luer *emend.* Folsom

Chapman's fringed orchis

Range: southeastern Georgia, Florida, and eastern Texas
Texas: Pineywoods—local in the Big Thicket area
Globally Threatened
Plant: terrestrial, to 100(110) cm tall
Leaves: 2–4; cauline, lanceolate 0.75–4.0 cm wide × 5.0–25.0 cm long, rapidly reduced to bracts within the inflorescence
Flowers: 30–75(-92); arranged in a dense terminal raceme; sepals ovate, petals linear, the apex erose to slightly fringed, enclosed within the sepals forming a hood; lip ovate with a delicately fringed margin; perianth brilliant orange; individual flower size 2 cm, not including the 0.8–1.7 cm spur, typically parallel to the ovary; column bent forward with a pronounced hook; orifice keyhole-shaped
Habitat: open wet meadows, roadside ditches and seeps, and pine/palmetto flatwoods
Flowering period: late July to early September

Not always easy to identify, **Chapman's fringed orchis**, *Platanthera chapmanii*, arose ancestrally as a hybrid between *Platanthera ciliaris*, the **orange fringed orchis,** and *P. cristata*, the **orange crested orchis.** Many years of adaptation have resulted in a pollinator-specific, stable, reproducing species. Many texts still cite it as *P.* ×*chapmanii*, referring to its perceived hybrid status (see Folsom, 1984; Brown and Folsom, 2004 for details). Because of its origins, this species falls morphologically between the two ancestors. The two best characters are the spur, equal in length to the lip, and the bent column. Also, unlike *P.* ×*channellii*, the true contemporary hybrid of *P. ciliaris* and *P. cristata*, *P. chapmanii* occurs in pure stands. From a global standpoint this is one of the rarest orchids we know. It has recently been classified as G1G2 by The Nature Conservancy. *Platanthera chapmanii* is known from two (historical) sites in southern Georgia, several scattered, although substantial, sites in northern Florida, and a few small stands in four counties of eastern Texas, where it was formerly more abundant. Hybrids with *P. cristata* are known as *P.* ×*apalachicola* and those with *P. ciliaris* as *P.* ×*osceola*. Hatch et al. (1990) also noted *P. chapmanii* for the High Plains region but it has never been vouchered from that area and suitable habitat does not exist for this rare species there. That region was omitted from the 2001 revision and Gulf Plains and Marshes was added. See page 279 for additional information.

Platanthera ciliaris (Linnaeus) Lindley

orange fringed orchis

Range: southern Michigan east to Massachusetts, south to Florida and Texas

Texas: Pineywoods, Gulf Prairies and Marshes, Post Oak Savannah, Blackland Prairies, Cross Timbers and Prairies— scattered and local

Plant: terrestrial, 25–100+ cm tall

Leaves: 2–5; cauline, lanceolate, 1–5 cm wide × 5–30 cm long, gradually reduced to bracts within the inflorescence

Flowers: 30–75; arranged in a dense terminal raceme; sepals ovate, petals linear, fringed at the tip, enclosed within the sepals forming a hood; lip ovate with a delicately fringed, filiform margin; perianth deep yellow to orange; individual flower size 4 cm, not including the 2.5–3.5 cm spur which typically is loosely descending; the column tapering to a point

Habitat: open wet meadows, roadside ditches and seeps, and pine flatwoods

Flowering period: late July and often into September in the south

The brilliant, deep yellow to orange plumes of the **orange fringed orchis**, *Platanthera ciliaris*, can be a meter in height. Scattered populations are well known from throughout eastern Texas. *Platanthera ciliaris* has a preference for areas that stay moist to damp in the hot, dry days of summer; the thriftiness of populations varies from year to year. Because the **southern white fringed orchis**, *P. conspicua*, is considered historical in Texas and then documented only from the Houston area, P. ×*lueri* would be most unlikely. Hybrids with *P. cristata*, the **orange crested orchis**, are known as *P.* ×*channellii* and have been found in Texas. Hatch et al. (1990) also noted *P. chapmanii* for the High Plains region but it has never been vouchered from that area. That region was omitted from the 2001 revision and Gulf Plains and Marshes was added.

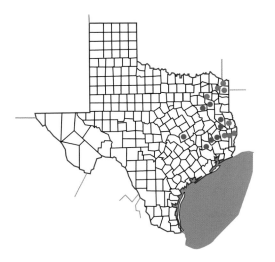

Platanthera conspicua (Nash) P.M. Brown

southern white fringed orchis

Range: southeastern North Carolina south along the Coastal Plain to eastern Texas
Texas: Gulf Prairies and Marshes—extirpated
Plant: terrestrial, 25–100 cm tall
Leaves: 2–4 cauline, lanceolate 1–5 cm wide × 5–35 cm long, rapidly reduced to bracts within the inflorescence
Flowers: 30–65; arranged in a dense terminal raceme; sepals ovate, petals linear, enclosed within the sepals forming a hood; lip ovate with a delicately fringed margin narrowed to a distinct isthmus at the base; perianth pure white; individual flower size 3 cm, not including the 3–4 cm spur
Habitat: open wet meadows, roadside ditches and seeps, and pine flatwoods
Flowering period: August to early October

One of a handful of species considered historical or of cryptic distribution in Texas, the **southern white fringed orchis,** Platanthera conspicua, would be unmistakable if rediscovered. The fringed orchids of eastern and central North America present some of the showiest orchids of the summer and the stately, snow-white plumes of the **southern white fringed orchis** are no exception. Widely scattered throughout the southeastern Coastal Plain and sparingly to southern Louisiana, this species, like other species of fringed orchids, has fallen victim to construction. Typically it prefers open damp meadows, pine flatwoods, and seeps; it is now most frequently found in narrow roadside ditches and open sphagnous areas within the woodlands. Plants flower over a long period of time in mid to late summer. See the entry for Platanthera hybrids on page 120 for plants with lemon or pale cinnamon-colored flowers.

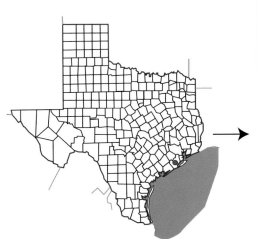

Platanthera cristata (Michaux) Lindley

orange crested orchis

forma *straminea* P.M. Brown—pale yellow-flowered form
North American Native Orchid Journal 1(1): 12. 1995, type: New Jersey

Range: southeastern Massachusetts south to Florida, and west to eastern Texas; primarily on the Coastal Plain

Texas: Pineywoods, Gulf Prairies and Marshes, Post Oak Savannah, Blackland Prairies, Cross Timbers and Prairies—rare and scattered throughout

Plant: terrestrial, to 80 cm tall

Leaves: 2–4; cauline, lanceolate, 1–3 × 5–20 cm, rapidly reduced to bracts within the inflorescence

Flowers: 30–80; arranged in a loose to dense terminal raceme; sepals ovate, petals spatulate with the margin of the apex crested, enclosed within the sepals forming a hood; lip long triangular-ovate with a coarsely lacerate margin; perianth deep yellow to orange or, in the forma *straminea*, pale yellow; individual flower size 5–7 mm, not including the 7 mm spur which is typically curved; the column is very short and the face flattened

Habitat: open wet meadows, roadside ditches and seeps, and pine flatwoods

Flowering period: late June to late September

A smaller and perhaps more refined version of the **orange fringed orchis**, *Platanthera ciliaris*, the **orange crested orchis**, *P. cristata*, is a common species of the southeastern Coastal Plain and often occurs without other related species nearby. In the prairies and plains plants have occasionally been found in open pine flatwoods, although it can also be found in damp meadows, ditches, and roadside seeps. The raceme is usually about 2.5 cm in diameter and the spur is always shorter than the lip and typically curved forward, whereas in *P. ciliaris* the loosely descending spur is always much longer than the lip, and the raceme is 4.5+ cm in diameter. Hatch et al. (1990) also noted *P. cristata* for the High Plains region but it has never been vouchered from that area and suitable habitat does not exist for this rare species there. That region was omitted from the 2001 revision and Gulf Plains and Marshes was added.

Hybrids with *Platanthera ciliaris*, the **orange fringed orchis**, are known as *P.* ×*channellii* and have been found in Texas. Hybrids with *P. conspicua*, *P.* ×*beckneri*, are exceedingly unlikely to be found, given the current status of *P. conspicua* in Texas (see page 120).

forma *straminea*

Platanthera flava (Linnaeus) Lindley var. *flava*

southern tubercled orchis

Range: southwestern Nova Scotia; Missouri, east to Maryland, south to Florida and Texas
Texas: Pineywoods, Gulf Prairies and Marshes—local and scattered throughout the area
Plant: terrestrial, 10–60 cm tall
Leaves: 2–4; cauline, nearly basal, lanceolate, 1–4 cm wide × 5–20 cm long, rapidly reduced to bracts within the inflorescence
Flowers: 10–40; arranged in a loose to dense terminal raceme; sepals and petals ovate, enclosed within the dorsal sepal forming a hood; lip ovate with a prominent tubercle in the center; perianth yellow-green; individual flower size 6–7 mm, not including the 8 mm spur
Habitat: open wet meadows, roadside ditches and seeps, swamps and shaded floodplains
Flowering period: late April in the south–July northward

Platanthera flava var. *flava*, the **southern tubercled orchis**, is equally at home in shaded, wet woodlands, streamsides, and bright and sunny, open, damp roadsides. Although the flowers are identical in both habitats, the habit of the plant varies greatly. Those in shaded habitats tend to be tall and slender, with flowers spaced out along the stem, whereas those in sunnier habitats have flower spikes and leaves that are very compact and crowded. The flowers in the shade tend to be very green in color and those in the sun much more yellow, tending toward chartreuse. However, in both instances, that distinctive tubercled lip is always prominent. Hatch et al. (1990) also noted *P. flava* for the High Plains region but it has never been vouchered from that area.

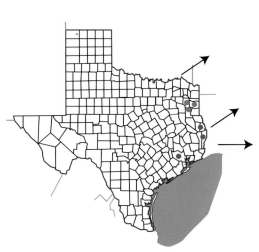

Platanthera flava (Linnaeus) Lindley var. *herbiola* (R. Brown) Luer

northern tubercled orchis

forma *lutea* (Boivin) Whiting & Catling—yellow-flowered form
Naturaliste Canadien 109(2): 278. 1982, type: Ontario

Range: Minnesota east to Nova Scotia, south to Texas and Georgia; south in the Appalachian Mountains

Texas: Sabine County; rare

Plant: terrestrial, 10–50 cm tall

Leaves: 3–5; cauline, nearly basal, lanceolate 2–5 cm wide × 8–20 cm long, rapidly reduced to bracts within the inflorescence

Flowers: 15–45; arranged in a loose to dense terminal raceme; sepals and petals ovate, enclosed within the dorsal sepal and forming a hood; lip oblong with a prominent tubercle near the base and triangular lobes on either side; perianth grass-green or, in the forma *lutea*, distinctly yellow; individual flower size 6–7 mm, not including the 5–7 mm spur

Habitat: open wet meadows, roadside ditches and seeps, swamps and shaded floodplains

Flowering period: late April into May

Platanthera flava var. *herbiola*, the **northern tubercled orchis**, is an obscure, grass-green, fragrant species that was once considered one of the rarer orchids in eastern North America. As the result of intensive field searches by many individuals, we now know of some large, stable populations in several states. The northern variety of the **tubercled orchis** is at the southwestern extreme of its range in Sabine County, Texas. Its sweet, perfume-like fragrance is often detected before the plant is actually seen. The nominate variety *flava* occurs primarily in the southeastern and south central United States with disjunct populations in southwestern Nova Scotia and southern Ontario.

Platanthera flava var. *herbiola*, the **northern tubercled orchis**, was found by Cliff and Sandee Pelchat in 2002. It differs from the nominate variety in having an oblong, rather than square, lip and the floral bracts exceed the flowers. Habitat and flowering period are the same as var. *flava*.

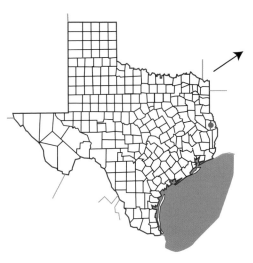

Platanthera lacera (Michaux) G. Don

green fringed orchis, ragged orchis

Range: Manitoba east to Newfoundland, south to Texas and Georgia

Texas: Pineywoods—very rare

Plant: terrestrial, 20–80 cm tall

Leaves: 3–6; cauline, lanceolate, keeled, 2.5–5.0 cm wide × 8.0–24.0 cm long, passing into bracts

Flowers: 12–40+, highly variable; arranged in a loose to dense terminal raceme; sepals obovate, the petals oblong, upright, usually with entire margins; lip three-parted and deeply lacerate; perianth varies from green to nearly yellow or white; individual flower size ca. 1.5–3.0 cm, not including the 1.6–2.3 cm spur, the orifice nearly square

Habitat: open wet meadows, roadside ditches and seeps, mountain meadows

Flowering period: June through mid-July

The least conspicuous of the fringed orchises, the **green fringed orchis**, *Platanthera lacera*, is one of the rarest orchids in Texas. Its discovery in 1946 by Donovan and Helen Correll remains as the only known record for the species in Texas. Flowering in early summer typically in damp meadows, open wet woods, and roadside ditches, the flower color is highly variable in many shades of green and some plants are nearly white.

Hybrids

Note: *Platanthera ×beckneri* and *P. ×lueri* are included here in the hopes that observations of these hybrids will eventually lead to the rediscovery of the white-flowered parent, *P. conspicua*.

Platanthera ×apalachicola P.M. Brown & S. Stewart
Apalachicola hybrid fringed orchis
(*P. chapmanii × P. cristata*)
> North American Native Orchid Journal 9: 35. 2003, type: Florida

Platanthera ×apalachicola is locally common in northern Florida where both parents frequently grow together. They usually occur as individuals and may appear within stands of *P. chapmanii* as smaller flowered, more slender plants, or within stands of *P. cristata* as larger flowered, more robust individuals. The hooked column of *P. chapmanii* is usually dominant but the spur is intermediate in length and position.

Platanthera ×beckneri P.M. Brown
Beckner's hybrid fringed orchis
(*P. conspicua × P. cristata*)
> North American Native Orchid Journal 8: 3–14. 2002, type: Florida

These small, pale yellow to cream-colored plants of *Platanthera ×beckneri* may be found as isolated individuals or in hybrid swarms. The TAMU *Digital Flora of Texas* (Hatch, ca. 2000) lists *P. ×canbyi*. At the time this name was posted on the Internet it would have been the correct name for the hybrid between *P. blephariglottis* var. *conspicua* and *P. cristata*, but because the former has not been seen in Texas since its original collection by Moyer in the early 1900s, evidence of the hybrid (*P. ×beckneri*) would be most encouraging in searches for a current site for *P. conspicua*.

Platanthera ×*channellii* Folsom
Channell's hybrid fringed orchis
(*P. ciliaris* × *P. cristata*)
> *Orquidea* (Mex.) 9(2): 344. 1984, type: Alabama

This hybrid and the species *Platanthera chapmanii* can be difficult to tell apart. One of the best ways is to look about and see which other species are growing nearby. If all the plants observed are the same, and within the range of *P. chapmanii*, it is most likely *P. chapmanii*, whereas if it is a colony of mixed species and only a few intermediate plants are present, it is more likely to be *P.* ×*channellii*.

Platanthera ×*lueri* P.M. Brown
Luer's hybrid fringed orchis
(*P. conspicua* × *P. ciliaris*)
> *North American Native Orchid Journal* 8: 3–14. 2002, type: Florida

Platanthera ×*lueri* is the southeastern counterpart to the more northern and inland *Platanthera* ×*bicolor*, with a similar range of color from rich cream and lemon to coffee. As mentioned above, this hybrid is included in hopes of leading to extant plants of *P. conspicua*.

Platanthera ×*osceola* P.M. Brown & S. Stewart
Osceola hybrid fringed orchis
(*P. chapmanii* × *P. ciliaris*)
> *North American Native Orchid Journal* 9: 35. 2003, type: Florida

This hybrid is known primarily from the Osceola National Forest in northern Florida where both parents are found growing together. Plants of the hybrid usually occur as individuals and may appear within stands of *Platanthera chapmanii* as larger flowered, more robust plants with decidedly longer spurs or within stands of *P. ciliaris* as smaller, more compactly flowered individuals. The hooked column of *P. chapmanii* is not as dominant as in *P.* ×*apalachicola*.

Pogonia

This is a small genus of only three species, found in both Asia and North America. Formerly the genus included those species, among others, that are now treated in *Triphora*, *Isotria*, and *Cleistes*, although some current authors are again including *Isotria* and *Cleistes*. We have only a single species in the United States and Canada, *Pogonia ophioglossoides*, which has one of the broadest ranges of any North American orchid.

Pogonia ophioglossoides Ker-Gawler

rose pogonia; snakemouth orchid

forma *albiflora* Rand & Redfield—white-flowered form
Flora of Mount Desert Island 152. 1894, type: Maine
forma *brachypogon* (Fernald) P.M. Brown—short-bearded
form
Rhodora 23: 245. 1922, type: Nova Scotia
Range: Manitoba east to Newfoundland, south to Texas and
Florida
Texas: Pineywoods, Post Oak Savannah—locally abundant,
especially in eastern counties
Plant: terrestrial, 8–35 cm tall
Leaves: 1, rarely 2; cauline, ovate, placed midway on the stem,
6–10 cm wide × 2 cm long
Flowers: 1–3(4); terminal; sepals and petals similar, lanceolate;
the sepals wide spreading; lip spatulate with a deeply fringed
margin and bright yellow beard or, in the forma *brachypogon*,
the beard reduced to a few colorless knobs, to 2 cm; perianth
from light to dark, rosy-pink or lavender or, in the forma *albiflora*, pure white; individual flower size ca. 4 cm
Habitat: moist meadows, open bogs and prairies, roadside
ditches, and sphagnous seeps
Flowering period: May and June

From Newfoundland to Florida and westward to the Mississippi Valley and eastern Texas, this little jewel adorns open bogs and meadows, roadside ditches, bor-
row pits, and sphagnous seeps. Their pink flowers and broad spatulate lip may
remind one of roseate spoonbills (*Ajaia ajaia*). Although variable in color, form,
and size, the **rose pogonias,** *Pogonia ophioglossoides*, are a true herald of a solid
season of wild orchids. They are often seen in the company of grass-pinks, *Calopogon*, and various ladies'-tresses, *Spiranthes*. Color and form vary greatly from
colony to colony. It is not unusual to find plants with the petals and sepals very
narrow and, within the same colony, individuals with the sepals and petals broad
and rounded. Plants with coloring from pale lilac to intense magenta occasionally have white-flowered plants among them. Although most plants have solitary
flowers, it can be interesting, especially in a large population, to search for those
with multiple flowers. Stems with two flowers are not that unusual and, upon rare
occasion, a three-flowered stem will be seen. Only once has the author seen a stem
with four flowers! The unusual forma *brachypogon*, although described originally
from Nova Scotia, has recently been seen, or more correctly detected, throughout
the range of the species.

forma *albiflora*

Ponthieva

Ponthieva is a genus of about fifty Neotropical species; members of the genus form herbaceous basal rosettes and a pubescent to puberulent raceme of flowers. The individual flowers are usually set at right angles to the axis. Two species are known from the United States and one, *P. racemosa*, from Texas.

Ponthieva racemosa (Walter) C. Mohr

shadow-witch

Range: southeastern Virginia south to
Florida, west to eastern Texas; West Indies,
Mexico, Central America, northern South
America
Texas: Pineywoods: rare and local
Plant: terrestrial, 8–60 cm tall
Leaves: 3–8, in a basal rosette; dark green,
elliptic, 1–5 cm wide × 3–15 cm long
Flowers: 8–30, non-resupinate; sepals light
green, veined with darker green; petals
white, veined with bright green; lip white
with a green, concave center; individual
flower size (0.6)0.8–.09(1.2) cm, the flow-
ers tipped out from the rachis at about
60° and the ovary brown in color
Habitat: damp to wet shaded woodlands,
swamps, and riverbanks
Flowering period: September to November

For the Corrells and their orchid hunting expeditions, 1946 was a banner year.
Ponthieva racemosa, **the shadow-witch orchid,** was one of their discoveries that
year. Plants can often form large patches in wet woods along seasonally flooded
stream banks. Rarely is it found without other orchids and most often is accompa-
nied by the fragrant ladies'-tresses, *Spiranthes odorata*, and, in nearby Louisiana,
the low ground orchid, *Platythelys querceticola*, and southern oval ladies'-tresses,
Spiranthes ovalis var. *ovalis*.

Schiedeella

A small genus of only nine species as currently defined, this is another of several genera that were once treated within the genus *Spiranthes* (Garay, 1980[1982]). Only one species occurs in the United States, and it has undergone a considerable taxonomic and nomenclatural history.

Schiedeella arizonica P.M. Brown

Indian braids; Arizona red-spot

forma *virescens* P.M. Brown—green-stemmed form
McAllen International Orchid Society Journal 7(12): 10–11, type: Arizona

Range: Arizona, New Mexico, Texas
Texas: Trans-Pecos—rare and local
Plant: to 20 cm tall; slender stems rosy white or, forma *virescens*, greenish yellow; with several bracts
Leaves: 3–5, in basal rosette, oval, to 3 cm wide × 6 cm long; not present at flowering
Flowers: 6–12, in slender, loose, 1-ranked spiral, whitish; floral bracts translucent white; lip oblong with crenulate margins (outer portion strongly recurved), apex with 3 green stripes; disc in center of lip, rich cinnabar-red or, in the forma *virescens*, pale yellow, especially if viewed from beneath; individual flower ca. 0.75–1.0 cm long
Habitat: dry coniferous forest, hillsides, creek canyons at moderate to high elevations (1,500–4,600 m)
Flowering Period: May into early July

Schiedeella arizonica, the **Arizona red-spot** or, locally, **Indian braids**, is one of the most inconspicuous orchids in the southwestern United States. The translucent stem and absence of leaves at flowering time led to the original applied species epithet of *parasitica*. The plant is not a parasite and certainly has abundant chlorophyll when the leaves appear. In Texas the species is known from two areas of the Trans-Pecos—scattered areas in the Davis Mountains in Jeff Davis County and in Guadeloupe Mountains National Park in northern Culberson County.

Plants of *Schiedeella arizonica* were addressed as *Spiranthes parasitica* A. Richard & Galeotti in Luer (1975), and as *Schiedeella parasitica* (A. Richard & Galeotti) Schlechter by Liggio and Liggio (1999). Meanwhile Brown (1996) treated them as *S. fauci-sanguinea* (Dod) Burns-Balogh. Neither of those species actually occurs in the United States, and Brown later described the taxon as a new species—*Schiedeella arizonica* (Brown and Coleman, 2000).

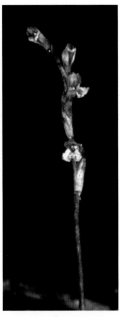

forma *virescens*

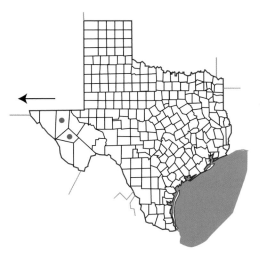

Spiranthes

Spiranthes is a cosmopolitan genus of about fifty species. Treated in the strictest sense it is one of the most easily identified genera of native orchids but includes some of the more difficult plants to identify to species. The relatively slender, often twisted stems and spikes of small white or creamy yellow (or pink in *S. sinensis*) flowers are universally recognizable. In the United States and Canada we have twenty-four species, and fifteen of these may be found in Texas.

Note: *Spiranthes cernua* is a compilospecies, i.e., with gene flow from several other species, depending on the plant's geographic location. Occasionally these plants prove problematic to key out. An unusual, nearly yellow-flowered cleistogamous/peloric race occurs in East Texas and western Louisiana.

Key to the ladies'-tresses, *Spiranthes*

1a leaves present or withering at flowering time . . . 6
1b leaves absent at flowering time . . . 2

2a flowers pure white with no trace or markings of yellow, cream, or green on the lip . . . . . **little ladies'-tresses,** *Spiranthes tuberosa,* p. 160
2b flowers with yellow, cream, or green lips or with green markings on the lip . . . 3

3a flowers white with green central portion of the lip . . . . . **southern slender ladies'-tresses,** *Spiranthes lacera* var. *gracilis,* p. 142
3b flowers white or cream with similar or deep cream or pale yellow lips . . . 4

4a floral bracts with distinctive white tips . . . . . **Navasota ladies'-tresses,** *Spiranthes parksii,* p. 154
4b floral bracts green . . . 5

5a sepals distinct, arching forward . . . . . **Great Plains ladies'-tresses,** *Spiranthes magnicamporum,* p. 148
5b sepals approximate, not arching . . . . . **nodding ladies'-tresses,** *Spiranthes cernua,* p. 136

6a leaves oval to oblong; arranged in a basal rosette . . . 7
6b leaves linear to oblanceolate, ascending the lower third of the stem . . . 9

7a flowers with green central portion on the lip; lateral sepals spatulate . . . . . **Eaton's ladies'-tresses,** *Spiranthes eatonii,* p. 138
7b flowers otherwise . . . 8

8a inflorescence and flowers pubescent . . . . . **Texas ladies'-tresses,** *Spiranthes brevilabris,* p. 134

8b inflorescence and flowers glabrous . . . . . **Florida ladies'-tresses,** *Spiranthes floridana,* p. 140

9a plants spring flowering . . . 10

9b plants summer/autumn flowering . . . 12

10a flower green to creamy green; lips and often the petals with green veining . . . . . **woodland ladies'-tresses,** *Spiranthes sylvatica,* p. 158

10b flowers white to pale cream . . . 11

11a lateral sepals appressed, lip white with green veining . . . . . **giant ladies'-tresses,** *Spiranthes praecox,* p. 156

11b lateral sepals spreading; lip often a deeper cream . . . . . **grass-leaved ladies'-tresses,** *Spiranthes vernalis,* p. 162

12a plants summer flowering; lip a contrasting deeper cream to yellow . . . . . **lace-lipped ladies'-tresses,** *Spiranthes laciniata,* p. 144

12b plants autumn flowering . . . 13

13a flowers arranged in a single rank . . . . . **long-lipped ladies'-tresses,** *Spiranthes longilabris,* p. 146

13b flowers arranged in multiple ranks . . . 14

14a plants of open prairies and grasslands; roadside areas . . . 15

14b plants of woodlands . . . 16

15a sepals distinct, arching forward . . . . . **Great Plains ladies'-tresses,** *Spiranthes magnicamporum,* p. 148

15b sepals approximate, not arching . . . . . *Spiranthes cernua,* **nodding ladies'-tresses,** p. 136

16a flowers ca. 1 cm long or longer, lip creamy yellow or greenish in the central trough; often plants of wet woods and roadside ditches . . . . . **fragrant ladies'-tresses,** *Spiranthes odorata,* p. 150

16b flowers ca. 5 mm long, pure white . . . . . **southern oval ladies'-tresses,** *Spiranthes ovalis* var. *ovalis,* p. 152

Spiranthes brevilabris Lindley

Texas ladies'-tresses

Range: Florida west to eastern Texas
Texas: Pineywoods, Blackland Prairies, Gulf Prairies and
Marshes—very rare with most historical populations extirpated
Globally Threatened
Plant: terrestrial, 20–40 cm tall; densely pubescent with
capitate hairs
Leaves: 3–6; ovate, 1–2 × 2–6 cm, yellow-green; withering at
flowering time
Flowers: 10–35; in a single rank, spiraled or secund; sepals
and petals similar, elliptic; perianth ivory to yellow with a
dense pubescence; lip oblong, with the apex undulate-lacerate;
individual flower size ca. 4–5 mm
Habitat: grassy roadsides, cemeteries
Flowering period: late February–April

This delicate, nearly ephemeral ladies'-tresses is one of four species that produce winter rosettes. The leaves of **Texas ladies'-tresses**, *Spiranthes brevilabris*, are more yellow-green than those of the other three species. Viewed from a moving vehicle, the creamy yellow, densely pubescent flowers are difficult to pick out on the roadsides, whereas the white-flowered species tend to stand out regardless of their size. Plants may flower erratically and are dependent on winter rainfall. Extant populations are few, with a 2007 discovery by Eric Keith in Walker County, and following up on reports from previous years does not always give an accurate accounting of the species. Hatch et al. (1990) also noted *S. brevilabris* for the High Plains region but it has never been vouchered from that area and the record may be based upon a misidentification of plants of *S. vernalis*. *Spiranthes brevilabris* was first collected by Drummond in 1840 and served as the type for the species.

Spiranthes cernua (Linnaeus) L.C. Richard

nodding ladies'-tresses

Range: South Dakota east to Nova Scotia, south to Texas and Florida
Texas: Pineywoods, Gulf Prairies and Marshes, Post Oak Savannah, Blackland Prairies, Cross Timbers and Prairies, South Texas Plains, Edwards Plateau—occasional to frequent in appropriate habitat
Plant: terrestrial, 10–50 cm tall
Leaves: 3–5; appearing basal or on the lower portion of the stem; linear-oblanceolate, up to 2 cm wide × 26 cm long; ascending to spreading; usually present at anthesis in most races, although in the Deep South and some prairie races they are absent
Flowers: 10–50; in a spike, tightly to loosely spiraled with 5 or more flowers per cycle, nodding from the base of the perianth or rarely ascending; sepals and petals similar, lanceolate; perianth white, ivory, or in some races greenish; lip oblong, broad at the apex, the central portion of the lip, in some races, creamy yellow or green; the sepals approximate and extending forward, sometimes arching above the flower; individual flower size 0.6–10.5 mm
Habitat: wet to dry open sites, lightly wooded areas, moist grassy roadsides, pine flatwoods, etc.
Flowering period: autumn flowering; late September through November (December)

Of all our native orchids in North America the **nodding ladies'-tresses**, *Spiranthes cernua*, is the most difficult to describe simply and concisely. Because it is a compilospecies, with gene flow from several different similar species, plants in different geographic areas have strong resemblances to the basic diploid species contributing that unidirectional gene flow. In other words, those plants growing along the southern states in close proximity to the **fragrant ladies'-tresses**, *S. odorata*, have a greater resemblance to *S. odorata*, whereas those from the drier northern and western portions of its range bear strong affinities to the **Great Plains ladies'-tresses**, *S. magnicamporum*. Plants in the northeastern states have gene flow from the **yellow ladies'-tresses**, *S. ochroleuca*.

In many areas, especially away from the Coastal Plain, this is the common autumn flowering *Spiranthes* to be found and is the most widespread species of *Spiranthes* in Texas. Those who are seriously interested in learning and determining the various races in their areas are urged to read Sheviak's entries for *S. cernua*, *S. odorata*, *S. magnicamporum*, and *S. ochroleuca* in volume 26 of *Flora of North America* (2002). Many plants of *S. cernua* seen throughout Texas will be similar to each other. Only in areas where the monoembryonic diploid species occur will there be plants that strongly emphasize the unidirectional gene flow. Sheviak (1982) illustrates several different ecotypes of *S. cernua* that may occur within Texas. The most unusual of these is a cleistogamous peloric type. The yellow-green flowers never really open and the floral parts are all similar, with the lip not well differentiated. Hatch et al. (1990) also noted *S. cernua* for the Trans-Pecos region but no species of *Spiranthes* (*sensu stricto*) has ever been vouchered from that area. That region was omitted from the 2001 revision and several other regions were added.

Spiranthes eatonii Ames *ex* P.M. Brown

Eaton's ladies'-tresses

Range: eastern Texas east through all of Florida, north to southeastern Virginia; restricted to the Coastal Plain

Texas: Pineywoods, Gulf Prairies and Marshes— apparently rare and local, although there are several herbarium vouchers; perhaps overlooked

Plant: terrestrial, 20–50 cm tall

Leaves: 3–6; oblanceolate-lanceolate, 0.75–1.0 cm wide × 5.5 cm long, withering quickly at flowering time

Flowers: 10–35; in a single rank, spiraled or secund; sepals spatulate, green at the base; petals lanceolate, green at the base; perianth white; lip oblong, centrally green with the apex undulate; individual flower size ca. 4–5 mm

Habitat: roadsides, cemeteries, drier pine flatwoods, sandy openings, damp saw palmetto scrub

Flowering period: late March into early May

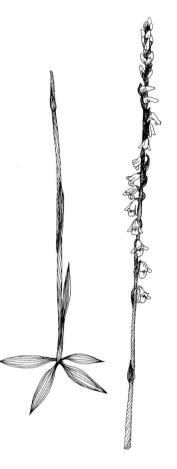

As herbarium specimens have been examined, *Spiranthes eatonii*, **Eaton's ladies'-tresses**, only recently described (Brown, 1999), has been easily confused with *Spiranthes lacera* var. *lacera* and var. *gracilis*, *S. floridana*, *S. brevilabris*, *S. tuberosa*, and (in Florida) *S. torta*. In the field it is easily identified as it is the only spring flowering, white-flowered, basal-leaved *Spiranthes* to be found. The narrow, oblanceolate leaves are distinctive within this basal-leaved group. For many years plants of *S. eatonii* were identified as *S. lacera* and its southern variety *gracilis*, but neither name is a synonym. The exceedingly slender stems and tiny flowers make it easy to overlook when in bloom. The photograph in Liggio and Liggio (1999) identified as *S. floridana* is that of *S. eatonii*.

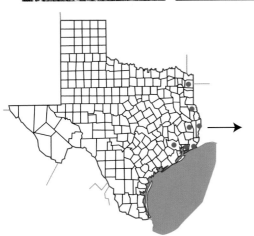

Spiranthes floridana (Wherry) Cory *emend.* P.M. Brown

Florida ladies'-tresses

Range: eastern Texas east through all of Florida and north to North Carolina, primarily on the Coastal Plain
Texas: Pineywoods, Gulf Prairies and Marshes, Post Oak Savannah—exceedingly rare and often misidentified
Globally Threatened
Plant: terrestrial, 20–40 cm tall; glabrous to sparsely pubescent
Leaves: 3–5; ovate, 1–2 cm wide × 2–6 cm long, yellow-green, withering at flowering time
Flowers: 10–35; in a single rank, spiraled or secund; sepals and petals similar; perianth creamy yellow; lip oblong, centrally yellow with the apex undulate; individual flower size ca. 4–5 mm
Habitat: roadsides, cemeteries, pine flatwoods
Flowering period: late March into early May

Spiranthes floridana, **Florida ladies'-tresses**, is often easily confused with *S. brevilabris*, **Texas ladies'-tresses**, although the degree of pubescence is an excellent diagnostic tool in the field. While abundant apparent habitat still exists, *S. floridana* has become very rare, with only recent populations seen in Mississippi (Sorrie, 1998) and northern Florida. Plants tend to be small and populations vary greatly from year to year. The photograph in Liggio and Liggio (1999) identified as *S. floridana* is that of *S. eatonii*. Hatch et al. (1990) also noted *S. floridana* (as *S. brevilabris* var. *floridana*) for the High Plains region but it has never been vouchered from that area and the record may be based upon a misidentification of *S. vernalis*.

Spiranthes lacera Rafinesque var. *gracilis* (Bigelow) Luer

southern slender ladies'-tresses

Range: Kansas, Michigan east to Maine, south to Texas and Georgia

Texas: Pineywoods, Gulf Prairies and Marshes, Post Oak Savannah, Blackland Prairies, Cross Timbers and Prairies, South Texas Plains, Edwards Plateau—widespread and relatively common in both open and lightly wooded areas

Plant: terrestrial, 15–65 cm tall, glabrous to sparsely pubescent

Leaves: 2–4; ovate, dark green, 1–2 cm wide × 2–5 cm long, usually absent at flowering time

Flowers: 10–35; in a single rank, spiraled or secund; sepals and petals similar, elliptic; perianth white; lip oblong, with the apex rounded; central portion green with a clearly defined crisp apron; individual flower size ca. 4.0–7.5 mm

Habitat: dry to moist meadows, grassy roadsides, cemeteries, open sandy areas in woodlands, lawns, old fields

Flowering period: summer flowering; July through August and often into early September

Spiranthes lacera var. *gracilis*, the **southern slender ladies'-tresses,** is the more southerly of the two varieties and found in nearly every state in the central and eastern United States. The small, white, green-throated flowers are very distinctive and the simple spiral of the inflorescence quite eye-catching. Plants are often encountered in lawns, and local cemeteries are usually a good place to search as well. The differences between this variety and the more northerly var. *lacera* are not great, but the more northern of the two has lower flowers well spaced out on the inflorescence and they appear to be much smaller because of the position of the sepals. Hybrids with *Spiranthes tuberosa* are known as *S. ×eamesii*.

The April (May, June) flowering dates in Liggio and Liggio (1999) refer to specimens of *S. eatonii*.

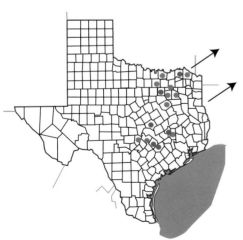

Spiranthes laciniata (Small) Ames

lace-lipped ladies'-tresses

Range: eastern Texas east through all of Florida and north to southern New Jersey; primarily on the Coastal Plain
Texas: Pineywoods, Gulf Prairies and Marshes—widely scattered and locally frequent in the southern wet prairies
Plant: terrestrial, 20–95 cm tall; densely pubescent with capitate hairs
Leaves: 3–5; lanceolate, 1.0–1.7 cm wide × 5–40 cm long
Flowers: 10–50; in a single rank, spiraled or secund; sepals and petals similar, elliptic; perianth white to ivory; lip oblong, with the apex undulate-lacerate, the central portion of the lip creamy yellow; individual flower size ca. 1 cm
Habitat: wet, grassy roadsides, ditches, swamps, and shallow open water
Flowering period: late June through July

Spiranthes laciniata, the **lace-lipped ladies'-tresses**, is easily distinguished from *Spiranthes vernalis*, the **grass-leaved ladies'-tresses**, which it superficially resembles, by its ball-tipped hairs, in contrast to the pointed articulate hairs on *S. vernalis*. It typically flowers later than *S. vernalis* where the two are sympatric. The tall, creamy white spikes may often be observed along the wet roadside ditches and open savannahs of the Gulf Coastal Plain counties. Hatch et al. (1990) also noted *S. laciniata* for the High Plains region but it has never been vouchered from that area. That region was omitted from the 2001 revision.

Spiranthes longilabris Lindley

long-lipped ladies'-tresses

Range: eastern Texas east through all of Florida, and north to south-eastern Virginia

Texas: Pineywoods, Gulf Prairies and Marshes—widely distributed but never frequent; most sites are local and with few plants

Plant: terrestrial, 20–50 cm tall; sparsely pubescent with clubbed hairs

Leaves: 3–5; linear-lanceolate, 0.5 cm wide × 8.0–15.0 cm long; often withered at flowering time

Flowers: 10–30; in a tight single rank, spiraled or secund; sepals and petals similar, lanceolate; perianth white to ivory; lip oblong, with the apex undulate-lacerate, the central portion of the lip yellow; the sepals wide-spreading; individual flower size 1.0–1.5 cm

Habitat: moist grassy roadsides, pine flatwoods

Flowering period: October–November

Spiranthes longilabris, the **long-lipped ladies'-tresses**, is perhaps the most handsome of all the ladies'-tresses. The close-ranked flowers spread their long sepals like wings and the narrow, creamy yellow lip descends from the front of the large flowers. The **long-lipped ladies'-tresses** is an unmistakable plant and easily identified. It often grows with *S. odorata* and occasionally the hybrid, *S. ×folsomii* can also be found. Hatch et al. (1990) also noted *S. longilabris* for the Blacklands Prairie region but it has never been vouchered from that area and suitable habitat most likely does not exist there.

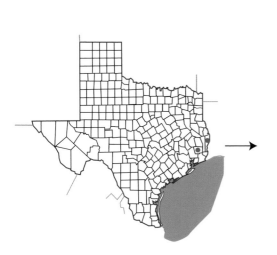

→

Spiranthes magnicamporum Sheviak

Great Plains ladies'-tresses

Range: Manitoba east to southern Ontario, south to New Mexico, Texas, Alabama, and Georgia
Texas: Post Oak Savannah, Blackland Prairies, Cross Timbers and Prairies, Edwards Plateau—widespread and scattered locales throughout the plains and prairies
Plant: terrestrial, 10–63 cm tall
Leaves: 2–4; appearing basal or on the lower portion of the stem; linear-oblanceolate, up to 1.5 cm wide × 16.0 cm long; ascending to spreading; leaves usually absent or withering at anthesis
Flowers: 12–54; in a spike, tightly to loosely spiraled with 3–4 flowers per cycle; abruptly nodding from the base; lateral sepals wide-spreading and usually arched above the flower, petals linear-lanceolate; perianth white, ivory, or cream; lip ovate to oblong, the apex crenulate, the central portion of the lip usually yellow; individual flower size 0.4–1.2 cm
Habitat: wet to dry alkaline prairies, bluffs, and fens
Flowering period: September through November southward

The **Great Plains ladies'-tresses,** *Spiranthes magnicamporum,* a typical prairie and plains species, reaches from southern Canada southward to central Texas. The **Great Plains ladies'-tresses** has a preference for limy bluffs and open prairies, whereas the **nodding ladies'-tresses,** *S. cernua,* may be found at the base of some of these bluffs in the damper ditches. *Spiranthes magnicamporum* is one of the several species of *Spiranthes* that contributes gene flow to the **nodding ladies'-tresses.** Several of these eastern element prairie sites may contain mixed populations of both *S. magnicamporum* and *S. cernua,* so the plants and, if absolutely necessary, the seeds need to be carefully examined to determine the correct species. Seeds from the basic diploid species, *S. magnicamporum, S. ochroleuca, S. odorata* and *S. ovalis,* are monoembryonic, whereas those of *S. cernua,* usually a polyploid species, are polyembryonic. This type of examination goes beyond the scope of this field guide and requires more sophisticated techniques. A compound microscope and the skills to use it are required. Hatch et al. (1990) also noted *S. magnicamporum* for the High Plains region but it has never been vouchered from that area, although its occurrence there is not illogical.

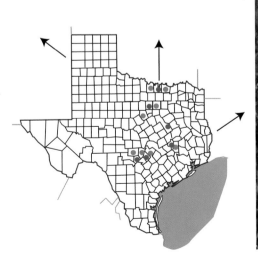

Spiranthes odorata (Nuttall) Lindley

fragrant ladies'-tresses

Range: eastern Texas north to Oklahoma and Arkansas, east to Florida, and north to (?)Delaware

Texas: Pineywoods, Gulf Prairies and Marshes, Post Oak Savannah, Blackland Prairies—widespread and locally common

Plant: terrestrial or semiaquatic, 20–110 cm tall, pubescent, stoloniferous

Leaves: 3–5; linear-oblanceolate, up to 4 cm wide × 52 cm long; rigidly ascending or spreading

Flowers: 10–30; in several tight ranks; sepals and petals similar, lanceolate; perianth white to ivory; lip oblong, tapering to the apex, the central portion of the lip creamy yellow or green; the sepals extending forward; individual flower size 1.0–1.8 cm

Habitat: moist grassy roadsides, pine flatwoods, cypress swamps, wooded river floodplains

Flowering period: October–early December

Spiranthes odorata, the **fragrant ladies'-tresses**, can be by far the largest of our native ladies'-tresses. Plants in wooded swamplands may reach a full meter in height. The **fragrant ladies'-tresses** occurs typically in seasonally inundated sites and may flower while emerging from shallow water. The rather thick, broad leaves give the plant a distinctive vegetative habit. The very long, wide-spreading roots produce vegetative offshoots often 30 cm from the parent shoot, giving rise to extensive clonal colonies. Despite the typical size of *S. odorata*, there is a very definable ecotype that occupies mowed road shoulders and can often be no more than 15 cm tall.

Spiranthes ovalis Lindley var. *ovalis*

southern oval ladies'-tresses

Range: Arkansas south to eastern Texas, east to Florida

Globally Threatened

Texas: Pineywoods, Post Oak Savannah, Blackland Prairies—very rare and local with few scattered populations

Plant: terrestrial, 20–40 cm tall; pubescent

Leaves: 2–4; basal and on the lower half of the stem, oblanceolate, 0.5–1.5 cm wide × 3.0–15.0 cm long; present at flowering time

Flowers: 10–50; in 3 tight ranks; sepals and petals similar, lanceolate; perianth white; lip oblong, tapering to the apex with a delicate undulate margin, the sepals extending forward; individual flower size 5.5–7.0 mm; rostellum and viscidium present, therefore the plants are fully sexual

Habitat: rich, damp woodlands and floodplains

Flowering period: October into November

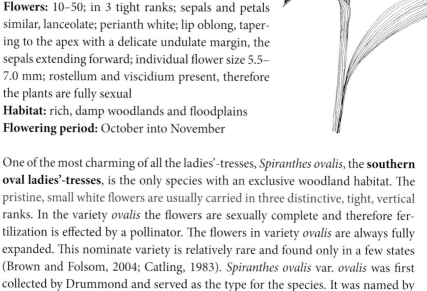

One of the most charming of all the ladies'-tresses, *Spiranthes ovalis*, the **southern oval ladies'-tresses**, is the only species with an exclusive woodland habitat. The pristine, small white flowers are usually carried in three distinctive, tight, vertical ranks. In the variety *ovalis* the flowers are sexually complete and therefore fertilization is effected by a pollinator. The flowers in variety *ovalis* are always fully expanded. This nominate variety is relatively rare and found only in a few states (Brown and Folsom, 2004; Catling, 1983). *Spiranthes ovalis* var. *ovalis* was first collected by Drummond and served as the type for the species. It was named by Lindley in 1840.

Spiranthes parksii Correll

Navasota ladies'-tresses

Range: east-central Texas
Federally Listed as Endangered
Texas: restricted to two areas within the Pineywoods and Post Oak Savannah regions
Plant: terrestrial, 15–33 cm tall, moderately to densely pubescent
Leaves: 2–3; appearing basal or on the lower portion of the stem; linear-lanceolate, up to 2 cm wide × 22 cm long; ascending to spreading; the leaves are usually absent or withering at anthesis
Flowers: 8–15; in a spike, loosely spiraled with 5 flowers per cycle; ascending; sepals lanceolate, white to pale green, directed forward; petals obovate, whitish to yellow-green with a prominent central green stripe, usually erose on the margin; lip oblong to obovate, centrally yellowish or green, the margins erose at the apex; individual flower size 0.5–0.6 mm
Habitat: thin soil, lightly shaded woodlands, usually with post oaks
Flowering period: late October well into November

The **Navasota ladies'-tresses**, *Spiranthes parksii*, is one of the rarest ladies'-tresses in North America. It is confined to two areas in eastern Texas. Plants of this species were first described in 1947 and then rarely seen until Paul Catling rediscovered them in 1986. *Spiranthes parksii* was one of the very few species that Luer, in the early 1970s, was unable to locate for photographs for his book (Luer, 1975). Subsequently, in 1986 Bridges and Orzell found a small population in Angelina National Forest in eastern Texas. The tiny flowers appear never to completely open, or at least are not wide-spreading like most *Spiranthes*, and appear to be apomictic. The plants are not unlike some cleistogamous and peloric forms of *S. cernua* found in the area, but the small flower size and shape of the lateral sepals is distinctive and the white-tipped floral bracts diagnostic. Like those of *S. cernua* the seeds of *S. parksii* appear to be polyembryonic. *Spiranthes parksii* was first collected by Parks in 1945 and named in his honor by Correll in 1947.

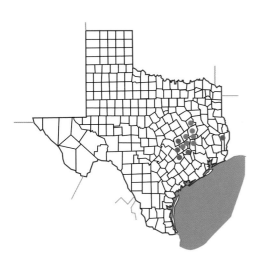

Spiranthes praecox (Walter) S. Watson

giant ladies'-tresses

forma *albolabia* P.M. Brown & C. McCartney, white-lipped form
North American Native Orchid Journal 1(1): 13. 1995, type: Florida

Range: Arkansas south to Texas, east to Florida, north to New Jersey; primarily on the Coastal Plain

Texas: Pineywoods, Gulf Prairies and Marshes, Post Oak Savannah—widespread and locally common, primarily along the Coastal Plain

Plant: terrestrial, 20–75 cm tall, sparsely pubescent

Leaves: 2–7; basal and on the lower half of the stem, linear-lanceolate, 1–7 cm wide × 10–25 cm long, present at flowering time

Flowers: 10–40; in either single or multiple ranks; sepals and petals similar, lanceolate; perianth typically white, but in some plants green; lip ovate-oblong, rounded to the apex with a delicate undulate margin with distinctive green veining or, in the forma *albolabia*, the lip appearing pure white and the veins actually a pale lemon yellow, the sepals appressed and extending forward to create a tubular flower; individual flower size 6–12 mm

Habitat: roadsides, meadows, prairies, open woodlands—just about anywhere that is not too shady

Flowering period: March into early June

Spiranthes praecox, the **giant ladies'-tresses**, is one of the most frequently encountered orchids in much of the Coastal Plain. It starts flowering shortly after *Spiranthes vernalis* and continues throughout the spring. The tubular flowers with their appressed sepals are distinctive and quickly help to separate it from *S. vernalis*. In rare situations the two hybridize, producing *Spiranthes ×meridionalis*. The small, slender, pure white flowers help in separating this species from the somewhat similar woodland ladies'-tress, *S. sylvatica*, which also has green veining in the lip. Plants mapped from the northern counties in the Pineywoods have proven to be *S. sylvatica*.

forma *albolabia*

Spiranthes sylvatica P.M. Brown

woodland ladies'-tresses

Range: eastern Texas to Florida, north to Arkansas and along the Coastal Plain to southeastern North Carolina

Texas: Pineywoods, Post Oak Savannah: local; under-collected and status not completely known

Plant: terrestrial, 25–75 cm tall, sparsely pubescent with capitate hairs

Leaves: 3–7; basal and on the lower third of the stem, linear-lanceolate, 0.8–1.6 cm wide × 10.0–35.0 cm long, present at flowering time

Flowers: 10–30; in a dense spike usually appearing as multiple ranks; sepals and petals similar, lanceolate; perianth creamy green; lip ovate-oblong, rounded and broadened to the apex with a delicate undulate or ruffled margin with distinctive darker green veining, the sepals slightly spreading; individual flower size 1.0–1.7(2.2) cm

Habitat: shaded roadsides, open woodlands, and dry live oak hammocks; rarely in wetlands

Flowering period: April through early May

Spiranthes sylvatica, the **woodland ladies'-tresses**, is the most recent *Spiranthes* species to be described from North America (Brown, 2001). Although the plants have been known for some time, sufficient evidence has only recently been available to separate this species satisfactorily from the **giant ladies'-tresses**, *Spiranthes praecox*. Although both typically have green-veined lips, all similarity ceases at that point. The **woodland ladies'-tresses** has been passed over for many years as a disappointing example of *S. praecox. Spiranthes sylvatica* is usually a plant of shaded and woodland habitats and its very distinctive, large, creamy green flowers are unlike any other *Spiranthes*. It is most frequently seen along roadside hedgerows bordering woodlands where the plants are tucked up into the border. There are many distinctive differences between the two species, but flower size, shape, and color are the most noticeable. Plants have the habit of producing long, slender leaves in the autumn that winter over until new growth commences in the early spring. Recent fieldwork has confirmed extant sites in Texas, as well as in Arkansas, Georgia, South Carolina, and North Carolina.

Wild Orchids of Texas

Spiranthes tuberosa Rafinesque

little ladies'-tresses

Range: Arkansas east to southern Michigan and Massachusetts, south to Florida and west to Texas

Texas: Pineywoods, Gulf Prairies and Marshes, Post Oak Savannah, Blackland Prairies—a common summer-flowering species, particularly in the southern states

Plant: terrestrial, 10–30 cm tall, glabrous

Leaves: 2–4; ovate, dark green, 1–2 cm wide × 2–5 cm long, absent at flowering time

Flowers: 10–35; in a single rank, spiraled or secund; sepals and petals similar, elliptic; perianth crystalline white; lip oblong, with the apex undulate-lacerate, exceeding the sepals; individual flower size ca. 3–4 mm

Habitat: grassy roadsides, cemeteries, open sandy areas in woodlands

Flowering period: highly variable from late June through early October

Spiranthes tuberosa, the **little ladies'-tresses**, is the only pure white *Spiranthes* to flower in early to midsummer. One of its favorite habitats is old, dry cemeteries. The nomenclatural history of this plant is rather complex, and among the names applied to it are *S. beckii* and *S. grayi*. See Correll (1950) for a discussion. This species is easily recognized by its pure white flowers, broad crisped lip, and absence of leaves at flowering time. Hybrids with *Spiranthes lacera* var. *gracilis* are known as *S. ×eamesii*.

Spiranthes vernalis Engelmann & Gray

grass-leaved ladies'-tresses

Range: Nebraska south to Texas, east to Florida and north to southern New Hampshire

Texas: Pineywoods, Gulf Prairies and Marshes, Post Oak Savannah, Blackland Prairies, Rolling Plains—the most common *Spiranthes* found in Texas

Plant: terrestrial, 10–85 cm tall, pubescent with sharp-pointed hairs

Leaves: 2–7; basal and on the lower third of the stem, linear-lanceolate, 1–2 cm wide × 5–25 cm long, present at flowering time

Flowers: 10–50; arranged in either a single or multiple ranks; sepals and petals similar, lanceolate; perianth typically creamy white; lip ovate-oblong, rounded to the apex with a delicate undulate margin, usually a deeper creamy yellow; the sepals wide-spreading; individual flower size 6–9 mm

Habitat: roadsides, meadows, prairies, cultivated lawns—just about anywhere that is sunny

Flowering period: April and May in the southeastern counties, often persisting until early July in the northern counties

Spiranthes vernalis, the **grass-leaved ladies'-tresses,** is perhaps our most variable *Spiranthes* in habit, although the flowers remain surprisingly consistent. Plants may vary greatly in size and vigor, as well as degree of spiraling, resulting in plants that are essentially secund to those that appear to be multiple-ranked. Plants are not consistent in habit from year to year. Color is somewhat variable, from nearly pure white to cream with a contrasting, yellower lip, and some individuals have two brown or orange spots on the lip. The most consistent diagnostic character is the presence in the inflorescence of copious articulate, pointed hairs; these readily distinguish *S. vernalis* from other species. *Spiranthes vernalis* was first collected by Lindheimer in 1843 and served as the type for the species.

Hybrids

Spiranthes ×eamesii P.M. Brown

Eames' hybrid ladies'-tresses

(*S. lacera* var. *gracilis* × *S. tuberosa*)
> *North American Native Orchid Journal.* 12: 60. 2006,
> type: Connecticut

The hybrid may not be that rare in Texas because counties where both parents overlap are numerous and have similar habitats.

Spiranthes ×folsomii P.M. Brown

(*S. longilabris* × *S. odorata*)

Folsom's hybrid ladies'-tresses
> *North American Native Orchid Journal.* 6(1): 16. 2000,
> type: Florida

Plants tend to be intermediate between the parents and to have shorter leaves and more slender wide-spreading sepals than *S. odorata*. These are expected where the two parental species grow together along the southern Gulf Coastal Plain in Hardin County.

Spiranthes ×intermedia Ames
intermediate hybrid ladies'-tresses
(*S. lacera* var. *gracilis* × *S. vernalis*)
  Rhodora 5: 262. 1903, type: Massachusetts

One of the first *Spiranthes* hybrids to be described, it occurs in only a few places, primarily in the Northeast, where both parents flower at the same time.

Although both parents occur in Texas and in many of the same counties, the spread in flowering time makes the possibility of this hybrid remote. However, in an unusual weather year such a combination may occur.

Spiranthes ×itchetuckneensis P.M. Brown
Ichetucknee hybrid ladies'-tresses
(*S. odorata* × *S. ovalis*)
  North American Native Orchid Journal 5(4): 368–69.

This hybrid is frequent in the Deep South and could occur in the few areas where the rare parent, *S. ovalis*, occurs.

Spiranthes ×meridionalis P.M. Brown
(*S. praecox* × *S. vernalis*)
southern hybrid ladies'-tresses
  North American Native Orchid Journal 6(2): 139. 2000, type: Florida

This is an apparently rare but distinctive hybrid that, despite the relative abundance of both parents in hospitable habitat, has been documented only a few times. Watch for *vernalis*-like plants with green veins in the lip or *praecox*-like plants with spreading sepals.

Tipularia

Tipularia is a small genus of only two species known from the Himalayas and eastern United States. The species are very similar to each other and differ in the shape of the lip. The genus is characterized by a series of tubers from which arises a single, annual leaf that remains green throughout the winter, then, in the summer, a leafless spike of flowers with the sepals and petals all drawn to one side. A single species in North America is the **crane-fly orchid**, *Tipularia discolor*.

Tipularia discolor (Pursh) Nuttall

crane-fly orchis

forma *viridifolia* P.M. Brown—green-leaved form
North American Native Orchid Journal (4): 336–37. 2000, type:
Florida

Range: eastern Texas, northeast to southern Michigan,
east to southeastern Massachusetts, south to Florida
Texas: Pineywoods—local in woodlands
Plant: terrestrial, 25–60 cm tall
Leaf: 1; basal, ovate, dark green above with raised purple
spots and dark purple beneath or, in the forma *viridifolia*,
green on both sides; 6–7 cm wide × 8–10 cm long, the
long petiole ca. 5 cm; leaf withering in the spring and
absent at flowering time
Flowers: 20–40; in a loose raceme; sepals and petals similar, oblanceolate; perianth greenish yellow, tinged and
mottled with pale purple; lip 3-lobed, the central lobe
slender, blunt, with a few shallow teeth; the sepals and
petals are asymmetrical and all drawn to one side; spur to
2.5–3.0 cm; individual flower size 2.0–3.0 × 3.0–3.5 cm,
not including spur
Habitat: deciduous and mixed woodlands
Flowering period: late June–early August

The **crane-fly orchis**, *Tipularia discolor*, is a very distinctive species that is most
easily found during the winter months when not in flower, and when the single
leaf is most apparent. The dark green leaf has a seersucker look with raised
purple spots on the upper surface. If one turns the leaf over, the satiny purple
underside can be seen—hence the name *discolor*, two colors. Leaves with no
purple present, forma *viridifolia*, have been seen in scattered locations. The
flower spike appears in midsummer and the coloring of the stem and flowers
makes it most difficult to see in the woodlands, although the spike and flowers
are not at all small. Spikes usually grow to 45–50+ cm tall.

Triphora

Consisting of about twenty species in North America, the West Indies, Mexico, and Central America, *Triphora* is a genus of small, delicate herbs, many largely mycotrophic. They all arise from swollen tuberoids. Some produce very colorful but small flowers, and several species have flowers that do not fully open. In Texas we have only a single species with two varieties.

Key to the three birds orchis, *triphora*

1a   plants (leaves, mostly on the reverse, and stems) suffused with purple; central lobe of lip ovate, the papillose green (or yellow) crests appearing to extend to the middle of the lip; flower color highly variable from white to deep pink . . . . . **three birds orchis,** *Triphora trianthophora* var. *trianthophora,* p. 172

1b   plants bright green (below ground portions may have a faint pink tinge); central lobe of the lip oval-oblong; bright green papillose crests extending to nearly the margin of the lip; flower bright white often with fine cerise edging; currently known only from Houston Co., Texas . . . . . **Texas three birds orchis; Pike's three birds orchis,** *Triphora trianthophora* var. *texensis,* p. 174

Triphora trianthophora (Swartz) Rydberg var. *trianthophora*

three-birds orchid

forma *albidoflava* Keenan—white-flowered form
Rhodora 94: 38–39. 1992, type: New Hampshire
forma *caerulea* P.M. Brown—blue-flowered form
North American Native Orchid Journal 7(1): 94–95. 2001, type:
Florida
forma *rossii* P.M. Brown—multi-colored form
North American Native Orchid Journal 5(1): 5. 1999, type: Florida

Range: Texas north to Minnesota, east to Maine, south to
Florida
Texas: Pineywoods—rare and local throughout
Plant: terrestrial, 8–25 cm tall
Leaves: 2–8; broadly ovate-cordate, with smooth margins,
dark green, often with a purple cast, or, in the forma *rossii*,
the stem and leaves white, pink, and yellow; 2–15 cm wide
× 10–15 mm long
Flowers: 1–8(12), nodding; from the axils of the upper
leaves; sepals and petals similar, oblanceolate; perianth white
to pink; lip 3-lobed, the central lobe with the margin sinu-
ate and 3 parallel green crests or, in the forma *albidoflava*,
the perianth pure white and the crests yellow or, in the forma *caerulea*, lilac-blue;
individual flower size ca. 1–2 cm
Habitat: deciduous and mixed woodlands, often with partridgeberry
Flowering period: varies from late July until mid-September

The **three-birds orchis**, *Triphora trianthophora*, is the largest-flowered and showiest of the genus *Triphora*. The plants are quite elusive and only appear for a few
days most years. The stunning little flowers open in midmorning and usually
close by midafternoon, leaving only a few hours for the eager eye to observe them.
Colonies are not at all consistent in their flowering habits from year to year and it
often takes a great deal of persistence on the part of the observer to catch them in
prime condition. Plants have a decided preference for live oak and beech woodlands and colonies are often widely scattered, few flowered, and may remain dormant for several years. Hatch et al. (1990) also noted *T. trianthophora* for the High
Plains region but it has never been vouchered from that area and suitable habitat
most likely does not exist there. That region was omitted from the 2001 revision
and Gulf Plains and Marshes was added.

Triphora trianthophora var. *mexicana* has not been documented from the United States. It is restricted to Mexico and Central America. *Triphora trianthophora*
var. *texensis* is endemic to east central Texas.

forma *rossii*　　　　　　forma *caerulea*

forma *albidoflava*

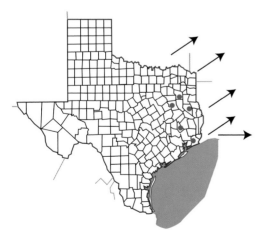

Triphora trianthophora (Swartz) Rydberg var. *texensis* P.M. Brown & R.B. Pike

Texas three-birds orchis, Pike's three-birds orchis

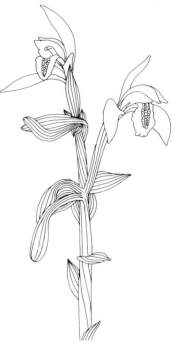

Range: Texas
Texas: endemic to Houston County
Plant: terrestrial, 8–15 cm tall
Leaves: 3–5; ovate-acuminate, bright emerald green, reduced to oblanceolate bracts within the inflorescence; 2–11 cm wide × 7–10 mm long
Flowers: 3–5; white with a green crest, the edges of the petals and sepals with a fine line of cerise; lip with a ruffled margin and notched at the apex; flower size 2 × 2 cm
Habitat: mixed hardwoods with scattered pines in open forest floor in deep leaf mulch
Flowering period: late July–early September

In 2005 Dick Pike, a biologist with the Texas Parks and Wildlife Department, discovered a population of what is now designated *Triphora trianthophora* var. *texensis*, the **Texas three-birds orchis**, in a small ravine in Davy Crockett National Forest, Houston County, Texas.

What first strikes one about these plants is the uniformity of the snowy white flowers and the large bright green area surrounding the three papillose crests. All the plants found by Pike in the Houston County population were sufficiently distinctive, and different from var. *trianthophora*, to warrant recognition at the varietal level. Like the nominate variety, var. *texensis* also flowers for only a few hours and at random intervals during a short season. Weather patterns, especially a drop in temperature after a rain, often trigger flowering.

Zeuxine

An African and Asiatic genus of about thirty species, *Zeuxine* is allied to *Spiranthes*, *Platythelys*, and *Goodyera*. One species, the lawn orchid, *Zeuxine strateumatica*, is naturalized in the New World. Plants appear to be both apomictic and annual. They often appear in greenhouses and potted nursery stock as well as throughout the landscape.

Zeuxine strateumatica (Linnaeus) Schlechter*

lawn orchid

Range: Texas, east to Florida and north to South Carolina; West Indies

Texas Pineywoods, Gulf Prairies and Marshes—a recent introduction possibly in potted nursery materials

Plant: terrestrial, 4–25 cm tall

Leaves: 5–12; lanceolate, green with purple or tan pigmentation (the stem as well); 0.3–1.0 cm wide × 1–8 cm long

Flowers: 5–50+; in a densely flowered terminal spike, the flowers twisted to an angle; sepals and petals similar, oblanceolate; perianth white; lip narrowed at the base and broadly spreading at the apex, bright yellow; individual flower size 6–8 mm

Habitat: lawns, shrub borders, roadsides, and now established in out-of-the-way natural areas

Flowering period: (late October) December into March

Originally attributed to potted nursery stock in its first record from Texas, the **lawn orchid**, *Zeuxine strateumatica*, may also appear in unlikely spots around homes. The plants vary greatly in size and vigor, but there is no other species in bloom at that time of year whose flowers resemble the distinctive white and yellow flowers of the **lawn orchid**. To some it may appear as a *Spiranthes*, but close examination reveals a very different lip. The plants are annuals that move around as the seed blows. Capsules mature in a matter of one to two weeks after flowering. Despite its widespread habits it is in no danger of being a threat to our native orchid populations.

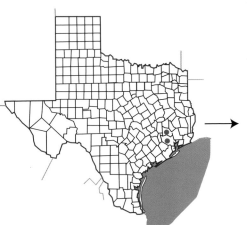

→

Bordering Species, Excluded Species, and Literature Reports

Perhaps because of the sheer size and diversity of Texas, more bordering species are of interest than are usually noted for other regions. Those species found in western Louisiana and southern Oklahoma are more likely to occur in eastern Texas, whereas those of the "sky-islands" of Arizona and New Mexico should be sought in the similar habitats of Trans-Pecos Texas.

Calopogon barbatus (Walter) Ames
bearded grass-pink
Previously considered to range west throughout Louisiana, east Texas, and southern Arkansas, most of those plants have proven to be *Calopogon oklahomensis* (Goldman, 1995). A few sites remain for *C. barbatus* in western Louisiana; listed by Hatch (ca. 2000).

Epidendrum magnoliae Mühlenberg
green-fly orchid
Louisiana
The only epiphyte in upper Gulf Coastal Plain is found within a few miles of the Texas line. This species has been sought, unsuccessfully, for many years in the coastal live oaks of nearby Texas.

Liparis loeselii (Linnaeus) Richard
Loesel's twayblade
Arkansas
Reported for Texas but never vouch-
ered; nearest location is in Garland
County, Arkansas.

Platythelys querceticola (Lindley)
Garay
low ground orchid
Louisiana
Reaching the western limit of its
range in Louisiana, this species has
been reported in the literature for
Texas for many years but without
any supporting herbarium specimen.

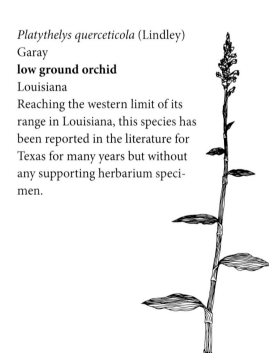

Pteroglossaspis ecristata
(Fernald) Rolfe
crestless plume orchid
Louisiana
Additional sites have recently been found in western Louisiana and are not far from the Texas border. This species often produces many vegetative plants and few inflorescences as well as dormant years.

The species found in bordering counties in southeastern Oklahoma (Magrath, 2001) are most impressive and they deserve intensive searches in nearby Texas. All are very distinctive species and should present no problems in identification.

Aplectrum hyemale
(Mühlenberg *ex* Willdenow) Nuttall
putty-root orchid
Produces a winter leaf and then as the leaf withers, a stem of 8–15 flowers.

Galearis spectabilis (Linnaeus) Rafinesque
showy orchis
The brilliant purple and white flowers on squat leafy plants are a real showstopper!

Goodyera pubescens (Willdenow)
R. Brown
downy rattlesnake orchis
The evergreen, beautifully marked leaves of this "jewel orchid" confirm identification year-round.

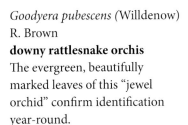

Liparis liliifolia (Linnaeus)
Richard *ex* Lindley
lily-leaved twayblade
Although the chocolate-purple flowers of this, the largest of the twayblades, may be excellent camouflage, the pair of bright green, keeled leaves is distinctive.

Three species of *Malaxis* are found in the "sky-islands" of southern Arizona and New Mexico. Whereas several other species from that area are found in western Texas, these should be carefully sought.

Malaxis abieticola Salazar & Soto Arenas
fir-loving adder's-mouth
Arizona, New Mexico
Restricted to high elevation coniferous forests in both Arizona and New Mexico, the habitat is very limited in the Trans-Pecos

Malaxis corymbosa (S. Watson) Kuntze
flat-topped adder's-mouth
Arizona
The rarest of this group of adder's-mouth orchids, although it is widespread in Mexico

Malaxis porphyrea (Ridley) Kuntze
purple adder's-mouth
Arizona, New Mexico
Similar to Wendt's adder's-mouth, purple-flowered plants encountered in the Trans-Pecos need to be carefully examined; listed by Hatch (ca. 2000); see p. 100 for details

Platanthera brevifolia (Greene) Kranzlein
short-leaved rein orchis
New Mexico
Curiously restricted to a few counties in southern New Mexico and widespread in northern Mexico, this distinctive plant favors cool southern-affinity woodlands.

Platanthera limosa Lindley
Thurber's rein orchis
Arizona, New Mexico
A widespread and not uncommon species in the cool mountains, it would be easy to spot as no other green-flowered *Platanthera* species occur in western Texas.

Microthelys minutiflora (A. Richard &
Galeotti) Garay
tiny-flowered ladies'-tresses
Reported by Cory and Parks (1937), based
on the account of Ed. Palmer (1880), this
species from the Trans-Pecos region has
never been vouchered or reported again for
Texas. Correll (1944) discounted it along
with several others species that have subsequently been found in Texas. The nearest
location vouchered for *M. minutiflora* is in
Coahuila, in north central Mexico, where
it has been collected by Gerardo Salazar.
At the time of the Texas report the genus
Microthelys was included in *Spiranthes*. No
similar spiranthoid species are found in the
Trans-Pecos region, which should elimi-
nate the possibility of confusion. Plants
recently collected in Nuevo Leon and described as *Galeottiella hintoniorum* Todzia
(1994), later transferred to *Microthelys hintoniorum* (Todzia) Szlachetko, Rutkowski,
& Mytnik (2004), are considered by Salazar
to be synonymous with *M. minutiflora*.
Both Coahuila and Nuevo Leon are states
in Mexico that border on Texas.

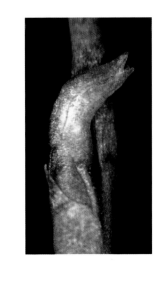

Microthelys rubrocallosa (Robinson &
Greenman) Garay
little red lip
In 2005 *Microthelys rubrocallosa* was
found for the first time in the United
States in southern New Mexico
(Coleman and Baker, 2006).

Epipactis helleborine (Linnaeus)
Cranz
broad-leaved helleborine*
Ranges from eastern North America, spreading westward to the Pacific Northwest and California; Europe
The habitat is highly variable, from shaded calcareous woodlands to front lawns and garden beds and even the crack in a concrete sidewalk; typically a lime-lover. Flowering in late July through August. Not currently known from Texas, this European visitor may easily show up in a variety of calcareous habitats, including recently disturbed building sites and shrub borders.

Some northern species are found in the Rocky Mountains of New Mexico at elevations and habitats that, although not that far from Texas, make them highly unlikely for the Trans-Pecos or High Plains regions of western Texas. These include:
Goodyera oblongifolia, **giant rattlesnake orchis**
Goodyera repens, **lesser rattlesnake orchis**
Piperia unalascensis, **Alaskan piperia**
Platanthera stricta, **slender rein orchis**
Spiranthes romanzoffiana, **hooded ladies'-tresses**
Not really bordering Texas, but erroneously reported earlier and perpetuated by Johnston (1990), *S. romanzoffiana* is a widespread species of northern North America and extends southward in the Rocky Mountains.

The TAMU *Digital Flora of Texas* and the *Texas Vascular Plant Checklist* (Hatch, ca. 2000) list *Corallorhiza striata* var. *vreelandii*, *Platanthera integrilabia*, and *Spiranthes ovalis* var. *erostellata*; none of these taxa have ever been vouchered for the state.

Part 3

References and Resources

Stan Folsom

Checklist of the Wild Orchids of Texas

Calopogon oklahomensis D.H. Goldman
Oklahoma grass-pink
   forma *albiflorus* P.M. Brown—white-flowered form

Calopogon tuberosus (Linnaeus) Britton, Sterns, & Poggenberg var. *tuberosus*
common grass-pink
   forma *albiflorus* Britton—white-flowered form

Cleistes bifaria (Fernald) Catling & Gregg
upland spreading pogonia

Corallorhiza maculata (Rafinesque) Rafinesque var. *occidentalis* (Lindley) Ames
western spotted coralroot
   forma *aurea* P.M. Brown—golden yellow/spotted form
   forma *immaculata* (Peck) Howell—yellow spotless form
   forma *intermedia* Farwell—brown-stemmed form
   forma *punicea* (Bartholomew) Weatherby & Adams—red-stemmed form

Corallorhiza odontorhiza (Willdenow) Nuttall var. *odontorhiza*
autumn coralroot
   forma *flavida* Wherry—yellow-flowered form

Corallorhiza striata Lindley var. *striata*
striped coralroot
   forma *eburnea* P.M. Brown—yellow/white form
   forma *fulva* Fernald—dusky tan form

Corallorhiza wisteriana Conrad
Wister's coralroot
   forma *albolabia* P.M. Brown—white-flowered form
   forma *cooperi* P.M. Brown—cranberry-pink colored form
   forma *rubra* P.M. Brown—red-stemmed form

Cypripedium kentuckiense C.F. Reed
ivory-lipped lady's-slipper
   forma *pricei* P.M. Brown—white-flowered form
   forma *summersii* P.M. Brown—concolorous yellow-flowered form

Cypripedium parviflorum Salisbury var. *pubescens* (Willdenow) Knight
large yellow lady's-slipper

Deiregyne confusa Garay
Hildago ladies'-tresses

Dichromanthus cinnabarinus (La Llave & Lexarza) Garay
cinnabar ladies'-tresses
    forma *aureus* P.M. Brown—golden-yellow flowered form

Dichromanthus michuacanus (La Llave & Lexarza) Salazar & Soto-Arenas
Michoacan ladies'-tresses

Epipactis gigantea Douglas *ex* Hooker
stream orchid
    forma *citrina* P.M. Brown—yellow-flowered form
    forma *rubrifolia* P.M. Brown—red-leaved form

Gymnadeniopsis clavellata (Michaux) Rydberg var. *clavellata*
little club-spur orchis
    forma *slaughteri* (P.M. Brown) P.M. Brown—white-flowered form
    forma *wrightii* (Olive) P.M. Brown—spurless form

Gymnadeniopsis integra (Nuttall) Rydberg
yellow fringeless orchis

Gymnadeniopsis nivea (Nuttall) Rydberg
snowy orchis

Habenaria quinqueseta (Michaux) Eaton
Michaux's orchid

Habenaria repens Nuttall
water-spider orchid

Hexalectris grandiflora (A. Richard & Galeotti) L.O. Williams
Greenman's crested coralroot
    forma *luteoalba* P.M. Brown—whitish-yellow form

Hexalectris nitida L.O. Williams
shining crested coralroot

Hexalectris revoluta Correll var. *revoluta*
recurved crested coralroot

Hexalectris spicata (Walter) Barnhardt var. *spicata*
crested coralroot
   forma *albolabia* P.M. Brown—white flowered form
   forma *lutea* P.M. Brown—yellow-flowered form
   forma *wilderi* P.M. Brown—albino form
Hexalectris spicata (Walter) Barnhardt var. *arizonica* (S. Watson) Catling & Engel
Arizona crested coralroot

Hexalectris warnockii Ames & Correll
Texas purple-spike
   forma *lutea* P.M. Catling—yellow-flowered form

Isotria verticillata Rafinesque
large whorled pogonia

Listera australis Lindley
southern twayblade
   forma *scottii* P.M. Brown—many-leaved form
   forma *trifolia* P.M. Brown—three-leaved form
   forma *viridis* P.M. Brown—green-flowered form

Malaxis soulei L.O. Williams
rat-tailed adder's-mouth

Malaxis unifolia Michaux
green adder's-mouth
   forma *bifolia* (Mousley) Fernald—two-leaved form
   forma *variegata* Mousley—variegated leaf form

Malaxis wendtii Salazar
Wendt's adder's-mouth

Platanthera chapmanii (Small) Luer *emend.* Folsom
Chapman's fringed orchis

Platanthera ciliaris Lindley
orange fringed orchis

Platanthera conspicua (Nash) P.M. Brown
southern white fringed orchis

Platanthera cristata (Michaux) Lindley
orange crested orchis
   forma *straminea* P.M. Brown—pale yellow-flowered form

Platanthera flava (Linnaeus) Lindley var. *flava*
southern tubercled rein orchis
Platanthera flava (Linnaeus) Lindley var. *herbiola* (R. Brown) Luer
northern tubercled rein orchis
   forma *lutea* (Boivin) Whiting & Catling—yellow-flowered form

Platanthera lacera (Michaux) G. Don
green fringed orchis; ragged orchis

Hybrids:
Platanthera ×apalachicola P.M. Brown & S. Stewart
Apalachicola hybrid fringed orchis
(*P. chapmanii* × *P. cristata*)

Platanthera ×channellii Folsom
Channell's hybrid fringed orchis
(*P. ciliaris* × *P. cristata*)

Platanthera ×osceola P.M. Brown & S. Stewart
Osceola hybrid fringed orchis
(*P. chapmanii* × *P. ciliaris*)

Pogonia ophioglossoides (Linnaeus) Ker-Gawler
rose pogonia
   forma *albiflora* Rand & Redfield—white-flowered form
   forma *brachypogon* (Fernald) P.M. Brown—short-bearded form

Ponthieva racemosa (Walter) Mohr
shadow-witch

Schiedeella arizonica P.M. Brown
Indian braids; red-spot ladies'-tresses
   forma *virescens* P.M. Brown—green stemmed form

Spiranthes brevilabris Lindley
Texas ladies'-tresses

Spiranthes cernua (Linnaeus) L.C. Richard
nodding ladies'-tresses

Spiranthes eatonii Ames *ex* P.M. Brown
Eaton's ladies'-tresses

Spiranthes floridana (Wherry) Cory *emend.* P.M. Brown
Florida ladies'-tresses

Spiranthes lacera Rafinesque var. *gracilis* (Bigelow) Luer
southern slender ladies'-tresses

Spiranthes laciniata (Small) Ames
lace-lipped ladies'-tresses

Spiranthes longilabris Lindley
long-lipped ladies'-tresses

Spiranthes magnicamporum Sheviak
Great Plains ladies'-tresses

Spiranthes odorata (Nuttall) Lindley
fragrant ladies'-tresses

Spiranthes ovalis Lindley var. *ovalis*
southern oval ladies'-tresses

Spiranthes parksii Correll
Navasota ladies'-tresses

Spiranthes praecox (Walter) S. Watson
giant ladies'-tresses
 forma *albolabia* Brown & McCartney—white-lipped form

Spiranthes sylvatica P.M. Brown
woodland ladies'-tresses

Spiranthes tuberosa Rafinesque
little ladies'-tresses

Spiranthes vernalis Englemann & Gray
grass-leaved ladies'-tresses

Hybrids:
Spiranthes ×eamesii P.M. Brown
Eames' hybrid ladies'-tresses
(*S. lacera* var. *gracilis* × *S. tuberosa*)

Spiranthes ×folsomii P.M. Brown
Folsom's hybrid ladies'-tresses
(*S. longilabris* × *S. odorata*)

Spiranthes ×itchetuckneensis P.M. Brown
Ichetucknee Springs hybrid ladies'-tresses
(*S. odorata* × *S. ovalis*)

Spiranthes ×intermedia Ames
intermediate hybrid ladies'-tresses
(*S. lacera* var. *gracilis* × *S. vernalis*)

Spiranthes ×meridionalis P.M. Brown
southern hybrid ladies'-tresses
(*S. praecox* × *S. vernalis*)

Tipularia discolor (Pursh) Nuttall
crane-fly orchis
    forma *viridifolia* P.M. Brown

Triphora trianthophora (Swartz) Rydberg var. *trianthophora*
three-birds orchis; nodding pogonia
    forma *albidoflava* Keenan—white and yellow-flowered form
    forma *caerulea* P.M. Brown—blue-flowered form
    forma *rossii* P.M. Brown—multicolor form
Triphora trianthophora (Swartz) Rydberg var. *texensis* P.M. Brown & R.B. Pike
Texas three-birds orchis

Zeuxine strateumatica (Linnaeus) Schlechter
lawn orchid*

Regional Distribution of the Wild Orchids of Texas

Because of the vast size of Texas, comprising 252 counties, distributional informa-tion is grouped by physiographic region. These regions often follow county lines, but in many cases they may bisect a county. Also, the makeup of the regions is not always as precise as we might like. Isolated islands of vegetation certainly occur well away from the main body of several of these regions and therefore selected species may occur as local disjuncts. See map 1.1, p. 2.

[ ] = unvouchered report
H = historic record

Pineywoods

39 species and varieties, including 1 unvouchered report
Located in eastern Texas, this region provides habitat for many of the typical southeastern swamp, coastal plain, and pine flatwoods species
Calopogon oklahomensis, Oklahoma grass-pink
Calopogon tuberosus, common grass-pink
Cleistes bifaria, upland spreading pogonia H
Corallorhiza odontorhiza, autumn coralroot
Corallorhiza wisteriana, Wister's coralroot
Cypripedium kentuckiense, ivory-lipped lady's-slipper
Gymnadeniopsis clavellata, little club-spur orchis
Gymnadeniopsis integra, yellow fringeless orchis
Gymnadeniopsis nivea, snowy orchis
Habenaria quinqueseta, Michaux's orchid
Habenaria repens, water spider orchid
Hexalectris spicata var. *spicata,* crested coralroot
Isotria verticillata, large whorled pogonia
Listera australis, southern twayblade
Malaxis unifolia, green adder's-mouth
Platanthera chapmanii, Chapman's fringed orchis
Platanthera ciliaris, orange fringed orchis
Platanthera cristata, orange crested orchis

Platanthera flava var. *flava*, southern tubercled orchis
Platanthera flava var. *herbiola*, northern tubercled orchis
Platanthera lacera, green fringed orchis; ragged orchis
[*Platytheles querceticola*, low ground orchid]
Pogonia ophioglossoides, rose pogonia
Ponthieva racemosa, shadow-witch
Spiranthes brevilabris, short-lipped ladies'-tresses; Texas ladies'-tresses
Spiranthes cernua, nodding ladies'-tresses
Spiranthes eatonii, Eaton's ladies'-tresses
Spiranthes floridana, Florida ladies'-tresses
Spiranthes lacera var. *gracilis*, southern slender ladies'-tresses
Spiranthes laciniata, lace-lipped ladies'-tresses
Spiranthes longilabris, long-lipped ladies'-tresses
Spiranthes odorata, fragrant ladies'-tresses
Spiranthes ovalis var. *ovalis*, southern oval ladies'-tresses
Spiranthes parksii, Navasota ladies'-tresses
Spiranthes praecox, giant ladies'-tresses
Spiranthes sylvatica, woodland ladies'-tresses
Spiranthes tuberosa, little ladies'-tresses
Spiranthes vernalis, grass-leaved ladies'-tresses
Tipularia discolor, crane-fly orchis
Triphora trianthophora var. *trianthophora*, three-birds orchis; nodding pogonia
Triphora trianthophora var. *texensis*, Texas three-birds orchis
Zeuxine strateumatica, lawn orchid*

Gulf Prairies and Marshes

23 species and varieties
Calopogon oklahomensis, Oklahoma grass-pink
Calopogon tuberosus, common grass-pink
Gymnadeniopsis nivea, snowy orchis
Habenaria repens, water spider orchid
Hexalectris spicata var. *spicata*, crested coralroot
Platanthera conspicua, southern white fringed orchis H
Platanthera ciliaris, orange fringed orchis
Platanthera flava var. *flava*, southern tubercled orchis
Pogonia ophioglossoides, rose pogonia
Spiranthes brevilabris, Texas ladies'-tresses
Spiranthes cernua, nodding ladies'-tresses
Spiranthes eatonii, Eaton's ladies'-tresses

Spiranthes floridana, Florida ladies'-tresses
Spiranthes lacera var. *gracilis*, southern slender ladies'-tresses
Spiranthes laciniata, lace-lipped ladies'-tresses
Spiranthes odorata, fragrant ladies'-tresses
Spiranthes ovalis var. *ovalis*, southern oval ladies'-tresses
Spiranthes parksii, Navasota ladies'-tresses
Spiranthes praecox, giant ladies'-tresses
Spiranthes sylvatica, woodland ladies'-tresses
Spiranthes tuberosa, little ladies'-tresses
Spiranthes vernalis, grass-leaved ladies'-tresses
Zeuxine strateumatica, lawn orchid*

Post Oak Savannah

15 species and varieties
Calopogon oklahomensis, Oklahoma grass-pink
Calopogon tuberosus, common grass-pink
Corallorhiza odontorhiza, autumn coralroot
Corallorhiza wisteriana, Wister's coralroot
Cypripedium kentuckiense, ivory-lipped lady's-slipper
Habenaria repens, water spider orchid
Hexalectris spicata var. *spicata*, crested coralroot
Spiranthes cernua, nodding ladies'-tresses
Spiranthes lacera var. *gracilis*, southern slender ladies'-tresses
Spiranthes magnicamporum, Great Plains ladies'-tresses
Spiranthes odorata, fragrant ladies'-tresses
Spiranthes ovalis var. *ovalis*, southern oval ladies'-tresses
Spiranthes praecox, giant ladies'-tresses
Spiranthes tuberosa, little ladies'-tresses
Spiranthes vernalis, grass-leaved ladies'-tresses

Blackland Prairies

16 species and varieties
Corallorhiza wisteriana, Wister's coralroot
Epipactis gigantea, stream orchid
Gymnadeniopsis nivea, snowy orchis
Habenaria repens, water spider orchid
Hexalectris grandiflora, Greenman's crested coralroot
Hexalectris spicata var. *spicata*, crested coralroot

Hexalectris spicata var. *arizonica*, Arizona crested coralroot
Hexalectris nitida, shining crested coralroot
Hexalectris warnockii, Texas purple-spike
Spiranthes brevilabris, Texas ladies'-tresses
Spiranthes cernua, nodding ladies'-tresses
Spiranthes lacera var. *gracilis*, southern slender ladies'-tresses
Spiranthes magnicamporum, Great Plains ladies'-tresses
Spiranthes odorata, fragrant ladies'-tresses
Spiranthes praecox, giant ladies'-tresses
Spiranthes tuberosa, little ladies'-tresses
Spiranthes vernalis, grass-leaved ladies'-tresses

Cross Timbers and Prairies

6 species and varieties
Corallorhiza wisteriana, Wister's coralroot
Epipactis gigantea, stream orchid
Hexalectris spicata var. *spicata*, crested coralroot
Spiranthes cernua, nodding ladies'-tresses
Spiranthes lacera var. *gracilis*, southern slender ladies'-tresses
Spiranthes magnicamporum, Great Plains ladies'-tresses

South Texas Plains

7 species and varieties
Corallorhiza wisteriana, Wister's coralroot
Epipactis gigantea, stream orchid
Hexalectris nitida, shining crested coralroot
Hexalectris spicata var. *spicata*, crested coralroot
Hexalectris spicata var. *arizonica*, Arizona crested coralroot
Hexalectris warnockii, Texas purple-spike
Spiranthes magnicamporum, Great Plains ladies'-tresses

Edwards Plateau

7 species and varieties
Epipactis gigantea, stream orchid
Hexalectris nitida, shining crested coralroot
Hexalectris warnockii, Texas purple-spike
Hexalectris spicata var. *spicata*, crested coralroot

Hexalectris spicata var. *arizonica*, Arizona crested coralroot
Corallorhiza wisteriana, Wister's coralroot
Spiranthes magnicamporum, Great Plains ladies'-tresses

Rolling Plains

2 species and varieties
Epipactis gigantea, stream orchid
Spiranthes vernalis, grass-leaved ladies'-tresses

High Plains

1 species
Cypripedium parviflorum var. *pubescens*, large yellow lady's-slipper H

Trans-Pecos Texas

15 species and varieties
Corallorhiza maculata var. *occidentalis*, western spotted coralroot
Corallorhiza striata var. *striata*, striped coralroot
Deiregyne confusa, rimrock ladies'-tresses
Dichromanthus cinnabarinus, cinnabar ladies'-tresses
Dichromanthus michuacanus, Michoacan ladies'-tresses
Epipactis gigantea, stream orchid
Hexalectris nitida, shining crested coralroot
Hexalectris grandiflora, Greenman's crested coralroot
Hexalectris revoluta, recurved crested coralroot
Hexalectris spicata var. *spicata*, crested coralroot
Hexalectris spicata var. *arizonica*, Arizona crested coralroot
Hexalectris warnockii, Texas purple-spike
Malaxis soulei, rat-tailed adder's-mouth
Malaxis wendtii, Wendt's adder's-mouth
Schiedeella arizonica, Indian braids

Comparative Taxonomy and Notes on Texas Orchid Publications

Because of numerous taxonomic changes over the past 175 years, nearly all earlier publications concerning the Orchidaceae of Texas contain misconceptions or misinformation. This is not to say that these publications are full of errors, although the occasional error may have occurred, but that taxonomic and distributional knowledge at the time of manuscript preparation became dated in the ensuing years. For the current student of Texas's native orchids, it can be very confusing to try to align Correll's work of 1944 or even that of 1950 with today's knowledge. Table 3.1, at the end of this description of publications, compares orchid names known from Texas at the time of publication with those used in this book. Correll's publications, specifically on the *Orchidaceae* of Texas from 1944 and 1947 and his contribution to Correll and Johnston (1979, below), are treated as a single unit.

The publication in 2002 of the Orchidaceae in *Flora of North America* helped to standardize much of the taxonomic and distributional information. But that information had been completed well before the publication date and, despite exhaustive editing and proofing, some errors in content were incorporated into the final version. Details of publication of the following sources can be found in the bibliography.

Coulter. 1894. *Botany of Western Texas.*

Includes only 9 species, primarily from western (defined liberally) Texas

It is here that *Achroanthes monophylla* (Lindley) Green is listed with *Microstylis monophyllos* Lindley as a synonym. This caused considerable early confusion because this plant as it reads is a species from northern latitudes of North America and was never recorded for such latitude or habitat as Texas. Correll (1944) states that this is an error and it was perpetuated and mapped by Small and others. Coulter's description and the specimens he based it upon are *Malaxis unifolia* Michaux.

Coulter's description of *Corallorhiza odontorhiza* Nuttall is clearly that of *C. wisteriana* Conrad. Although cited from Texas by several authors and mapped by Luer (1975), *Corallorhiza odontorhiza* was not found in Texas until 1979.

Cory and Parks. 1937. *Catalogue of the flora of the state of Texas.*

This first comprehensive list for Texas included 34 species, but several are synonyms. The publication presents several interesting citations.

A major error was in the listing of *Blephariglottis tricholepis* (Torrey) Nash, which apparently is *Blepharoneuron tricholepis* (Torrey) Nash in the *Poaceae*, a grass known primarily from the Trans-Pecos region. Both *Corallorhiza odontorhiza* and *C. wisteriana* are included, as are *Malaxis monophyllos* and *M. unifolia*. Apart from some standard synonyms used then, Cory and Parks also list *Liparis loeselii, Physurus querceticola, Spiranthes brevifolia, S. minutiflora, S. ochroleuca,* and *S. reverchonii. Spiranthes reverchonii* has proven to be *S. vernalis,* and *S. brevifolia* is a synonym for *S. longilabris.* Also, given the habitat listed for *S. ochroleuca,* the plants are most likely a cream-colored prairie form of *S. cernua* or *S. magnicamporum,* but certainly not *S. ochroleuca* from northeastern North America.

Spiranthes minutiflora presents the most intriguing record of all. By today's nomenclature this would be *Microthelys minutiflora* (Garay, 1980[1982]; Szlachetko et al., 2005), a small, inconspicuous spiranthoid species known from northern Mexico. Cory and Parks noted it from the Trans-Pecos region based on a report of Ed. Palmer from his expedition in 1880. Until 2005 this would have been discounted, as no specimen has ever been found to substantiate this listing. But in 2005 *Microthelys rubrocallosa,* a similar and closely related species from northern Mexico, was found for the first time in the United States in southwestern New Mexico (Coleman and Baker, 2006)! *Liparis loeselii,* subsequently mapped for Texas by several authors but discounted by Correll and the Liggios, has been found fewer than 200 miles away to the north and the east in Kansas, Arkansas, and Mississippi. This species was mentioned in an informal verbal report on the plants of Caddo Lake on the Texas/Louisiana border, and the habitat certainly exists there for it. Apparently no specimen exists for Texas.

Physurus querceticola (*Platythelys querceticola*) is included most likely on the basis of the range given for Texas in Ames (1924). Again, no specimen of this species has ever been located for Texas, nor have plants ever been reported, but they do occur not far away in southern Louisiana. Curious typos are Canefly for Cranefly and, in the following family, Saururaceae, the genus *Tipularia* for *Saururus.*

Correll. 1944. Orchidaceae. Vol. 3, pt. 3, *Flora of Texas.*

Correll's initial work on the Orchidaceae of Texas cleared up most of these problems in both taxonomy and distribution, and mention is made of some of the claims by Cory and Parks for species not recorded from Texas. Two excluded species are mentioned for the first time: *Habenaria* (*Platanthera*) *limosa* from nearby New Mexico and *Epidendrum conopseum* (*E. magnoliae*) from just over the state line in Louisiana. Although Correll was optimistic about finding both of these in Texas, they have never been reported or vouchered for the state. Correll's species concepts in 1944 did not include the yet-to-be-described *Cypripedium kentuckiense, Calopogon oklahomensis,* or *Cleistes bifaria.*

Correll. 1947. *Additions to the Orchids of Texas.*

Several additional species were added to the flora of Texas in this publication and a few taxonomic changes were made.

Correll. 1962. Orchidaceae, in *Texas Plants: A Checklist and Ecological Summary*

List similar to that of Correll 1944 and 1947.

Gould. 1969. *Texas Plants: A Checklist and Ecological Summary* with supplement (Orchidaceae contributed by Correll)

Calopogon barbatus appears for the first time in the supplement

Gould. 1975. *Texas Plants: A Checklist and Ecological Summary* (Orchidaceae contributed by Correll)

List similar to that of previous Correll lists

Correll and Johnston. 1979. *Manual of Vascular Flora of Texas.*

Taxonomy essentially the same as previous Correll publications, with the addition of *Calopogon barbatus* and *Malaxis ehrenbergii,* and comments on *Triphora trianthophora* var. *schaffneri.*

Hatch, Gandhi, and Brown. 1990. *Checklist of the vascular plants of Texas.*

Both the original 1990 publication and the Web version indicate several regional records that do not appear elsewhere. The 2001 revised version corrected some of those records, but several well-documented species have been omitted from both versions.

1990. http://www.csdl.tamu.edu/FLORA/cgi/plants?type= boolean&query=orchidaceae&rform=full

2001. http://www.csdl.tamu.edu/FLORA/cgi/msproj/shao/ frame.pl?query=orchidaceae&rform=list&type=Boolean

In or about 2000 Hatch/TAMU published the *Digital Flora of Texas* and the *Texas Vascular Plant Checklist* on the Internet. Orchidaceae contains several curious entries that have never been substantiated for Texas, as well as several perpetuated errors and a few omissions. Most notable as discounted species are *Calopogon barbatus, Corallorhiza striata* var. *vreelandii, Malaxis porphyrea, Plat-*

anthera integrilabia, and *Spiranthes ovalis* var. *erostellata. Spiranthes eatonii* and *Cypripedium parviflorum* var. *pubescens* were omitted. Several other synonyms or misapplied names also were used. Perhaps the most interesting is the inclusion of *Platanthera* ×*canbyi* (see page 118 for a discussion of this hybrid).

Jones, Wipff, and Montgomery. 1997. *Vascular plants of Texas: A comprehensive checklist including synonymy, bibliography, and index.*

Includes a wealth of synonyms, many obscure, and two non-natives, *Phaius* and *Bletilla,* noted as cultivated but no indication whether they are escaped, introduced, or naturalized

Diggs, Lipscomb, and O'Kennon. 1999. *Shinner's and Mahler's Illustrated Flora of North Central Texas.*

Calopogon barbatus, although treated at the full species level, is noted as not being a component of the Texas flora. *Spiranthes longilabris* is reported but has not been vouchered from north central Texas. It was included based upon a report by Hatch et al., 1990.

Liggio and Liggio. 1999. *Wild Orchids of Texas.*

More than a decade was spent in preparing the manuscript for this work, and to enable a 1999 publication, although primary research continued through 1997. At that time several new taxa had not been described, although they are illustrated in the text. The description and photographs of *Schiedeella parasitica* are *S. arizonica*; the photograph captioned *S. praecox* is *S. sylvatica*; the photograph captioned *S. floridana* is *S. eatonii*. The latter two species are not treated in the book. The photograph of *Corallorhiza maculata* is the variety *occidentalis* and the photograph labeled *Malaxis wendtii* is *M. porphyrea* from New Mexico (Carr, 2005).

Turner, Nichols, Denny, and Doron. 2003. *Atlas of the Vascular Plants of Texas.*

Several taxa are not treated, including *Spiranthes sylvatica* and *S. eatonii*

Maps are duplicated for *Dichromanthus cinnabarinus* (as *Spiranthes cinnabarina*) and several others are based upon synonyms and/or misapplied names. Included are several additional county records not cited in Liggio and Liggio.

Diggs, Lipscomb, Reed, and O'Kennon. 2006. *Illustrated Flora of East Texas.*

This is the most up-to-date and complete treatment of the orchids in a regional Texas publication.

Four continental publications treat the orchids of Texas:

Correll. 1950. *Native Orchids of North America.*
Follows the taxonomy set forth in his previous publications.

Luer. 1972. *The Native Orchids of Florida.*
———. **1975. *The Native Orchids of the United States and Canada excluding Florida.***
Texas species are included in each publication. Numerous taxonomic changes are provided, especially in *Habenaria/Platanthera* and *Spiranthes*.

***Flora of North America North of Mexico*. 2002. Vol. 26, Orchidaceae.** This publication contains extensive taxonomic and distributional revisions; erroneous distributional information excluded the following from Texas: *Cypripedium parviflorum* var. *pubescens*; *Cleistes bifaria*; *Zeuxine strateumatica*; *Platanthera flava* var. *herbiola* (in text but not mapped); *Corallorhiza maculata*; *Spiranthes sylvatica* was not yet published at this time.

Brown and Folsom. 2003. *The Wild Orchids of North America, North of Mexico.*
Follows *FNA* closely and also omits *Cypripedium parviflorum* var. *pubescens*, *Platanthera flava* var. *herbiola*, and *Corallorhiza maculata* from Texas

Regional works that treat portions of Texas

Brown and Folsom. 2004. *Wild Orchids of the Southeastern United States.*
Also omits the general distribution of the above three species from Texas; the map for *Corallorhiza odontorhiza* var. *odontorhiza* is too expansive; included is the restoration of *Platanthera conspicua* and the genus *Gymnadeniopsis*.

Brown and Folsom. 2006c. *Wild Orchids of the Prairies and Great Plains Region of North America.*
Consistent with the present volume.

Table 3.1, on the following two pages, compares the taxonomy of the seven major statewide publications; only those species historically known by two or more names are included.

Note:
Reports of excluded species: *Liparis loeselii*, *Microstylis monophyllos*, *Physurus querceticola*, *Spiranthes minutiflora*, *Spiranthes ochroleuca*, *Spiranthes reverchonii* (=*S. vernalis*)
Horticultural records: *Bletilla striata*, *Phaius tankervilliae*
Cryptic citation: *Blephariglottis tricholepis-Blepharoneuron tricolepis* (Poaceae)

Brown 2008

nt = not treated

Brown 2008	Cory & Parks 1937	Correll 1944/1947	Hatch et al. 1990, 2000, 2001
Calopogon oklahomensis	nt	C. barbatus	C. barbatus
Calopogon tuberosus	C. tuberosus	C. pulchellus	C. tuberosus
Cleistes bifaria	nt	nt '44; C. divaricata '47	C. divaricata
Corallorhiza odontorhiza	nt	nt	C. odontorhiza
Cypripedium kentuckiense	nt	C. calceolus var. pubescens	C. calceolus var. pubescens
Cypripedium parviflorum var. pubescens	C. calceolus var. pubescens	C. calceolus var. pubescens	C. calceolus var. pubescens
Deiregyne confusa	Spiranthes saltensis	Spiranthes durangensis	Spiranthes durangensis
Dichromanthus cinnabarinus	Spiranthes cinnabarina	Spiranthes cinnabarina	Spiranthes cinnabarina
Dichromanthus michuacanus	Spiranthes michuacana	Spiranthes michuacana	Spiranthes michuacana
Gymnadeniopsis clavellata	nt	Habenaria clavellata	Habenaria clavellata
Gymnadeniopsis integra	Habenaria integra	Habenaria integra	Habenaria integra
Gymnadeniopsis nivea	Habenaria nivea	Habenaria nivea	Habenaria nivea
Hexalectris grandiflora	nt	H. mexicana	H. grandiflora
Hexalectris spicata var. spicata	H. spicata	H. spicata	H. spicata
Hexalectris spicata var. arizonica	nt	nt	nt
Malaxis soulei	M. montana	M. soulei	M. soulei
Malaxis wendtii	nt	nt	nt
Platanthera chapmanii	nt	XHabenaria chapmanii	Habenaria xchapmanii
Platanthera ciliaris	Blephariglottis ciliaris	Habenaria ciliaris	Habenaria ciliaris
Platanthera conspicua	nt	Habenaria blephariglottis	Habenaria blephariglottis
Platanthera cristata	nt	Habenaria cristata	Habenaria cristata
Platanthera flava var. flava	nt	nt	Habenaria flava var. flava
Platanthera flava var. herbiola	nt	nt	nt
Platanthera lacera	nt	Habenaria lacera ('47)	Habenaria lacera
Schiedeella arizonica	nt	Spiranthes parasitica	Spiranthes parasitica
Spiranthes brevilabris	nt	S. gracilis var. brevilabris	S. gracilis var. brevilabris
Spiranthes eatonii	nt	nt	nt
Spiranthes floridana	S. floridana	S. gracilis var. floridana	S. gracilis var. floridana
Spiranthes lacera var. gracilis	S. gracilis	S. gracilis var. gracilis	S. gracilis var. gracilis
Spiranthes longilabris	S. brevifolia	S. longilabris	S. longilabris
Spiranthes magnicamporum	nt	nt	nt
Spiranthes odorata	S. odorata	S. cernua var. odorata	S. cernua var. odorata
Spiranthes ovalis var. ovalis	S. ovalis	nt	S. ovalis
Spiranthes parksii	nt	S. parksii	S. parksii
Spiranthes sylvatica	nt	nt	nt
Spiranthes tuberosa	S. beckii	S. beckii '44/S. grayi('47)	S. beckii / S. grayi
Triphora trianthophora var. texensis	nt	nt	nt
Zeuxine strateumatica	nt	nt	nt

Jones 1997	Liggio 1999	Turner 2003	Brown 2008
C. oklahomensis	*C. oklahomensis*	*C. oklahomensis*	*Calopogon oklahomensis*
C. tuberosus	*C. tuberosus*	*C. tuberosus*	*Calopogon tuberosus*
C. bifaria	*C. bifaria*	*C. divaricata*	*Cleistes bifaria*
C. odontorhiza	*C. odontorhiza*	*C. odontorhiza*	*Corallorhiza odontorhiza*
C. kentuckiense	*C. kentuckiense*	*C. kentuckiense*	*Cypripedium kentuckiense*
C. pubescens	*C. parviflorum* var. *pubescens*	*C. pubescens*	*Cypripedium parviflorum* var. *pubescens*
Spiranthes saltensis	*D. confusa*	*D. confusa*	*Deiregyne confusa*
Dicromanthus cinnabarinus	*D. cinnabarinus*	*D. cinnabarinus* (*Spiranthes*)	*Dichromanthus cinnabarinus*
Stenorrhynchos michuacanus	*Stenorrhynchos michuacanus*	*Spiranthes michuacana*	*Dichromanthus michuacanus*
Platanthera clavellata	*Platanthera clavellata*	*Platanthera clavellata*	*Gymnadeniopsis clavellata*
Platanthera integra	*Platanthera integra*	*Platanthera integra*	*Gymnadeniopsis integra*
Platanthera nivea	*Platanthera nivea*	*Platanthera nivea*	*Gymnadeniopsis nivea*
H. grandiflora	*H. grandiflora*	*H. grandiflora*	*Hexalectris grandiflora*
H. spicata	*H. spicata* var. *spicata*	*H. spicata*	*Hexalectris spicata* var. *spicata*
H. spicata var. *arizonica*	*H. spicata* var. *arizonica*	nt	*Hexalectris spicata* var. *arizonica*
M. macrostachya	*M. macrostachya*	*M. macrostachya*/*M. soulei*	*Malaxis soulei*
M. wendtii	*M. wendtii*	*M. wendtii*	*Malaxis wendtii*
nt	*P. chapmanii*	*P. chapmanii*	*Platanthera chapmanii*
P. ciliaris	*P. ciliaris*	*P. ciliaris*	*Platanthera ciliaris*
P. blephariglottis var. *conspicua*	*P. blephariglottis* var. *conspicua*	*P. blephariglottis*	*Platanthera conspicua*
P. cristata	*P. cristata*	*P. cristata*	*Platanthera cristata*
P. flava	*P. flava*	*P. flava* var. *flava*	*Platanthera flava* var. *flava*
nt	nt	nt	*Platanthera flava* var. *herbiola*
P. lacera	*P. lacera*	*P. lacera*	*Platanthera lacera*
Schiedeella parasitica	*Schiedeella parasitica*	*Schiedeella parasitica*	*Schiedeella arizonica*
S. brevilabris var. *brevilabris*	*S. brevilabris*	*S. gracilis* var. *brevilabris*	*Spiranthes brevilabris*
nt	nt	nt	*Spiranthes eatonii*
S. brevilabris var. *floridana*	*S. floridana*	nt	*Spiranthes floridana*
S. lacera var. *gracilis*	*S. lacera* var. *gracilis*	*S. lacera*	*Spiranthes lacera* var. *gracilis*
S. longilabris	*S. longilabris*	*S. longilabris*	*Spiranthes longilabris*
S. magnicamporum	*S. magnicamporum*	*S. magnicamporum*	*Spiranthes magnicamporum*
S. odorata	*S. odorata*	*S. odorata*	*Spiranthes odorata*
S. ovalis	*S. ovalis*	*S. ovalis*	*Spiranthes ovalis*
S. parksii	*S. parksii*	*S. parksii*	*Spiranthes parksii*
nt	nt	nt	*Spiranthes sylvatica*
S. tuberosa	*S. tuberosa*	*S. tuberosa*	*Spiranthes tuberosa*
nt	nt	nt	*Triphora trianthophora* var. *texensis*
Z. strateumatica	*Z. strateumatica*	*Z. strateumatica*	*Zeuxine strateumatica*

Some Facts about the Wild Orchids of Texas

10 species and varieties are known from only 1 county:
Cleistes bifaria, upland spreading pogonia
Cypripedium parviflorum var. *pubescens*, large yellow lady's-slipper
Deiregyne confusa, rimrock ladies'-tresses
Dichromanthus cinnabarinus, cinnabar ladies'-tresses
Habenaria quinqueseta, Michaux's orchid
Malaxis wendtii, Wendt's adder's-mouth
Platanthera conspicua, southern white fringed orchis
Platanthera flava var. *herbiola*, northern tubercled orchis (report)
Platanthera lacera, green fringed orchis; ragged orchis
Triphora trianthophora var. *texensis*, Texas three-birds orchis

10 species are known from only 2 counties:
Corallorhiza maculata var. *occidentalis*, western spotted coralroot
Corallorhiza odontorhiza, autumn coralroot
Corallorhiza striata, striped coralroot
Dichromanthus michuacanus, Michoacan ladies'-tresses
Hexalectris revoluta, recurved crested coralroot
Malaxis soulei, rat-tailed adder's-mouth
Ponthieva racemosa, shadow-witch
Schiedeella arizonica, Indian braids; Arizona red-spot
Spiranthes longilabris, long-lipped ladies'-tresses
Zeuxine strateumatica, lawn orchid*

2 species are known from only 3 counties:
Gymnadeniopsis integra, yellow fringeless orchis
Hexalectris grandiflora, Greenman's crested coralroot

4 species are considered historical or extirpated:
Cleistes bifaria, upland spreading pogonia
Cypripedium parviflorum var. *pubescens*, large yellow lady's-slipper
Habenaria quinqueseta, Michaux's orchid
Platanthera conspicua, southern white fringed orchis

3 species previously considered historical have recently been rediscovered:
Deiregyne confusa, rimrock ladies'-tresses 2004
Gymnadeniopsis integra, yellow fringeless orchis 1988
Spiranthes parksii, Navasota ladies'-tresses 1978

1 species, not based upon taxonomic changes, was recently discovered in Texas:
Corallorhiza odontorhiza, autumn coralroot 1979

34 species and varieties reach the western limit of their range in Texas:
Calopogon oklahomensis, Oklahoma grass-pink
Calopogon tuberosus, common grass-pink
Cleistes bifaria, upland spreading pogonia
Cypripedium kentuckiense, ivory-lipped lady's-slipper
Gymnadeniopsis clavellata, little club-spur orchis
Gymnadeniopsis integra, yellow fringeless orchis
Gymnadeniopsis nivea, snowy orchis
Habenaria quinqueseta, Michaux's orchid
Habenaria repens, water spider orchid
Isotria verticillata, large whorled pogonia
Listera australis, southern twayblade
Malaxis unifolia, green adder's-mouth
Platanthera chapmanii, Chapman's fringed orchis
Platanthera ciliaris, orange fringed orchis
Platanthera conspicua, southern white fringed orchis
Platanthera cristata, orange crested orchis
Platanthera flava var. *flava,* southern tubercled orchis
Platanthera flava var. *herbiola*, northern tubercled orchis
Platanthera lacera, green fringed orchis; ragged orchis
Pogonia ophioglossoides, rose pogonia
Ponthieva racemosa, shadow-witch
Spiranthes brevilabris, short-lipped ladies'-tresses; Texas ladies'-tresses
Spiranthes eatonii, Eaton's ladies'-tresses
Spiranthes floridana, Florida ladies'-tresses
Spiranthes laciniata, lace-lipped ladies'-tresses
Spiranthes longilabris, long-lipped ladies'-tresses
Spiranthes odorata, fragrant ladies'-tresses
Spiranthes ovalis var. *ovalis*, southern oval ladies'-tresses
Spiranthes praecox, giant ladies'-tresses
Spiranthes sylvatica, woodland ladies'-tresses

Spiranthes tuberosa, little ladies'-tresses
Tipularia discolor, crane-fly orchis
Triphora trianthophora, three-birds orchis; nodding pogonia
Zeuxine strateumatica, lawn orchid*

12 species and varieties reach the eastern limit of their range in Texas:
Deiregyne confusa, rimrock ladies'-tresses
Dichromanthus cinnabarinus, cinnabar ladies'-tresses
Dichromanthus michuacanus, Michoacan ladies'-tresses
Hexalectris grandiflora, Greenman's crested coralroot
Hexalectris nitida, shining crested coralroot
Hexalectris revoluta, recurved crested coralroot
Hexalectris spicata var. *arizonica*, Arizona crested coralroot
Hexalectris warnockii, Texas purple-spike
Malaxis soulei, rat-tailed adder's-mouth
Malaxis wendtii, Wendt's adder's-mouth
Schiedeella arizonica, Indian braids; Arizona red-spot
Spiranthes parksii, Navasota ladies'-tresses

8 species reach the northern limit of their range in Texas and are more frequent in Mexico:
Deiregyne confusa, rimrock ladies'-tresses
Dichromanthus cinnabarinus, cinnabar ladies'-tresses
Dichromanthus michuacanus, Michoacan ladies'-tresses
Hexalectris grandiflora, Greenman's crested coralroot
Hexalectris nitida, shining crested coralroot
Hexalectris revoluta, recurved crested coralroot
Malaxis soulei, rat-tailed adder's-mouth
Malaxis wendtii, Wendt's adder's-mouth

1 species and 1 variety are endemic to Texas:
Spiranthes parksii, Navasota ladies'-tresses
Triphora trianthophora var. *texensis*, Texas three-birds orchis

2 species are endemic to the southwestern United States (Texas, New Mexico, Arizona):
Schiedeella arizonica, Indian braids; Arizona red-spot
Spiranthes parksii, Navasota ladies'-tresses

5 species and 2 varieties are found in the United States only in Texas:
Deiregyne confusa, rimrock ladies'-tresses
Dichromanthus cinnabarinus, cinnabar ladies'-tresses
Hexalectris grandiflora, Greenman's crested coralroot
Hexalectris revoluta var. *revoluta*, recurved crested coralroot
Malaxis wendtii, Wendt's adder's-mouth
Spiranthes parksii, Navasota ladies'-tresses
Triphora trianthophora var. *texensis*, Texas three-birds orchis

6 species have been reported in the literature from Texas but without supporting herbarium specimens:
Calopogon barbatus, bearded grass-pink: east Texas; all specimens proved to be *C. oklahomensis*
Cleistes bifaria (as *C. divaricata*). Upland rosebud orchid: specimen collected by Palmer was seen by Correll (1937) but never relocated
Liparis loeselii, Loesel's twayblade: cited by Cory and Parks (1937) but without any information
Microthelys minutiflora (as *Spiranthes*), tiny-flowered ladies'-tresses: cited by Cory and Parks (1937) but without any information
Platytheles querceticola, low ground orchid: reported in Ames (1924) but never vouchered or seen
Spiranthes romanzoffiana, hooded ladies'-tresses: included by Johnson (1990) but further research indicates it may have been a labeling error (Liggio and Liggio, 1999)

6 species found in Texas have recently been described and were often merged with other established species:
Calopogon oklahomensis, Oklahoma grass-pink [*C. barbatus*]
Deiregyne confusa, rimrock ladies'-tresses [*Spiranthes durangensis*; *D. durangensis*]
Malaxis wendtii, Wendt's adder's-mouth [*M. ehrenbergii*; *M. porphyrea*]
Schiedeella arizonica, Indian braids; Arizona red-spot [*Spiranthes parasitica*, *S. fauci-sanguinea*; *Schiedeella parasitica*, *S. fauci-sanguinea*]
Spiranthes eatonii, Eaton's ladies'-tresses [*S. floridana*, *S. lacera* var. *gracilis*]
Spiranthes sylvatica, woodland ladies'-tresses [*S. praecox*]

3 species honor prominent Texas botanists:
Hexalectris warnockii, Texas purple-spike: Barton Warnock
Malaxis wendtii, Wendt's adder's-mouth: Tom Wendt
Spiranthes parksii, Navasota ladies'-tresses: Haliburton Parks

1 species is non-native
Zeuxine strateumatica, lawn orchid: Asia

Spiranthes is the largest genus in Texas with 15 species; 4 additional species, in various concepts, have also been treated as *Spiranthes*:
Deiregyne confusa, rimrock ladies'-tresses
Dichromanthus cinnabarinus, cinnabar ladies'-tresses
Dichromanthus michuacanus, Michoacan ladies'-tresses
Schiedeella arizonica, red-spot ladies'-tresses

3 taxa traditionally (Correll, Luer) treated at the varietal level are again recognized at the species level:
Cleistes bifaria, upland spreading pogonia
Platanthera conspicua, southern white fringed orchis
Spiranthes floridana, Florida ladies'-tresses

3 taxa originally described as species are treated at the varietal level:
Cypripedium parviflorum var. *pubescens*, large yellow lady's-slipper
Corallorhiza maculata var. *occidentalis*, western spotted coralroot
Hexalectris spicata var. *arizonica*, Arizona crested coralroot

5 species and 1 variety were originally described from Texas:
Hexalectris warnockii, Texas purple-spike Wimberley 1925 (Warnock 1937 type)
Spiranthes brevilabris, Texas ladies'-tresses Drummond 1840 type
Spiranthes ovalis var. *ovalis*, southern oval ladies'-tresses Drummond (Lindley) 1840 type
Spiranthes parksii, Navasota ladies'-tresses Parks 1945
Spiranthes vernalis, grass-leaved ladies'-tresses Lindheimer 1843 type
Triphora trianthophora var. *texensis*, Texas three-birds orchis 2007 based upon discovery in 2005 by Pike type

Chronology of Orchid Discoveries in Texas

Because of the wealth of publication on the flora of Texas, collection details have been recorded for many species of orchids found in the state. Several were found prior to 1844, and a few were collected and then unidentified until many years later. Some species that were identified under older recognized names have proven to be new species more recently described. In a few instances, recently reported species had not been seen since their original discovery/collection. Those dates are noted as well. The remaining species do not have precise discovery/collection dates.

Calopogon oklahomensis. Oklahoma grass-pink (as *C. tuberosus*), Lindheimer 1842

Calopogon tuberosus, common grass-pink, Lindheimer 1842

Cleistes bifaria, upland spreading pogonia, Palmer 193?

Corallorhiza maculata var. *occidentalis*, western spotted coralroot, Palmer 193?

Corallorhiza odontorhiza, autumn coralroot, Ajilvsgi 1979

Corallorhiza striata var. *striata*, striped coralroot, Hinckley

Corallorhiza wisteriana, Wister's coralroot, prior to 1898

Cypripedium parviflorum var. *pubescens*, large yellow lady's- slipper, Tharp 1929

Deiregyne confusa, Durango ladies'-tresses, Moore and Steyermark 1931, relocated 2004

Dichromanthus cinnabarinus, cinnabar ladies'-tresses, Harvard 1883

Dichromanthus michuacanus, Michoacan ladies'-tresses, Harvard 1880

Gymnadeniopsis integra, yellow fringeless orchis, Hooks 1950

Gymnadeniopsis nivea, snowy orchis, Lindheimer 1843

Habenaria quinqueseta, Michaux's orchid, Wright 1837–44

Hexalectris grandiflora, Greenman's crested coralroot, Wimberley 1925

Hexalectris nitida, shining crested coralroot, Warnock 1940

Hexalectris revoluta, recurved crested coralroot, Warnock 1937

Hexalectris spicata var. *arizonica*, Arizona crested coralroot, Meuller 1932

Platanthera ciliaris, orange fringed orchis, Neally 1884

Platanthera conspicua, southern white fringed orchis, Moyer 1900?

Platanthera flava var. *flava,* southern tubercled orchis, Drummond 1832

Platanthera flava var. *herbiola*, northern tubercled orchis, Pelchat 2002

Platanthera lacera, green fringed orchis; ragged orchis, Correll and Correll 1946

Ponthieva racemosa, shadow-witch Correll and Correll 1946

Schiedeella arizonica, Indian braids Palmer 1926

Spiranthes cernua, nodding ladies'-tresses Lindheimer 1842

Spiranthes eatonii, Eaton's ladies'-tresses Cory 1950/Brown 2001

Spiranthes floridana, Florida ladies'-tresses Hall 1872

Spiranthes lacera var. *gracilis*, southern slender ladies'-tresses Lindheimer 1839

Spiranthes laciniata, lace-lipped ladies'-tresses Neally 1939

Spiranthes longilabris, long-lipped ladies'-tresses Cory 1945

Spiranthes odorata, fragrant ladies'-tresses Lindheimer 1842

Spiranthes parksii, Navasota ladies'-tresses Parks 1945 type

Spiranthes sylvatica, woodland ladies'-tresses Brown 2002 based upon earlier specimens of *S. praecox*

Spiranthes tuberosa, little ladies'-tresses Hall 1872

Triphora trianthophora var. *texensis*, Texas three-birds orchis; Pikes three-birds orchis Pike 2005

Zeuxine strateumatica, lawn orchid 1989

Recent Literature References for New Taxa, Combinations, and Additions

Calopogon oklahomensis D.H. Goldman
Oklahoma grass-pink
Goldman, D. H. 1995. *Lindleyana* 10(1): 37–42.

Corallorhiza maculata (Rafinesque) Rafinesque var. *occidentalis* (Lindley) Ames
western spotted coralroot
Freudenstein, J. V. 1986. *Contributions from the University of Michigan Herbarium* 16: 145–53.

Cypripedium kentuckiense C.F. Reed
ivory-lipped lady's-slipper
Atwood, J. T., Jr. 1984. *AOS Bulletin* 53(8): 835–41.
Brown, P. M. 1995. *NANOJ* 1(3): 255.
———. 1998. *NANOJ* 4(1): 45.
Reed, C. 1981. *Phytologia* 48(5): 426–28.
Weldy, T. W., H. T. Mlodozeniec, L. E. Wallace, and M. A. Case. 1996. *Sida* 17(2): 423–35.

Cypripedium parviflorum Salisbury var. *pubescens*
large yellow lady's-slipper
Sheviak, C. J. 1994. *AOS Bulletin* 63(6): 664–69.
———. 1995. *AOS Bulletin* 64(6): 606–12.
———. 1996. *NANOJ* 2(4): 319–343.

Deiregyne confusa Garay
rimrock ladies'-tresses
Ambs, S. 2006. *Native Orchid Conference Journal* 3(2): 1–5.

Gymnadeniopsis Rydberg
Brown, P.M. 2002. *North American Native Orchid Journal* 8: 32–40.
Rydberg, P.A. 1901. in Britton, *Manual of the Flora of the Northeastern United States*, p. 293.

Gymnadeniopsis clavellata (Michaux) Rydberg var. *clavellata*
  forma *wrightii* (Olive) P.M. Brown—spurless form
Brown, P. M., and S. N. Folsom. 2006. *Wild Orchids of the Canadian Maritimes and Northern Great Lakes Region*, p. 284.
Brown, P. M. 2006. *North American Native Orchid Journal* 12: 30.

Hexalectris
Catling, P. M. 2004. *Native Orchid Conference Journal* 2: 5–25.

Hexalectris grandiflora, Greenman's crested coralroot
Brown-Marsden, M., and A. B. Collins. 2006. *Sida* 22(2): 1239–44.

Hexalectris revoluta Correll var. *revoluta*
recurved crested coralroot
Catling, P. M. 2004. *Native Orchid Conference Journal* 1(2): 5–25.

Hexalectris spicata (Walter) Barnhardt var. *arizonica* (S. Watson) Catling & Engel
Arizona crested coralroot
Catling, P. M., and V. S. Engel. 1993. *Lindleyana* 8(3): 119–25.

Hexalectris warnockii Ames & Correll forma *lutea* P.M. Catling
Catling, P. M. 2004. *Native Orchid Conference Journal* 2: 5–25.

Malaxis wendtii Salazar
Wendt's adder's-mouth
Salazar, G. A. 1993. *Orquidea* (Mexico) 13(1–2): 281–84.

Platanthera chapmanii (Small) Luer *emend.* Folsom
Chapman's fringed orchis
Brown, P. M. 2004. *Sida* 21: 853–59.
Folsom, J. P. 1984. *Orquidea* (Mexico) 9(2): 337–45.

Platanthera conspicua (Nash) P.M. Brown
southern white fringed orchis
Brown, P. M. 2002. *North American Native Orchid Journal* 8(2002): 3–14.

Pogonia ophioglossoides (Linnaeus) Ker-Gawler
rose pogonia
   forma *brachypogon* (Fernald) P.M. Brown—short-bearded form
Brown, P. M. 1998. *North American Native Orchid Journal* 6(4): 339.

Schiedeella arizonica P.M. Brown
Indian braids; Arizona red-spot
Brown, P. M. 1996. *North American Native Orchid Journal* 2(1): 66–68.

Spiranthes cernua (Linnaeus) L.C. Richard
nodding ladies'-tresses
Sheviak, C. J. 1991. *Lindleyana* 6(4): 228–34.

Spiranthes eatonii Ames *ex* P.M. Brown
Eaton's ladies'-tresses
Brown, P. M. 1999. *North American Native Orchid Journal* 5(1): 3–15.

Spiranthes floridana (Wherry) Cory *emend* P.M. Brown
Florida ladies'-tresses
Brown, P. M. 2001. *North American Native Orchid Journal* 7(1): 91–93.

Spiranthes magnicamporum Sheviak
Great Plains ladies'-tresses
Sheviak, C. J. 1973. *Botanical Museum Leaflet* [Harvard University] 23: 285–97.

Spiranthes ovalis Lindley
oval ladies'-tresses
Catling, P. M. 1983. *Brittonia* 35: 120–25.

Spiranthes sylvatica P.M. Brown
woodland ladies'-tresses
Brown, P. M. 2001. *North American Native Orchid Journal* 7(3): 193–205.

Triphora trianthophora var. *texensis* P.M. Brown & R.B. Pike
Brown, P. M. 2006. *North American Native Orchid Journal* 12: 4–10.

Rare, Threatened, and Endangered Species

In the United States each state has a somewhat different system for listing and ranking rare plants, whereas the Natural Heritage Programs and NatureServe have a uniform system for ranking species. The list of the orchids for each state may also be influenced by the presence or lack thereof of persons with a particular interest in the Orchidaceae. The list for Texas is surprisingly short and very conservative. It does not include species that are considered extirpated or several *Spiranthes* that are perhaps not well known. The following rankings and their definitions should enable the reader to understand the current status of the listed species. This information was provided by The Nature Conservancy and printed exactly as they list the species, with current synonyms in parentheses.

S1 or SE   Extremely rare throughout its range in the state or province (typically 5 or fewer occurrences or very few remaining individuals). May be especially vulnerable to extirpation.

S2 or ST   Rare throughout its range in the state or province (6–20 occurrences or few remaining individuals). May be vulnerable to extirpation due to rarity or other factors.

S3 or SR   Uncommon throughout its range in the state or province or found only in a restricted range even if abundant at some locations. (21–100 occurrences).

S#S#   Numeric range rank: A range between two consecutive numeric ranks. Denotes uncertainty about the exact rarity of the species; for example, S1S2.

SH   Historical: Species occurred historically throughout its range in the state or province (with expectation that it may be rediscovered) perhaps having not been verified in the past 20–70 years (depending on the species) and suspected to be still extant; used in many states but not in Texas.

NR; SNR   Species is not yet ranked; may be under review

T   Degree of threat from least at T4 to greatest at T1

State rankings indicate the relative rarity of the species within Texas. National and global rankings indicate the rarity within a larger area. Most species within the scope of this field guide are ranked as G4 or G5, indicating that globally they are considered secure. Fifteen are ranked otherwise.

Cypripedium kentuckiense G3 S1
southern lady's-slipper
Cypripedium calceolus var. *pubescens* G3S1 SH
Large yellow lady's-slipper
(*C. parviflorum* var. *pubescens*)
Epipactis gigantea G3S3
Chatterbox orchid
Hexalectris nitida G3S3
Glass Mountains coral-root, shining coral-root
Hexalectris revoluta G1G2 S1
Chisos coral-root
Hexalectris warnockii G2G3 S2
Warnock's coral-root
Malaxis wendtii G2 S1
Wendt's Malaxis
Platanthera chapmanii G2 S1
Chapman's fringed orchid
Platanthera integra G3G4S1
Golden frog arrow (*Gymnadeniopsis integra*)
Spiranthes parksii G3 S3 LE
Navasota ladies'-tresses
Spiranthes longilabris G3S1
Giant spiral-orchid

Source: http://www.nature.org/wherewework/northamerica/states/texas/files/
listofrareplants.pdf

Based on the criteria used for the above species, the following might also be considered for rare, threatened, or endangered status. Global and State ranking, when specified, are per NatureServe. All species are known from fewer than four locations and/or counties and two are considered historical.

Corallorhiza maculata var. *occidentalis* G5 SNR
western spotted coralroot
Corallorhiza odontorhiza var. *odontorhiza* G5 SNR
autumn coralroot
Deiregyne confusa G2 SNR
Hildago ladies'-tresses
Dichromanthus cinnabarinus G5 SNR
cinnabar ladies'-tresses
Habenaria quinqueseta S1 G4 SH

Michaux's orchid
Hexalectris grandiflora G4 S2
Greenman's crested coralroot
Malaxis soulei G4? SNR
rat-tailed adder's-mouth
Platanthera conspicua G3G4 S2 (SH)
southern white fringed orchis
Platanthera lacera G5 SNR
green fringed orchis
Schiedeella arizonica G4? SNR
Indian braids; red-spot ladies'-tresses
Spiranthes brevilabris G3 SNR T1
Texas ladies'-tresses
Spiranthes eatonii G2 SNR
Eaton's ladies'-tresses
Spiranthes floridana G3 SNR T1
Florida ladies'-tresses
Spiranthes ovalis G4 T3 SNR
southern oval ladies'-tresses
Spiranthes sylvatica NR
woodland ladies'-tresses
Stenorrhynchos michuacanum G4 SNR
Michoacan ladies'-tresses
(*Dichromanthus michuacanus*)

Source: http://www.nature.org/wherewework/northamerica/states/texas/
files/g3taxaabstracts720044.pdf http://www.natureserve.org/explorer/servlet/
NatureServe?init=Species

Synonyms and Misapplied Names

Synonyms and misapplied names are often confused both in the literature and in the understanding of orchid enthusiasts. A synonym is simply an alternate name for a previously published plant name. From among the synonyms each author must select a name that he or she feels best suits the currently accepted genus and specific epithet for a given plant. Although the genus may vary, the specific epithet may often be the same. In such large groups as the spiranthoid orchids (*Spiranthes* and its allied genera) many synonyms may exist for the same species—all within different genera.

The rules of priority, as set forth in the *International Code of Botanical Nomenclature* (Greuter et al., 2000), dictate that the earliest validly published specific epithet within the chosen genus must be used. A good example would be that of the common grass-pink, *Calopogon tuberosus* (Linnaeus) Britton, Sterns & Poggenberg, which was originally published by Linnaeus in 1753 as *Limodorum tuberosum*, with a new combination by Britton et al. in 1888. *Calopogon pulchellus* (Salisbury) R. Brown (1853) was based upon *Limodorum pulchellum* Salisbury (1796). Although the latter name as *Calopogon pulchellus* was in widespread usage for many years, priority indicates that the former is the valid name. It rarely comes down to months in determining what name was published first; usually the year of publication is sufficient for determining the valid name.

Orchis spectabilis would be a synonym for *Galearis spectabilis*, *Galearis* being the currently accepted genus for the North American species. *Habenaria* is another group that has undergone a great deal of scrutiny in the past twenty-five years. Several groups of species formerly included within *Habenaria* are now treated as distinct genera. This is not always so much a case of correct or incorrect names, as it is of the preference of the author for one genus over another. The recent trend of molecular, i.e., DNA, analysis of species has resulted in the placement of several species or groups of species within other genera. Although this is tempting to accept as the end-all and be-all of taxonomy, it is still only one tool to help in formulating an opinion.

A misapplied name is an incorrect name for a given plant that may have resulted from a reassessment of the genus or species, resulting in two or more species being described from within the original species, or it may simply be a wrong name assigned to the plants. This is especially common in geographic areas at the edge of a group's range. The most frequently encountered example is *Cypripedium calceolus*. For many years our North American yellow lady's-slippers have been treated as a geographic variant of the Eurasian species. Many years of work by Sheviak have demonstrated that this is not the case and that the North American plants are a distinct species: *Cypripedium parviflorum*. Therefore, the name *C. calceolus* is a misapplied name for the North American plants. The term *auct.* (*auctorum*, i.e., of authors) is used to indicate a misapplied name and occasionally an author will incorrectly append the phrase "in part" after a name listed under synonymy. Misapplied names are not synonyms and refer only to the specific geographic area being treated—in this case the state of Texas. An issue can arise as to whether a name is a synonym or misapplied, and that depends on a broad or narrow view of the taxonomy—the lumpers vs. the splitters. Such a situation would best be described thusly: if *Cypripedium parviflorum* var. *pubescens* is considered synonymous with *Cypripedium calceolus*, *Cypripedium parviflorum* var. *pubescens* becomes a synonym of *Cypripedium calceolus*; but, if *Cypripedium parviflorum* var. *pubescens* is considered a good species/variety on its own, *Cypripedium calceolus* becomes a misapplied name for *Cypripedium parviflorum* var. *pubescens*. At times this appears to be an endless argument and each author must make his or her own decision as to synonymy and misapplied names. In Texas there are very few misapplied names. Cross-references to all taxa with synonyms and misapplied names can be found at the end of this chapter.

In addition to occasional references to specific journal articles, sources of synonyms and misapplied names include:

Brown, P. M., and S. N. Folsom. 2003. *The Wild Orchids of North America, North of Mexico.*

———. 2004. *Wild Orchids of the Southeastern United States, North of Peninsular Florida.*

Correll, D. S. 1944. Orchidaceae. Vol. 3, pt. 3, *Flora of Texas.*

———. 1947. Additions to the orchids of Texas.

———. 1950. *Native Orchids of North America.*

Correll, D. S., and M.C. Johnston. 1979. *Manual of vascular flora of Texas.*

Diggs, G. M., Jr., B. Lipscomb, and R. J. O'Kennon. 1999. *Shinner's and Mahler's Illustrated Flora of North Central Texas.*

Diggs, G. M., Jr., B. Lipscomb, M. D. Reed, and R. J. O'Kennon. 2006. *Illustrated Flora of East Texas.*

Flora of North America North of Mexico, vol. 26. 2002. Orchidaceae.

Jones, S. D., J. K. Wipff, and P. Montgomery. 1997. *Vascular plants of Texas: A comprehensive checklist including synonymy, bibliography, and index.*

Liggio, J., and A. O. Liggio. 1999. *Wild Orchids of Texas.*

Luer, C. A. 1975. *The Native Orchids of the United States and Canada excluding Florida.*

Petrie, W. 1981. *Guide to the Orchids of North America.*

Turner, B. L., H. Nichols, G. Denny, and O. Doron. 2003. *Atlas of the vascular plants of Texas.*

Williams, J. G., A. E. Williams, and N. Arlott. 1983. *A Field Guide to the Orchids of North America.*

Segregate Genera

Three genera within the range of this book have been historically treated within the genus *Habenaria*, and are currently treated differently by various authors. Those are:

Gymnadeniopsis
Platanthera
Habenaria

Synonyms

Most current taxonomic treatments recognize the numerous segregate genera of the spiranthoid orchids (Garay, 1980[1982]). Volume 26 of *Flora of North America* (2002) treats all of the following taxa as well.

Calopogon barbatus (Walter) Ames
SYNONYM
Limodorum parviflorum (Lindley) Nash

Calopogon tuberosus (Linnaeus) Britton, Sterns & Poggenberg var. *tuberosus*
SYNONYMS
Calopogon pulchellus (Salisbury) R. Brown
Calthea tuberosa (Linnaeus) Salisbury

Cleistes bifaria (Fernald) Catling & Gregg
SYNONYMS
Cleistes divaricata (Linnaeus) Ames var. *bifaria* Fernald
Pogonia bifaria (Fernald) P.M. Brown & Wunderlin

Corallorhiza maculata (Rafinesque) Rafinesque var. *occidentalis* (Lindley) Ames
SYNONYM
Corallorhiza maculata (Rafinesque) Rafinesque subsp. *occidentalis* (Lindley) Cockerell

Cypripedium kentuckiense C.F. Reed
SYNONYM
C. daultonii V. Soukup *nom. nud.*

Cypripedium parviflorum Salisbury var. *pubescens* (Willdenow) Knight
SYNONYMS
Cypripedium calceolus Linnaeus var. *planipetalum* (Fernald) Victorin & Rousseau
Cypripedium calceolus Linnaeus var. *pubescens* (Willdenow) Correll
Cypripedium flavescens de Candolle
Cypripedium parviflorum var. *planipetalum* Fernald
Cypripedium pubescens Willdenow
Cypripedium veganum Cockerell & Barber
MISAPPLIED
Cypripedium calceolus Linnaeus

Deiregyne confusa Garay
SYNONYM
Spiranthes confusa (Garay) Kartesz & Gandhi
MISAPPLIED
Deiregyne durangensis (Ames & Schweinfurth) Garay
Spiranthes durangensis Ames & Schweinfurth

Dichromanthus cinnabarinus (La Llave & Lexarza) Garay
SYNONYMS
Spiranthes cinnabarina (La Llave & Lexarza) Hemsley
Stenorrhynchos cinnabarina (La Llave & Lexarza) Lindley

Dicromanthus michuacanus (La Llave & Lexarza) Salazar & Soto-Arenas
SYNONYMS
Spiranthes michuanica (La Llave & Lexarza) Hemsley
Stenorrhynchos michuacanum (Llave & Lexarza) Lindley

Epipactis gigantea Douglas *ex* Hooker
SYNONYMS
Amesia gigantea (Douglas) A. Nelson & Macbride
Helleborine gigantea (Douglas) Druce
Peramium giganteum (Douglas) Salisbury

Epipactis helleborine (Linnaeus) Cranz*
SYNONYM
Epipactis latifolia (Linnaeus) Allioni

Gymnadeniopsis clavellata (Michaux) Rydberg *ex* Britton
SYNONYMS
Habenaria clavellata (Michaux) Sprengel
Platanthera clavellata (Michaux) Luer

Gymnadeniopsis nivea (Nuttall) Rydberg
SYNONYMS
Habenaria nivea (Nuttall) Sprengel
Platanthera nivea (Nuttall) Luer

Hexalectris grandiflora (A. Richard & Galeotti) L.O. Williams
SYNONYM
Hexalectris mexicana Greenman

Hexalectris spicata (Walter) Barnhardt
SYNONYM
Hexalectris aphyllus Rafinesque

Hexalectris spicata (Walter) Barnhardt var. *arizonica* (S. Watson) Catling & Engel
SYNONYM
Corallorhiza arizonica S. Watson

Isotria verticillata (Mühlenberg *ex* Willdenow) Rafinesque
SYNONYM
Pogonia verticillata (Mühlenberg *ex* Willdenow) Nuttall

Listera australis Lindley
SYNONYM
Neottia australis (Lindley) Szlachetko

Malaxis porphyrea (Ridley) Kuntze
SYNONYM
Microstylis porphyrea Ridley
MISAPPLIED
Malaxis ehrenbergii (Reichenbach f.) Kuntze

Malaxis wendtii Salazar
MISAPPLIED
Malaxis ehrenbergii (Reichenbach f.) Kuntze
Malaxis porphyrea (Ridley) Kuntze

Malaxis soulei L.O. Williams
SYNONYMS
Malaxis macrostachys (Lexarza) Kuntze
Malaxis unifolia Lindley
Achroanthes monophylla (Lindley) Greene

Platanthera conspicua (Nash) P.M. Brown
SYNONYMS
Blephariglottis conspicua (Nash) Small
Habenaria blephariglottis var. *conspicua* (Nash) Ames
Habenaria conspicua Nash
Platanthera blephariglottis (Willdenow) Lindley var. *conspicua* (Nash) Luer

Platanthera chapmanii (Small) Luer *emend.* Folsom
SYNONYMS
Blephariglottis chapmanii Small
Habenaria ×chapmanii (Small) Ames
Platanthera ×chapmanii (Small) Luer

Platanthera ciliaris (Linnaeus) Lindley
SYNONYMS
Blephariglottis ciliaris (Linnaeus) Rydberg
Habenaria ciliaris (Linnaeus) R. Brown

Platanthera cristata (Michaux) Lindley
SYNONYMS
Blephariglottis cristata (Michaux) Rafinesque
Habenaria cristata (Michaux) R. Brown

Platanthera flava (Linnaeus) Lindley var. *flava*
SYNONYM
Habenaria flava (Linnaeus) R. Brown

Platanthera flava (Linnaeus) Lindley var. *herbiola* (R. Brown) Luer
SYNONYMS
Habenaria flava var. *herbiola* (R. Brown *ex* Aiton) Ames & Correll
Habenaria flava var. *virescens sensu* Fernald
Habenaria herbiola R. Brown *ex* Aiton

Platanthera lacera (Michaux) G. Don
SYNONYM
Habenaria lacera (Michaux) R. Brown

Platytheles querceticola (Lindley) Garay
SYNONYMS
Erythrodes querceticola (Lindley) Ames
Physurus querceticola Lindley

Schiedeella arizonica P.M. Brown
MISAPPLIED
Schiedeella fauci-sanguinea (Dod) Burns-Balog
Schiedeella parasitica (A. Richard & Galeotti) Schlechter
Spiranthes fauci-sanguinea Dod
Spiranthes parasitica A. Richard & Galeotti

Spiranthes brevilabris Lindley
SYNONYM
Spiranthes gracilis (Bigelow) Beck var. *brevilabris* (Lindley) Correll

Spiranthes cernua (Linnaeus) Richard
SYNONYM
Ibidium cernuum (Linnaeus) House

Spiranthes floridana (Wherry) Cory *emend.* P.M. Brown
SYNONYMS
Ibidium floridanum Wherry
Spiranthes brevilabris Lindley var. *floridana* (Wherry) Luer
Spiranthes gracilis (Bigelow) Beck var. *floridana* (Wherry) Correll

Spiranthes lacera Rafinesque var. *gracilis* (Bigelow) Luer
SYNONYMS
Ibidium beckii (Lindley) House
Ibidium gracile (Bigelow) House
Neottia gracilis Bigelow
Spiranthes beckii Lindley
Spiranthes gracilis (Bigelow) Beck

Spiranthes laciniata (Small) Ames
SYNONYM
Ibidium laciniatum (Small) House

Spiranthes longilabris Lindley
Ibidium longilabre (Lindley) House

Spiranthes odorata (Nuttall) Lindley
Ibidium odoratum (Nuttall) House
Spiranthes cernua (Linnaeus) L.C. Richard var. *odorata* (Nuttall) Correll

Spiranthes ovalis Lindley var. *ovalis*
Ibidium ovale (Lindley) House

Spiranthes praecox (Walter) S. Watson
Ibidium praecox (Walter) House

Spiranthes sylvatica P.M. Brown
Spiranthes praecox (Walter) S. Watson

Spiranthes tuberosa Rafinesque
Spiranthes beckii Lindley
Spiranthes grayi Ames

Spiranthes tuberosa var. *grayi* (Ames) Fernald
Ibidium beckii House

Spiranthes vernalis Engelmann & A. Gray
Ibidium vernale (Engelmann & A. Gray) House

Stenorrhynchos michuacanum (La Llave & Lexarza) Lindley
Spiranthes michuacana (La Llave & Lexarza) Hemsley

Triphora trianthophora (Swartz) Rydberg var. *trianthophora*

Pogonia pendula (Mühlenberg *ex* Willdenow) Lindley

The synonym is given first, followed by the currently acceptable names used in this work.
= synonym
≠ misapplied name

Achroanthes monophylla (Lindley) Greene = *Malaxis unifolia* Lindley

Amesia gigantea (Douglas) A. Nelson & Macbride = *Epipactis gigantea* Douglas *ex* Hooker

Blephariglottis blephariglottis (Willdenow) Rydberg = *Platanthera blephariglottis* (Willdenow) Lindley

Platanthera blephariglottis (Willdenow) Lindley var. *conspicua* (Nash) Luer = *Platanthera conspicua* (Nash) P.M. Brown

Blephariglottis chapmanii Small = *Platanthera chapmanii* (Small) Luer *emend.* Folsom

Blephariglottis ciliaris (Linnaeus) Rydberg = *Platanthera ciliaris* (Linnaeus) Lindley

Blephariglottis conspicua (Nash) Small = *Platanthera conspicua* (Nash) P.M. Brown

Blephariglottis cristata (Michaux) Rafinesque = *Platanthera cristata* (Michaux) Lindley

Blephariglottis flaviflora Rafinesque = *Platanthera ciliaris* (Linnaeus) Lindley

Calopogon pulchellus (Salisbury) R. Brown = *Calopogon tuberosus* (Linnaeus) Britton, Sterns, & Poggenberg

Calthea tuberosa (Linnaeus) Salisbury = *Calopogon tuberosus* (Linnaeus) Britton, Sterns, & Poggenberg

Cleistes divaricata (Linnaeus) Ames var. *bifaria* Fernald = *Cleistes bifaria* (Fernald) Catling & Gregg

Corallorhiza arizonica S. Watson = *Hexalectris spicata* (Walter) Barnhardt var. *arizonica* (S. Watson) Catling & Engel

Corallorhiza grandiflora Richard & Galeotti = *Hexalectris grandiflora* (Richard & Galeotti) L.O. Williams

Corallorhiza maculata subsp. *occidentalis* (Lindley) Cockerell = *Corallorhiza maculata* (Rafinesque) Rafinesque var. *occidentalis* (Lindley) Ames

Corallorhiza micrantha A. Chapman = *Corallorhiza odontorhiza* (Willdenow) Nuttall

Corallorhiza multiflora Nuttall = *Corallorhiza maculata* (Rafinesque) Rafinesque

Cypripedium calceolus Linnaeus ≠ *Cypripedium parviflorum* Salisbury var. *pubescens* (Willdenow) Knight

Cypripedium calceolus Linnaeus var. *pubescens* (Willdenow) Correll = *Cypripedium parviflorum* Salisbury var. *pubescens* (Willdenow) Knight

Cypripedium daultonii V. Soukup *nom. nud.* = *Cypripedium kentuckiense* C.F. Reed

Cypripedium flavescens de Candolle = *Cypripedium parviflorum* Salisbury var. *pubescens* (Willdenow) Knight

Cypripedium pubescens Willdenow = *Cypripedium parviflorum* Salisbury var. *pubescens* (Willdenow) Knight

Cypripedium veganum Cockerell & Barber = *Cypripedium parviflorum* Salisbury var. *pubescens* (Willdenow) Knight

Deiregyne durangensis (Ames & Schweinfurth) Garay ≠ *Deiregyne confusa* Garay

Epipactis latifolia (Linnaeus) Allioni = *Epipactis helleborine* (Linnaeus) Cranz

Erythrodes querceticola (Lindley) Ames = *Platytheles querceticola* (Lindley) Garay

Habenaria blephariglottis (Willdenow) Hooker = *Platanthera blephariglottis* (Willdenow) Lindley var. *blephariglottis*

Habenaria blephariglottis var. *conspicua* (Nash) Ames = *Platanthera conspicua* (Nash) P.M. Brown

Habenaria ciliaris (Linnaeus) R. Brown = *Platanthera ciliaris* (Linnaeus) Lindley

Habenaria clavellata (Michaux) Sprengel = *Gymnadeniopsis clavellata* (Michaux) Rydberg

Habenaria conspicua Nash = *Platanthera conspicua* (Nash) P.M. Brown

Habenaria cristata (Michaux) R. Brown = *Platanthera cristata* (Michaux) Lindley

Habenaria flava (Linnaeus) R. Brown *ex* Sprengel = *Platanthera flava* (Linnaeus) Lindley var. *flava*

Habenaria flava var. *herbiola* (R. Brown *ex* Aiton) Ames & Correll = *Platanthera flava* (Linnaeus) Lindley var. *herbiola* (R. Brown) Luer

Habenaria flava var. *virescens sensu* Fernald = *Platanthera flava* (Linnaeus) Lindley var. *herbiola* (R. Brown) Luer

Habenaria herbiola R. Brown *ex* Aiton = *Platanthera flava* (Linnaeus) Lindley var. *herbiola* (R. Brown) Luer

Habenaria lacera (Michaux) R. Brown = *Platanthera lacera* (Michaux) G. Don

Habenaria nivea (Nuttall) Sprengel = *Gymnadeniopsis nivea* Nuttall

Habenaria ×chapmanii (Small) Ames = *Platanthera chapmanii* (Small) Luer *emend.* Folsom

Helleborine gigantea (Douglas) Druce = *Epipactis gigantea* Douglas *ex* Hooker

Hexalectris aphyllus Rafinesque = *Hexalectris spicata* (Walter) Barnhardt

Hexalectris mexicana Greenman = *Hexalectris grandiflora* (A. Richard & Galeotti) L.O. Williams

Ibidium beckii (Lindley) House = *Spiranthes lacera* Rafinesque var. *gracilis* (Bigelow) Luer

Ibidium beckii House = *Spiranthes tuberosa* Rafinesque

Ibidium cernuum (Linnaeus) House = *Spiranthes cernua* (Linnaeus) L.C. Richard

Ibidium gracile (Bigelow) House = *Spiranthes lacera* (Rafinesque) Rafinesque var. *gracilis* (Bigelow) Luer

Ibidium laciniatum (Small) House = *Spiranthes laciniata* (Small) Ames

Ibidium odoratum (Nuttall) House = *Spiranthes odorata* (Nuttall) Lindley

Ibidium plantagineum (Rafinesque) House = *Spiranthes lucida* (H.H. Eaton) Ames

Ibidium vernale (Engelmann & A. Gray) House = *Spiranthes vernalis* Engelmann & A. Gray

Limodorum parviflorum (Lindley) Nash = *Calopogon barbatus* (Walter) Ames

Limodorum tuberosum Linnaeus = *Calopogon tuberosus* (Linnaeus) Britton, Sterns, & Poggenberg

Malaxis ehrenbergii (Reichenbach f.) Kuntze ≠ *Malaxis porphyrea* (Ridley) Kuntze

Malaxis macrostachys (Lexarza) Kuntze = *Malaxis soulei* L.O. Williams

Malaxis wendtii Salazar ≠ *Malaxis porphyrea* (Ridley) Kuntze

Microstylis macrostachys Lexarza = *Malaxis soulei* L.O. Williams

Microstylis porphyrea Ridley = *Malaxis porphyrea* (Ridley) Kuntze

Microstylis unifolia (Michaux) Britton, Sterns, & Poggenberg = *Malaxis unifolia* Michaux

Neottia australis (Lindley) Szlachetko = *Listera australis* Lindley

Neottia cinnabarina La Lave & Lexarza = *Dichromanthus cinnabarinus* (La Lave & Lexarza) Garay

Neottia gracilis Bigelow = *Spiranthes lacera* Rafinesque var. *gracilis* (Bigelow) Luer

Peramium giganteum (Douglas) Salisbury = *Epipactis gigantea* Douglas *ex* Hooker

Physurus querceticola Lindley = *Platytheles querceticola* (Lindley) Garay

Platanthera blephariglottis (Willdenow) Lindley var. *conspicua* (Nash) Luer = *Platanthera conspicua* (Nash) P.M. Brown

Platanthera clavellata (Michaux) Luer = *Gymnadeniopsis clavellata* (Michaux) Rydberg *ex* Britton

Platanthera nivea (Nuttall) Luer = *Gymnadeniopsis nivea* Nuttall

Platanthera repens (Nuttall) Wood = *Habenaria repens* Nuttall

Platanthera ×*chapmanii* (Small) Luer = *Platanthera chapmanii* (Small) Luer emend. Folsom

Pogonia bifaria (Fernald) P.M. Brown & Wunderlin = *Cleistes bifaria* (Fernald) Catling & Gregg

Pogonia verticillata (Mühlenberg *ex* Willdenow) Nuttall = *Isotria verticillata* (Mühlenberg *ex* Willdenow) Rafinesque

Schiedeella fauci-sanguinea (Dod) Burns-Balog ≠ *Schiedeella arizonica* P.M. Brown

Spiranthes beckii Lindley = *Spiranthes lacera* (Rafinesque) Rafinesque var. *gracilis* (Bigelow) Luer

Spiranthes cernua (Linnaeus) Richard var. *odorata* (Nuttall) Correll = *Spiranthes odorata* (Nuttall) Lindley

Spiranthes cinnabarina (Llave & Lexarza) Hemsley = *Dichromanthus cinnabarinus* (Llave & Lexarza) Garay

Spiranthes confusa (Garay) Kartesz & Gandhi = *Deiregyne confusa* Garay

Spiranthes durangensis Ames & Schweinfurth ≠ *Deiregyne confusa* Garay

Spiranthes gracilis (Bigelow) Beck = *Spiranthes lacera* (Rafinesque) Rafinesque var. *gracilis* (Bigelow) Luer

Spiranthes grayi Ames = *Spiranthes tuberosa* Rafinesque

Spiranthes michuacana (La Llave & Lexarza) Hemsley = *Dichromanthus michuacanus* (La Llave & Lexarza) Salazar & Soto-Arenas

Stenorrhynchos michuacanum (La Llave & Lexarza) Lindley = *Dichromanthus michuacanus* (La Llave & Lexarza) Salazar & Soto-Arenas

Spiranthes parviflora (Chapman) Ames = *Spiranthes ovalis* Lindley

Spiranthes tuberosa var. *grayi* (Ames) Fernald = *Spiranthes tuberosa* Rafinesque

Stenorrhynchos cinnabarina (La Llave & Lexarza) Lindley = *Dichromanthus cinnabarinus* (La Llave & Lexarza) Garay

Cross-references for Common Names

Most species normally have only a few different common names, but in Texas there are many regional common names. They are presented here, and in the index, to assist the reader in finding species by common names that may be more familiar. Undoubtedly, there are more common names in very limited regional usage.

Boldface type indicates names used in this book.

adder's-mouth = *Pogonia ophioglossoides*
adder's-tongue-leaved pogonia = *Pogonia ophioglossoides*
American valerian = *Cypripedium parviflorum* var. *pubescens*
Arizona crested coralroot = *Hexalectris cristata* var. *arizonica*
beard flower = *Pogonia ophioglossoides*
bearded grasspink = *Calopogon barbatus*
Beck's ladies'-tresses = *Spiranthes tuberosa*
bog torch = *Gymnadeniopsis nivea*
brooding pogonia = *Triphora trianthophora*
Chapman's finger orchid = *Platanthera chapmanii*
Chapman's fringed orchis = *Platanthera chapmanii*
Chapman's orchid = *Platanthera chapmanii*
chatterbox = *Epipactis gigantea*
Chiricahua adder's mouth orchid = *Malaxis soulei*
cinnabar ladies'-tresses = *Dichromanthus cinnabarinus*
Cochise adder's mouth orchid = *Malaxis porphyrea*
cock's-comb = *Hexalectris spicata*
common ladies'-tresses = *Spiranthes vernalis*
crane-fly orchis = *Tipularia discolor*
creeping orchid = *Habenaria repens*
creeping water spider orchid = *Habenaria repens*
crested coralroot = *Hexalectris cristata*
crested finger orchid = *Platanthera cristata*
crested fringed orchid = *Platanthera cristata*
crested yellow orchid = *Platanthera cristata*
crippled crane-fly orchid = *Tipularia discolor*
downy lady's-slipper = *Cypripedium parviflorum* var. *pubescens*

early southern coralroot = *Corallorhiza wisteriana*
Eaton's ladies'-tresses = *Spiranthes eatonii*
elfin-spur = *Tipularia discolor*
fall coralroot = *Corallorhiza odontorhiza*
false rein orchid = *Habenaria repens*
five-leaf orchid = *Isotria verticillata*
floating orchid = *Habenaria repens*
Florida ladies'-tresses = *Spiranthes floridana*
fragrant ladies'-tresses = *Spiranthes odorata*
fragrant tresses = *Spiranthes odorata*
frog spear = *Gymnadeniopsis integra*
frog-arrow = *Gymnadeniopsis integra*
frog-spike = *Gymnadeniopsis integra*
giant helleborine = *Epipactis gigantea*
giant ladies'-tresses = *Spiranthes praecox*
giant spiral ladies'-tresses = *Spiranthes praecox*
giant spiral orchid = *Spiranthes praecox*
glandular Neottia = *Ponthieva racemosa*
Glass Mountain coralroot = *Hexalectris nitida*
Glass Mountain crested coralroot = *Hexalectris nitida*
golden fret-lip = *Gymnadeniopsis integra*
golden fringe orchid = *Platanthera ciliaris*
golden frog-arrow = *Gymnadeniopsis integra*
golden slipper = *Cypripedium parviflorum* var. *pubescens*
grass-leaved ladies'-tresses = *Spiranthes praecox; S. vernalis*
Gray's ladies'-tresses = *Spiranthes tuberosa*
Great Plains ladies'-tresses = *Spiranthes magnicamporum*
green adder's-mouth = *Malaxis unifolia*
green fringed orchis = *Platanthera lacera*
green rein orchid = *Platanthera flava*
green wood orchid = *Gymnadeniopsis clavellata*
green woodland orchid = *Gymnadeniopsis clavellata*
Greenman's crested coralroot = *Hexalectris grandiflora*
green-veined ladies'-tresses = *Spiranthes praecox*
hairy shadow-witch = *Ponthieva racemosa*
ivory lady's-slipper = *Cypripedium kentuckiense*
jug orchid = *Platythelys querceticola*
lace-lipped ladies'-tresses = *Spiranthes laciniata*
large white fringed orchid = *Platanthera conspicua*
large whorled pogonia = *Isotria verticillata*

late coralroot = *Corallorhiza odontorhiza*

late southern coralroot = *Corallorhiza odontorhiza*

lawn orchid = *Zeuxine strateumatica*

leafless orchid = *Hexalectris spicata*

lesser ladies'-tresses = *Spiranthes tuberosa*

little club-spur orchis = *Gymnadeniopsis clavellata*

little elephants = *Spiranthes ovalis*

little ladies'-tresses = *Spiranthes tuberosa*

little pearl twist = *Spiranthes tuberosa*

long-lipped ladies'-tresses = *Spiranthes longilabris*

low Erythrodes= *Platythelys querceticola*

low ground orchid = *Platythelys querceticola*

marsh ladies'-tresses = *Spiranthes praecox*

Michaux's orchid = *Habenaria quinqueseta*

Michoacan ladies'-tresses = *Dichromanthus michuacanus*

Navasota ladies'-tresses = *Spiranthes parksii*

Noah's ark = *Cypripedium parviflorum* var. *pubescens*

nodding ladies'-tresses = *Spiranthes cernua*

nodding pogonia = *Triphora trianthophora*

northern oval ladies'-tresses = *Spiranthes ovalis*

northern tubercled orchis = *Platanthera flava*

Nuttall's habenaria = *Habenaria repens*

October ladies'-tresses = *Spiranthes ovalis*

orange crested orchis = *Platanthera cristata*

orange fringed orchis = *Platanthera ciliaris*

orange rein orchid = *Platanthera ciliaris*

orange-crest = *Platanthera cristata*

orange-crest orchid = *Platanthera cristata*

orange-fringe = *Platanthera ciliaris*

orange-plume = *Platanthera ciliaris*

pale green orchis = *Platanthera flava*

parks' ladies'-tresses = *Spiranthes parksii*

pine habenaria = *Habenaria quinqueseta*

plume of Navarre = *Platanthera conspicua*

Ponthieu's orchid = *Ponthieva racemosa*

prairie ladies'-tresses = *Spiranthes magnicamporum*

purloined lady's-slipper = *Cypripedium kentuckiense*

purple five-leaf orchid = *Isotria verticillata*

Rafinesque's lady's-slipper = *Cypripedium kentuckiense*

ragged orchid = *Platanthera lacera*

ragged orchis = *Platanthera lacera*

rat-tailed adder's-mouth = *Malaxis soulei*

rattlesnake's-master = *Cypripedium parviflorum* var. *pubescens*

recurved crested coralroot = *Hexalectris revoluta*

red-spot ladies'-tresses = *Schiedeella arizonica*

rimrock ladies'-braids = *Deiregyne confusa*

rimrock ladies'-tresses = *Deiregyne confusa*

rose orchid = *Cleistes bifaria*

rose pogonia = *Pogonia ophioglossoides*

rose-crested orchid = *Cleistes bifaria*

rose-wings = *Pogonia ophioglossoides*

smaller rosebud orchid = *Cleistes bifaria*

savannah orchid = *Gymnadeniopsis nivea*

shadow-witch = *Ponthieva racemosa*

shining cock's-comb = *Hexalectris nitida*

shining coralroot = *Hexalectris nitida*

shining crested coralroot = *Hexalectris nitida*

short-lipped ladies'-tresses = *Spiranthes brevilabris*

small green wood orchid = *Gymnadeniopsis clavellata*

small southern yellow orchis = *Gymnadeniopsis integra*

small rosebud orchid = *Cleistes bifaria*

small wood orchid = *Gymnadeniopsis clavellata*

smaller spreading pogonia = *Cleistes bifaria*

small-flowered coralroot = *Corallorhiza odontorhiza*

snake-mouth orchid = *Pogonia ophioglossoides*

snowy habenaria = *Gymnadeniopsis nivea*

snowy orchis = *Gymnadeniopsis nivea*

soldier's orchid = *Zeuxine strateumatica*

southern lady's-slipper = *Cypripedium kentuckiense*

southern oval ladies'-tresses = *Spiranthes ovalis*

southern rein orchid = *Gymnadeniopsis flava*

southern slender ladies'-tresses = *Spiranthes lacera* var. *gracilis*

southern small white orchid = *Gymnadeniopsis nivea*

southern tubercled orchis = *Platanthera flava*

southern twayblade = *Listera australis*

southern white fringed orchis = *Platanthera conspicua*

spiked crest coralroot = *Hexalectris spicata*

spreading pogonia = *Cleistes bifaria*

spreading rosebud orchid = *Cleistes bifaria*

spring coralroot = *Corallorhiza wisteriana*

spring tresses = *Spiranthes vernalis*
stream Epipactis = *Epipactis gigantea*
stream orchid = *Epipactis gigantea*
swamp tresses = *Spiranthes odorata*
swamp-pink = *Calopogon tuberosus*
sweet ladies'-tresses = *Spiranthes odorata*
Texas crested-coralroot = *Hexalectris warnockii*
Texas ladies'-tresses = *Spiranthes brevilabris*
Texas purple-spike = *Hexalectris warnockii*
three-birds orchis = *Triphora trianthophora*
tidal ladies'-tresses = *Spiranthes odorata*
tubercled finger orchid = *Platanthera flava*
tuberous grass-pink = *Calopogon tuberosus*
twisted ladies'-tresses = *Spiranthes tuberosa*
upland ladies'-tresses = *Spiranthes vernalis*
water orchid = *Habenaria repens*
water-spider orchid = *Habenaria repens*
water stealer = *Cypripedium parviflorum* var. *pubescens*
Wendt's adder's-mouth = *Malaxis wendtii*
whippoorwill-shoe = *Cypripedium parviflorum* var. *pubescens*
white finger orchid = *Platanthera conspicua*
white frog arrow = *Gymnadeniopsis nivea*
white nodding ladies'-tresses = *Spiranthes cernua*
white rein orchid = *Platanthera conspicua*
woodland ladies'-tresses = *Spiranthes sylvatica*
yellow finger orchid = *Platanthera ciliaris*
yellow fringed orchid = *Platanthera ciliaris*
yellow fringeless orchis = *Gymnadeniopsis integra*
yellow moccasin flower = *Cypripedium parviflorum* var. *pubescens*

Using Luer

Additions, corrections, nomenclatural changes, and comments for Luer (1975), *The Native Orchids of the United States and Canada excluding Florida* as pertaining to *Wild Orchids of Texas*

For those fortunate enough to own or have access to a copy of Carlyle Luer's original work on the orchids of the United States and Canada, the following additions, corrections, and comments are assembled. These should in no way detract from the usefulness of this book but simply allow for more than twenty-five years of research and nomenclatural changes as well as for the addition of several species that had not been described as of the date of Luer's publication. Names of authors may be found in the text and checklist of this book. No attempt has been made to completely rework the keys or the index.

Introduction

p. 12 for *Cypripedium calceolus* var. *pubescens* read *Cypripedium parviflorum* var. *pubescens*

Text

p. 39 couplets 7 & 8 see *Cypripedium* key in present text, p. 39
pp. 40, 41, pl. 1:3,4 forma *albiflorum*
pp. 42, 43, pl. 2: 1 forma *albiflorum*
p. 44 for *Cypripedium calceolus* Linnaeus var. *pubescens* (Willdenow) Correll read *Cypripedium parviflorum* Salisbury var. *pubescens* (Willdenow) Knight
pp. 44, 45, pl. 3, p. 46, 47, pl. 4 for *Cypripedium calceolus* var. *pubescens* read *Cypripedium parviflorum* var. *pubescens*
p. 48 for *Cypripedium calceolus* Linnaeus var. *parviflorum* Salisbury read *Cypripedium parviflorum* Salisbury var. *makasin* (Farwell) Sheviak
pp. 76, 77, pl. 15:3 forma *viridens*
pp. 82, 83, pl. 17:5 forma *viridis*
pp. 84, 85, pl. 18:4 forma *viridens*
p. 114 read var. *ovalis*

pp. 128, 129, pl. 4–9 for *Spiranthes parasitica* A. Richard & Galeotti read *Schiedeella arizonica* P.M. Brown

pp. 130, 131, pl. 30 1–8 read *Deiregyne durangensis*—this species does not occur in Texas or the United States. See *Deiregyne confusa* on p. 000 in this work for details.

pp. 132–33, pl. 31 1–3 for *Spiranthes cinnabarina* (Lexarza) Hemsley read *Dichromanthus cinnabarinus* (La Llave & Lexarza) Garay

pp. 133, pl. 31: 4–6; 134 for *Spiranthes michuacana* (Lexarza) Hemsley read *Dichromanthus michuacanus* (La Llave & Lexarza) Salazar & Soto-Arenas

pp. 185, 195, pl. 45: 1–3 for *Platanthera blephariglottis* var. *conspicua* (Nash) Luer read *Platanthera conspicua* (Nash) P.M. Brown; pl. 4 for *Platanthera ×bicolor* read *Platanthera ×lueri*

pp. 187, 188, pl. 46 for *Platanthera ×chapmanii* read *Platanthera chapmanii*; for *Platanthera ×canbyi* read *Platanthera ×beckneri*.

pp. 202, 203, pl. 52 for *Platanthera integra* (Nuttall) Gray *ex* Beck read *Gymnadeniopsis integra* (Nuttall) Rydberg

pp. 204, 205, pl. 53 for *Platanthera nivea* (Nuttall) Luer read *Gymnadeniopsis integra* (Nuttall) Rydberg

pp. 206, 207, pl. 54 for *Platanthera clavellata* (Michaux) Luer read *Gymnadeniopsis clavellata* (Michaux) Rydberg

pp. 270, 271, pl. 74:1 forma *albolabia*

pp. 300, 301, pl. 83 for *Malaxis macrostachya* (La Lave & Lexarza) Kuntze read *Malaxis soulei* L.O. Williams

pp. 318, 319, pl. 89:1, 9 *Corallorhiza maculata* var. *occidentalis* forma *immaculata*

pp. 320, 321, pl. 90:3 forma *albolabia*

pp. 324, 325, pl. 92:4 forma *eburnea*

pp. 338, 339, pl. 96 forma *albiflora*

The following taxa found within Texas are not treated in *The Native Orchids of the United States and Canada excluding Florida*

Calopogon oklahomensis

Corallorhiza maculata var. *occidentalis*

Cypripedium kentuckiense

Spiranthes eatonii

Spiranthes sylvatica

Triphora trianthophora var. *texensis*

Cryptic Species, Species Pairs, Varietal Pairs, and Complexes

When two species or varieties appear to be very closely related and have a similar morphology, they are often referred to as species pairs. Although not necessarily a scientific or taxonomic term, the designation is often helpful in recognizing two species that are often difficult to determine, whether in the field or in the herbarium. Their taxonomic history usually involves synonyms and/or recognition at different taxonomic levels, i.e. subspecies, varieties, or rarely forma. Validation of the two taxa at species level usually involves studies of pollinators, habit, habitat, range, morphology, and, in more recent years, DNA analyses. Few true species pairs exist for Texas but several varietal pairs are found in the state. Fortunately a few simple morphological characters easily separate the taxa. In each case these are characters that can be found within the key to the species. Also, range and habitat are often well separated.

Hexalectris nitida L.O. Williams
shining crested coralroot
Hexalectris revoluta Correll
recurved crested coralroot
very similar at first glance, but *H. revoluta* is restricted to Trans-Pecos and *H. nitida* is more widespread in its distribution; *H. nitida* has a smaller flower with a difference in lip size and position of the petals

H. nitida   *H. revoluta*

Platanthera ciliaris Lindley
orange fringed orchis
Platanthera chapmanii (Small) Luer *emend.* Folsom
Chapman's fringed orchis
Platanthera cristata (Michaux) Lindley
orange crested orchis
Three apparently similar species that differ in overall size, spur length and shape
of the orifice (the spur opening)
see page 279 for full details

P. ciliaris   P. chapmanii   P. cristata

Platanthera flava (Linnaeus) Lindley var. *flava*
southern tubercled orchis
Platanthera flava (Linnaeus) Lindley var. *herbiola* (R. Brown) Luer
northern tubercled orchis
Similar in overall appearance, the two varieties are distinguished by the shape of
the lip and length of the bracts. Range overlap is minimal in most of the bordering states.
see page 112–14 for full details

P. flava var. *flava*   P. flava var. *herbiola*

Spiranthes brevilabris Lindley
Texas ladies'-tresses
Spiranthes floridana (Wherry) Cory *emend*. P.M. Brown
Florida ladies'-tresses
Both species are very rare and are significantly different in degree of pubescence: *S. brevilabris* is densely pubescent within the inflorescence and *S. floridana* is essentially glabrous. This gives the former species a whitish green cast and the latter, a yellow-green cast.

S. *brevilabris*   S. *floridana*

Spiranthes cernua (Linnaeus) L.C. Richard
nodding ladies'-tresses
Spiranthes magnicamporum Sheviak
Great Plains ladies'-tresses
Spiranthes odorata (Nuttall) Lindley
fragrant ladies'-tresses
Spiranthes magnicamporum and *S. odorata* occupy vastly different habitats and ranges in Texas. Morphologically the arching position of the sepals on *S. magnicamporum* is diagnostic and the long, prominently troughed lip on *S. odorata* equally so. *Spiranthes cernua* is not so easy to define as it occupies a variety of habitats and, as a compilospecies, exhibits gene flow from both of the previously

mentioned basic diploid species. Careful examination of individual plants is critical to identification and problematic specimens of *S. cernua* are often found.

S. cernua *S. magnicamporum* *S. odorata*

Spiranthes eatonii Ames *ex* P.M. Brown
Eaton's ladies'-tresses
Spiranthes lacera Rafinesque var. *gracilis*
(Bigelow) Luer
southern slender ladies'-tresses
Both species exhibit white flowers with green central portions on the lip, basal leaves, and slender inflorescences; *S. eatonii* is spring flowering and the leaves are oblanceolate, whereas *S. lacera* var. *gracilis* is summer/autumn flowering and the leaves are more ovate. The inflorescence in *S. eatonii* is a slender, attenuated spike with the lower flowers often disproportionately spaced out, whereas in *S. lacera* var. *gracilis* the inflorescence tends to be more compact with little or no space evident between the flowers.

S. eatonii *S. lacera* var. *gracilis*

Spiranthes praecox (Walter) S. Watson
giant ladies'-tresses
Spiranthes sylvatica P.M. Brown
woodland ladies'-tresses
The only real similarity is that both species have distinctive green veining on the lips; otherwise there are critical differences in size, color, habitat, and position of the sepals.

S. praecox

S. sylvatica

Part 4
Orchid Hunting

1. East Texas and the Big Thicket

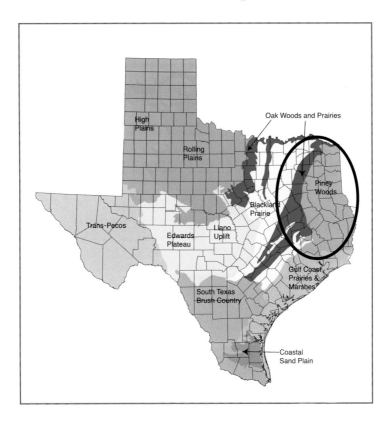

East Texas falls primarily into the Pineywoods and Post Oak Savannah regions. These two areas combined account for more than 70 percent of the known species of orchids found in Texas. Apart from the Big Thicket area, East Texas is abundant in riparian habitat and open meadows. It is in these areas that most of the orchids occur. The Big Thicket area of eastern Texas once comprised nearly 200,000 acres. Today it covers a much smaller area, set aside as Big Thicket National Preserve. The boundaries of the historical Big Thicket have always been in dispute; the national preserve consists of twelve disjunct units of different sizes totaling 84,500 acres. The preserve located near Beaumont, Texas, east of Interstate 45, is bordered on the east by Louisiana. Although many will lament the endless wildflowers, including orchids, that abounded in this area, there are still many species to be found. Roads may be few but exploration is unlimited. All of Texas east of I-45 presents a larger array of species than found in the Big Thicket. This area includes the Angelina National Forest, home to several species not found elsewhere in eastern Texas.

Species found in eastern Texas including the Big Thicket:

Calopogon oklahomensis, Oklahoma grass-pink
Calopogon tuberosus, common grass-pink
Cleistes bifaria, upland spreading pogonia H
Corallorhiza odontorhiza, autumn coralroot
Corallorhiza wisteriana, Wister's coralroot
Cypripedium kentuckiense, ivory-lipped lady's-slipper
Gymnadeniopsis clavellata, little club-spur orchis
Gymnadeniopsis integra, yellow fringeless orchis
Gymnadeniopsis nivea, snowy orchis
Habenaria quinqueseta, Michaux's orchid
Habenaria repens, water spider orchid
Hexalectris spicata var. *spicata,* crested coralroot
Isotria verticillata, large whorled pogonia
Listera australis, southern twayblade
Malaxis unifolia, green adder's-mouth
Platanthera chapmanii, Chapman's fringed orchis
Platanthera ciliaris, orange fringed orchis
Platanthera cristata, orange crested orchis
Platanthera flava var. *flava,* southern tubercled orchis
Platanthera flava var. *herbiola,* northern tubercled orchis
Platanthera lacera, green fringed orchis; ragged orchis
[*Platythelys querceticola,* low ground orchid]
Pogonia ophioglossoides, rose pogonia
Ponthieva racemosa, shadow-witch
Spiranthes brevilabris, short-lipped ladies'-tresses; Texas ladies'-tresses
Spiranthes cernua, nodding ladies'-tresses
Spiranthes eatonii, Eaton's ladies'-tresses
Spiranthes floridana, Florida ladies'-tresses
Spiranthes lacera var. *gracilis,* southern slender ladies'-tresses
Spiranthes laciniata, lace-lipped ladies'-tresses
Spiranthes longilabris, long-lipped ladies'-tresses
Spiranthes odorata, fragrant ladies'-tresses
Spiranthes ovalis var. *ovalis,* southern oval ladies'-tresses
Spiranthes parksii, Navasota ladies'-tresses
Spiranthes praecox, giant ladies'-tresses
Spiranthes sylvatica, woodland ladies'-tresses
Spiranthes tuberosa, little ladies'-tresses
Spiranthes vernalis, grass-leaved ladies'-tresses
Tipularia discolor, crane-fly orchis
Triphora trianthophora var. *trianthophora,* three-birds orchis; nodding pogonia

Triphora trianthophora var. *texensis*, Texas three-birds orchis; Pike's three-bird's orchis

Zeuxine strateumatica, lawn orchid*

Spring in eastern Texas produces the most prolific show of native orchids in the state. As in many other areas of the Southeast, spring starts with *Corallorhiza wisteriana*, Wister's coralroot, soon to be followed by *Listera australis*, the southern twayblade. *Isotria verticillata*, the large whorled pogonia, and, although a bit rarer, *Malaxis unifolia*, the green adder's-mouth, also come into early spring flower. All four of these species are found in mixed woodlands, although the *Listera* certainly prefers moister areas than the others.

The open prairies and wetlands will then be painted in various shades of pink and white by *Calopogon oklahomensis*, the Oklahoma grass-pink, soon to be followed by the more frequently encountered *C. tuberosus*, the common grass-pink. Plants from eastern Texas previously identified as *C. barbatus*, the bearded grass-pink, have all proven to be the recently described Oklahoma grass-pink.

By the time spring is fully underway, ladies'-tresses start to appear along the roadways and even in the woodlands. *Spiranthes vernalis*, the grass-leaved ladies'-tresses, is the most frequently seen member of the genus and found throughout the Southeast. Less abundant but still well distributed are *S. praecox*, the giant ladies'-tresses, and *S. sylvatica*, the woodland ladies'-tresses. The latter has recently been described and is characterized by a preference for shaded woodlands, and is often tucked up under the outer edge of thickets. Both species have the distinctive green veining in the lip. Three additional ladies'-tresses also flower at this time, and all are apparently very rare and their status uncertain. *Spiranthes brevilabris*, the Texas ladies'-tresses, *S. floridana*, the Florida ladies'-tresses, and *S. eatonii*, Eaton's ladies'-tresses, all have similar morphologies but distinctive characters that separate them. Read the three species descriptions carefully, for despite their extreme rarity, any or all may still be found in East Texas.

The absolute gem of the late spring woodlands is the rare *Cypripedium kentuckiense*, the ivory-lipped lady's-slipper. The largest-flowered of any of our yellow lady's-slippers, this spectacular species was once a common component of the spring woodland flora of western Arkansas, northwestern Louisiana, and eastern Texas. Development and logging have greatly reduced the number of locations for this choice orchid, but it can still be seen in several places both within and apart from the Big Thicket.

Early summer certainly begins the peak season for the many fringed orchises and their cousins. This group runs the gamut, from the very rarest to the most common. The first to show itself is *Gymnadeniopsis nivea*, the snowy orchis. Often favoring broad, mowed roadsides and damp grassy savannas, these small, fat spikes of stark white flowers stand out among surrounding vegetation. A short foray to nearby woodlands may be rewarded with a pleasant surprise of *Hexalec-*

tris spicata, the crested coralroot—a surprise only because it is unpredictable in its flowering from year to year. Back in the open roadside ditches and swamps, stands of *Platanthera flava*, the southern tubercled orchis, may sometimes be found in colonies of more than a hundred plants.

Platanthera chapmanii, Chapman's fringed orchis, *P. ciliaris*, the orange fringed orchis, and *P. cristata*, the orange crested orchis, make up a colorful midsummer trio and are well distributed throughout the Big Thicket but not necessarily as a threesome. The rarest of these, Chapman's fringed orchis, is one of the most geographically restricted orchids we have in North America. Apart from the central Panhandle of Florida and two historic sites in southern Georgia, the only other known area for this species is eastern Texas, primarily the Big Thicket. The other two orange orchises are found in a much wider area. Farther afield from the Big Thicket area, but still in East Texas, is the lone historic site for *Platanthera lacera*, the green fringed or ragged orchis. It was first recorded from here in 1946 and has not been seen since in Texas, but elsewhere to the northeast it can be a common species.

Gymnadeniopsis integra, the yellow fringeless orchis, holds a similar record, as it was not found in Texas until 1987, in the Angelina National Forest. Prior to that it had been documented but once, and that documentation was mislabeled as *G. nivea*, whereas an earlier collection that was labeled *G. integra* was actually *G. nivea*!

At the end of the summer two woodland species, both scattered and rare, pose no problems of identification. *Tipularia discolor*, the crane-fly orchis, and *Triphora trianthophora*, the three-birds orchis, both reach the western limit of their ranges in eastern Texas, and both occupy similar niches in the rich woodlands, with *Tipularia* the more frequently seen of the two. *Triphora* is not only rarer but also much more difficult to locate in flower. The flowering period lasts for only a few hours each day and for only a few days. It takes both diligence and patience to capture the three birds at their best! One of the newest taxons to be described is *Triphora trianthophora* var. *texensis*, the Texas three-birds orchis or Pike's three-birds orchis. It was discovered by Dick Pike in the Crockett National Forest and differs from the typical three-birds in its snowy white flowers with an emerald-green throat.

Autumn is the time for *Corallorhiza odontorhiza*, the autumn coralroot, and *Ponthieva racemosa*, the shadow-witch. The coralroot is a slender and obscure denizen of deciduous woodlands and often flowers under fallen leaves with its tiny cleistogamous blooms. The shadow-witch prefers shaded moist river floodplains and slopes.

Autumn is also the time for more ladies'-tresses. *Spiranthes lacera* var. *gracilis*, the southern slender ladies'-tresses, *S. cernua*, the nodding ladies'-tresses, and *S. odorata*, the fragrant ladies'-tresses, are all species in this genus that are frequently seen. Southern slender ladies'-tresses usually grows in dry, short-grass fields, lawns, and old cemeteries, whereas the fragrant ladies'-tresses is a wetland species and may be found in both sun and shade, often in shallow standing water. *Spiranthes cernua* is the most widespread and frequently seen ladies'-tresses in North America and occurs in many regional races. Here in eastern Texas one of the most unusual races is a cleistogamous/peloric race with yellow or green unopened flowers. Typically *S. cernua* has crystalline, nodding, white to ivory flowers, often with the fragrance of vanilla.

Our year-long tour of orchids in eastern Texas concludes with the federally endangered *Spiranthes parksii*, the Navasota ladies'-tresses. Known primarily from the Post Oak Savannah region near College Park, Texas, this very unusual species was discovered in 1945, declared extinct in 1975, and rediscovered in 1978 within the same Post Oak Savannah area and not more than ten miles from where it was originally found. In October 1986 the species was found for the first time in Angelina National Forest in the Pineywoods region of Jasper County, more than a hundred miles east of the original sites. *Spiranthes parksii*, with its partially open, off-white flowers, certainly is not the most attractive of our ladies'-tresses, but does demand a pilgrimage for those enslaved by the genus!

2. Gulf Coastal Plain

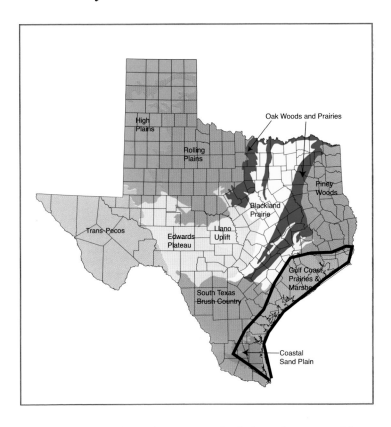

The Gulf Coastal Plain of Texas provides habitat for many of the same species found in the Pineywoods region to the north and inland; many of those species are reaching the southern limit of their range here and are therefore found in fewer places.

Species found within the Gulf Coastal Plain (Coastal Plain and Prairies):

Calopogon oklahomensis, Oklahoma grass-pink
Calopogon tuberosus, common grass-pink
Gymnadeniopsis nivea, snowy orchis
Habenaria repens, water spider orchid
Hexalectris spicata var. *spicata*, crested coralroot
Platanthera conspicua, southern white fringed orchis H
Platanthera flava var. *flava*, southern tubercled orchis
Spiranthes brevilabris, Texas ladies'-tresses
Spiranthes cernua, nodding ladies'-tresses
Spiranthes eatonii, Eaton's ladies'-tresses

Spiranthes floridana, Florida ladies'-tresses
Spiranthes lacera var. *gracilis*, southern slender ladies'-tresses
Spiranthes laciniata, lace-lipped ladies'-tresses
Spiranthes odorata, fragrant ladies'-tresses
Spiranthes praecox, giant ladies'-tresses
Spiranthes tuberosa, little ladies'-tresses
Spiranthes vernalis, grass-leaved ladies'-tresses
Zeuxine strateumatica, lawn orchid*

Calopogon oklahomensis, the Oklahoma grass-pink, *Hexalectris spicata* var. *spicata*, the crested coralroot, *Platanthera flava* var. *flava*, the southern tubercled orchis, and *Spiranthes lacera* var. *gracilis*, the southern slender ladies'-tresses, are all examples of species found more plentifully to the north and sparingly along this coastal strip.

Spring is the season for ladies'-tresses and grass-pinks. A selection of slender spirals may be observed in many areas, but apart from the last two species, the other three are very rare, and precise distribution is not known. *Spiranthes brevilabris*, the Texas ladies'-tresses, *S. eatonii*, Eaton's ladies'-tresses, and *S. floridana*, the Florida ladies'-tresses, are all superficially similar and careful examination is needed to determine the correct identification. All three grow in open grass habitats, often favoring roadsides and old cemeteries, and all have basal rosettes of pale, often yellowish, green leaves.

In contrast to the rarity of the previous trio, both *Spiranthes praecox*, the giant ladies'-tresses, and *S. vernalis*, the grass-leaved ladies'-tresses, are widespread and relatively common in this region. They often flower on common roadsides and are easily distinguished by the position of the sepals and presence, or lack thereof, of pointed hairs (see pages 156 and 162).

Spiranthes odorata, the fragrant ladies'-tresses, is the common ladies'-tresses of the autumn in a variety of open wet and woodland habitats. Perhaps the rarest species in this region, and certainly the most elusive, is *Platanthera conspicua*, the southern white fringed orchis. Known in Texas only from a collection made in the early 1900s in Galveston County, it has never been seen again. A trio of ladies'-tresses round out the native orchids of the region, each in its own season: *Spiranthes cernua*, the nodding ladies'-tresses, flowering in a variety of damp, often disturbed, habitats in the autumn; *Spiranthes laciniata*, the lace-lipped ladies'-tresses, bringing forth tall, slender, twisted spikes in wetlands, often while partly immersed, in early summer; and *Spiranthes tuberosa*, the little ladies'-tresses, a delicate and purest white spike of large-lipped flowers that prefers open sandy soil with little vegetation, like that often found along country roadsides and in old fields and cemeteries.

The final Texas orchid in the list is the Asian *Zeuxine strateumatica*, the lawn or helmet orchid. This alien species first came to the United States in the early twentieth century and has established itself throughout much of Florida and, more recently, in flowerbeds and container plants in both Texas and South Carolina. *Zeuxine* is an annual and offers no competition to our natives. It is a pleasant surprise in the winter flower garden when it springs forth in late December through March!

3. Edwards Plateau/Balcones Canyonlands

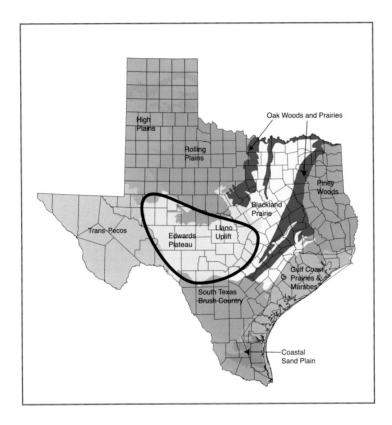

The Edwards Plateau and Balcones Canyonlands, the well-known Texas Hill Country, offers not only spectacular scenery, rivers, streams and waterfalls, and exciting birding, but also a selection of wild orchids. Roads wind through the area, and hiking and riding trails abound.

Species recorded from the Edwards Plateau and Balcones Canyonlands include:

Corallorhiza wisteriana, Wister's coralroot
[*Corallorhiza maculata*, spotted coralroot] report
Epipactis gigantea, stream orchid
Hexalectris nitida, shining crested coralroot
Hexalectris spicata var. *spicata*, crested coralroot
Hexalectris spicata var. *arizonica*, Arizona crested coralroot
Hexalectris warnockii, Texas purple-spike
Spiranthes cernua, nodding ladies'-tresses
Spiranthes magnicamporum, Great Plains ladies'-tresses

The northern and eastern portions of the Edwards Plateau give rise to the Balcones Canyonlands, and it is here that we find the selection of orchids noted for this region. The most frequently encountered is the summer-flowering *Epipactis gigantea*, the stream orchid. Although a typical western U.S. species, it is easily found along many of the streams and pools within the canyonlands. Equally at home in the open woodlands is *Corallorhiza wisteriana*, Wister's coralroot, an early spring bloomer and usually our first orchid of the season. These rocky wooded slopes repeat the array of crested coralroots found at the northern extreme in Dallas County in the White Rock Escarpment, although the latter now claims *H. grandiflora*, Greenman's crested coralroot, and further searching here in the Edwards Plateau may very well reveal this species here also. One of the problems with the crested coralroots is that in fruit many of the species are very similar. For now we have to be contented with plants of *Hexalectris nitida*, the shining crested coralroot; *H. spicata* var. *spicata*, the crested coralroot; *H. spicata* var. *arizonica*, the Arizona crested coralroot, and *H. warnockii*, Texas purple-spike. Although very rare elsewhere, *H. nitida* has been reported by Bill Carr to be frequent in the juniper/oak woodlands of the plateau. An additional species has been reported from here but without any documentation. That is the spotted coralroot, *Corallorhiza maculata*. It presents an interesting problem: if it is a southeastern extension of the western population of var. *occidentalis*, then it is the same taxon that has been recorded from the Trans-Pecos; but if it turns out to be var. *maculata*, more commonly found in the few southeastern/southern prairies and plains records, it would represent a new taxon for Texas.

Autumn and early winter bring two ladies'-tresses to the area: *Spiranthes cernua*, the nodding ladies'-tresses, and the more frequent *Spiranthes magnicamporum*, the Great Plains ladies'-tresses. Although relatively abundant in suitable habitat of limestone flats and seasonal seeps, they can be very difficult to tell apart.

Orchid hunting here in the Edwards Plateau should offer many challenges; excellent habitat abounds, thus additional species of wild orchids are certain to be found.

4. Dallas/Ft. Worth Area

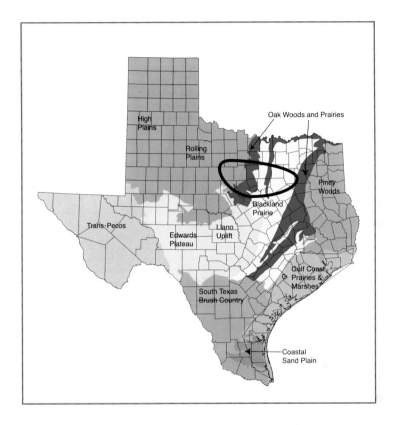

Despite the extensive development and urban sprawl of these twin Texas cities, several large, excellent nature preserves and county parks can be found within an hour's drive of downtown. It is here in the preserved lands that a dozen species and varieties of wild orchids may be easily found. Many of the parklands offer guided nature walks for both bird watchers and plant fanciers, and tagging along is a great way to search for orchids. Some of the rarest have shown up along the trails!

Species found in the Dallas/Ft. Worth area include:

Corallorhiza wisteriana, Wister's coralroot

Epipactis gigantea, stream orchid

Hexalectris grandiflora, Greenman's crested coralroot

Hexalectris nitida, shining crested coralroot

Hexalectris spicata var. *spicata*, crested coralroot

Hexalectris spicata var. *arizonica*, Arizona crested coralroot

Hexalectris warnockii, Texas purple-spike

Spiranthes cernua, nodding ladies'-tresses
Spiranthes lacera var. *gracilis*, southern slender ladies'-tresses
Spiranthes ovalis, southern oval ladies'-tresses
Spiranthes magnicamporum, Great Plains ladies'-tresses
Spiranthes vernalis, grass-leaved ladies'-tresses

Latest winter and early spring bring forth the first orchids of the season, including the only coralroot that is widespread in Texas, *Corallorhiza wisteriana*, Wister's coralroot. Its fondness for open woodland and even edges of cultivated lawns in lightly wooded habitats makes it a species that is not difficult to seek out. Following this somewhat less than showy orchid is the cosmopolitan *Spiranthes vernalis*, the grass-leaved ladies'-tresses, an indiscriminating species that may pop up most anywhere that is grass, including the center strip in a busy highway. It is the earliest and largest of the ladies'-tresses to be found in this region.

If the spring rains are cooperative, a June visit to some of the parklands west of Dallas should yield several of the crested coralroots: *Hexalectris grandiflora*, Greenman's crested coralroot; *H. nitida*, the shining crested coralroot; *H. spicata* var. *spicata*, the crested coralroot; *H. spicata* var. *arizonica*, the Arizona crested coralroot, and *H. warnockii*, the Texas purple-spike. With the recent addition of *H. grandiflora*, this quintet is matched only in the Trans-Pecos region. All are found in a few parks and conservation areas.

Reaching the eastern limit of its range (it also occurs in South Dakota and Oklahoma), *Epipactis gigantea*, the stream orchid, favors seepage slopes and streamside shores and is scattered throughout the area. Late summer and autumn bring us back to the ladies'-tresses, and four species are found here: *Spiranthes cernua*, the nodding ladies'-tresses of damp seeps and roadsides; *S. lacera* var. *gracilis*, the southern slender ladies'-tresses of open lawns, cemeteries, and meadows; *S. magnicamporum*, the Great Plains ladies'-tresses, of typical prairie habitat; and the rarest, at home in rich woodlands, *S. ovalis*, the southern oval ladies'-tresses.

5. The Panhandle and Great Plains

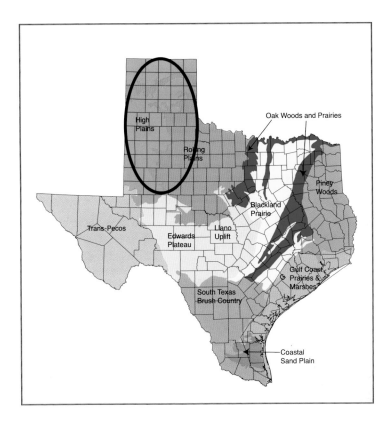

The geographically isolated but expansive area of northwestern Texas has little (remaining) wild orchid habitat. The short-grass prairie is heavily grazed and typically much drier than the tall-grass prairies that are so orchid rich to the east and north.

Only three orchid species have been recorded for this region:

Cypripedium parviflorum var. *pubescens*, the large yellow lady's-slipper
Epipactis gigantea, the stream orchid
Spiranthes vernalis, the grass-leaved ladies'-tresses

The grass-leaved ladies'-tresses is reaching the western limit of its range here and although it often favors disturbed grasslands, it remains a rare species of this region and is known only from Hemphill County in the northeastern portion of the Panhandle. The stream orchid may be found in Garza County at the base of the Panhandle. The large yellow lady's-slipper, certainly the most attractive and showiest of the trio from this region, is known only from a historical record based upon a collection made in 1929 by B. C. Tharp. This is the only collection for this species in Texas (all other yellow-flowering species of *Cypripedium* are *C. kentuck-iense* from eastern Texas). There are (were) several water holes in this semiarid area that could have supported such an orchid but the nearest known locations are at much higher elevations in New Mexico.

6. West Texas and the Big Bend

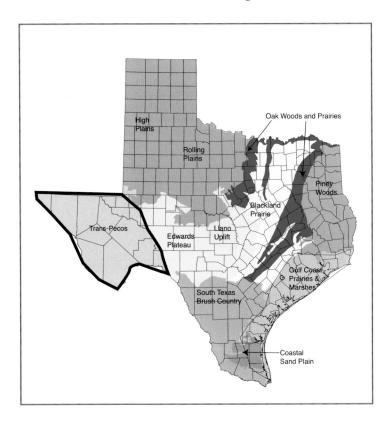

For the native orchid enthusiast the lure of the western Texas parklands means the remote, rugged high elevations of Big Bend and the oft-distant canyons of the Glass and Guadalupe Mountains. It is here within these national and state parks that nine species of wild orchids may be found that do not occur elsewhere in Texas, and four taxa that are not found elsewhere in the United States. Travel is at times difficult, the hiking arduous, and the timing rain-dependent. All include equally long trips and often chance discoveries. Three well-defined areas have been well explored and those are now where most of the orchids can be found: the Chisos Mountains in Big Bend National Park, the Glass Mountains in Glass Mountain State Park, and the Guadalupe Mountains, which are shared among The Nature Conservancy, the National Park Service, and the State of Texas.

Species recorded from West Texas parklands:

Corallorhiza maculata var. *occidentalis*, western spotted coralroot

Corallorhiza striata var. *striata*, striped coralroot

Deiregyne confusa, rimrock ladies'-tresses

Dichromanthus cinnabarinus, cinnabar ladies'-tresses
Dichromanthus michuacanus, Michoacan ladies'-tresses
Epipactis gigantea, stream orchid
Hexalectris nitida, shining crested coralroot
Hexalectris grandiflora, Greenman's crested coralroot
Hexalectris revoluta, recurved crested coralroot
Hexalectris spicata var. *spicata*, crested coralroot
Hexalectris spicata var. *arizonica*, Arizona crested coralroot
Hexalectris warnockii, Texas purple-spike
Malaxis soulei, rat-tailed adder's-mouth
Malaxis wendtii, Wendt's adder's-mouth
Schiedeella arizonica, Arizona red-spot; Indian braids

Late spring, or more appropriately early summer, in these rugged, high-elevation parklands brings the first flush of native orchids to this region of the Trans-Pecos. Most have very limited distribution in Texas and often are known only from one or two counties. Both *Corallorhiza maculata* var. *occidentalis*, the western spotted coralroot, and *C. striata*, the striped coralroot, are found in widely scattered, often coniferous woodlands. The western spotted coralroot has been found in both the Davis and the Chisos Mountains, and the showy striped coralroot in the Chianti and Guadalupe Mountains.

Epipactis gigantea, the stream orchid, is the most widely distributed orchid in the Trans-Pecos and favors seepages and streamsides, often forming large colonies. Late June to early July brings the first orchid bonanza to Big Bend National Park.

The recently rediscovered *Deiregyne confusa*, the rimrock ladies'-tresses, is found at elevations of 7,500 feet and favors pockets in the rimrock of the Chisos Mountains within the park. Of the quartet of early flowering crested coralroots—*Hexalectris nitida*, the shining or Glass Mountain coralroot, *H. revoluta* var. *revoluta*, the recurved crested coralroot, *H. spicata* var. *spicata*, the crested coralroot, and *H. spicata* var. *arizonica*, the Arizona crested coralroot—only the recurved crested coralroot is restricted in Texas to the slopes and ridges of the Chisos and Glass Mountains. It is not found elsewhere in the United States (plants from Arizona and New Mexico are var. *colemanii*). The final specialty of the area for this time of year is *Schiedeella arizonica*, Indian braids or red-spot ladies'-tresses. Diminutive in comparison to most of the other orchids in the region, this delightful little species has undergone many taxonomic changes in its life (see p. 000) and has been found in Texas in only a few spots in the Davis and Guadalupe Mountains on coniferous forest slopes usually above 7,000 feet. In the Guadalupe Mountains it is found growing with the rat-tail adder's-mouth, *Malaxis soulei*, although when the *Malaxis* is in flower in August, the only sign of the *Schiedeella* is the small basal rosette of leaves.

Late summer and early autumn feature only five species, but they are the specialties of the region and several are very showy. In the same areas of Big Bend National Park where one searched for (and hopefully found) rimrock ladies-tresses earlier in the season, the fiery torches of *Dichromanthus cinnabarinus*, the cinnabar ladies'-tresses, hold forth in rocky, often roadside, crags. The brilliant orange inflorescences are unmistakable! In much of this same area, watch carefully for the well-camouflaged spikes of *D. michuacanus*, the Michoacan ladies'-tresses. They tend to grow more out in the open, in grassy areas and along intermittent streams in open woodlands rather than in the rocky outcrops.

Perhaps the showiest of the crested coralroots, *Hexalectris warnockii*, the Texas purple-spike, is prime in August although it has been found flowering earlier, especially at lower elevations. Although not confined to the Trans-Pecos, the Texas purple-spike was first discovered in Love Peak Basin in the Chisos Mountains in 1932 and then again in 1937 in Upper Blue Creek Canyon by Barton Warnock, for whom the species is named.

A trek to the Boot Spring area in Big Bend National Park in early September may reward the explorer with a few plants of *Malaxis wendtii*, Wendt's adder's-mouth, in its only known location in the United States. The rich garnet spikes of tiny flowers rise from a single leaf and it takes a watchful eye to spot the plants. *Malaxis soulei*, the rat-tailed adder's-mouth, prefers a very different habitat and is usually confined to the cooler high-elevation coniferous woodlands of the Davis Mountains.

At the Limit

Nearly all of the fifty-nine species and varieties found in Texas are at one of their geographical limits. Only *Spiranthes parksii*, the Navasota ladies'-tresses, and *Triphora trianthophora* var. *texensis*, the Texas three-birds orchis, are endemics and therefore do not expand their range in any direction outside of Texas. A few other species such as *Spiranthes vernalis*, the grass-leaved ladies'-tresses, and *Ponthieva racemosa*, the shadow-witch, extend into Mexico for their southern limits.

Eastern Texas, in the greatest sense, is the western limit of the range for most of the species found in the Pineywoods and Coastal Prairies and Marshes regions. That would include:

Calopogon tuberosus, common grass-pink
Cleistes bifaria, upland spreading pogonia
Cypripedium kentuckiense, ivory-lipped lady's-slipper
Gymnadeniopsis clavellata, little club-spur orchis
Gymnadeniopsis integra, yellow fringeless orchis
Gymnadeniopsis nivea, snowy orchis
Habenaria quinqueseta, Michaux's orchid
Isotria verticillata, large whorled pogonia
Listera australis, southern twayblade
Platanthera chapmanii, Chapman's fringed orchis
Platanthera ciliaris, orange fringed orchis
Platanthera conspicua, southern white fringed orchis
Platanthera cristata, orange crested orchis
Platanthera flava var. *flava,* southern tubercled orchis
Platanthera flava var. *herbiola*, northern tubercled orchis
Platanthera lacera, green fringed orchis; ragged orchis
Pogonia ophioglossoides, rose pogonia
Spiranthes brevilabris, short-lipped ladies'-tresses; Texas ladies'-tresses
Spiranthes eatonii, Eaton's ladies'-tresses
Spiranthes floridana, Florida ladies'-tresses
Spiranthes laciniata, lace-lipped ladies'-tresses
Spiranthes longilabris, long-lipped ladies'-tresses
Spiranthes odorata, fragrant ladies'-tresses
Spiranthes ovalis var. *ovalis*, southern oval ladies'-tresses
Spiranthes praecox, giant ladies'-tresses

Spiranthes sylvatica, woodland ladies'-tresses
Spiranthes tuberosa, little ladies'-tresses
Tipularia discolor, crane-fly orchis
Zeuxine strateumatica, lawn orchid*

On the other side of the state the Trans-Pecos region is both the eastern and/or northern limit of the range for several western and Mexican species:

Deiregyne confusa, rimrock ladies'-tresses
Dichromanthus cinnabarinus, cinnabar ladies'-tresses
Dichromanthus michuacanus, Michoacan ladies'-tresses
Hexalectris revoluta, recurved crested coralroot
Malaxis wendtii, Wendt's adder's-mouth
Schiedeella arizonica, Arizona red-spot; Indian braids

Four crested coralroots—*Hexalectris grandiflora,* Greenman's crested coralroot, *H. nitida,* the shining crested coralroot, *H. spicata* var. *arizonica,* the Arizona crested coralroot, and *H. warnockii,* the Texas purple-spike—all reach their eastern limit in the Dallas area. No species of orchids that might be considered typically "northern" in their distribution ever reach Texas, nor do any classic "south Floridian" species come this far west. Environment and habitat may play the greater role here.

Tips and Trips

Many places to go and times to visit are described in this book. Here are some tips to make your trips more pleasurable.

Orchids, as tough as they might seem at times, are vulnerable to disturbance, so tread as lightly as you are able and respect both the plants and the habitat. In many areas the orchids are protected, especially if they are in local, state, or national parks—do not pick or dig up the plants!

Late May and early June in East Texas are usually best for the spring species, and late June and early July for some of the western higher elevations. The summer months bring little into flower throughout much of the state other than in the Pineywoods/Big Thicket area from mid-July to early August for the fringed orchis species, and on into September for the myriad of ladies'-tresses. With the advent of the fall rains, searching becomes good again in the Trans-Pecos in September and October and along the Gulf Coast and Pineywoods for several species of ladies'-tresses. Many of the areas are popular with tourists and require advance reservations to ensure accommodations. If you are photographing, bring twice as much film as you plan to use or ample memory cards for your digital camera. Purchasing the film that you want may not always be a possibility while on the road. The weather is bound to be variable but a hat and sunscreen are almost always in order. In the wetlands insects may abound, so come prepared. Enjoy the regional cuisines and customs and meet wonderful local people, who are often more than happy to either grant permission to cross their lands or guide you to a special spot. Stop and talk with the local populace. They will appreciate it.

What Next?

Although it may seem, between the work of the Liggios (1999) and this publication, that all of the information on Texas orchids has been exhausted, the recent rediscovery of *Deiregyne confusa* opens the possibility of more rediscoveries and even new species for the state. Three species first come to mind for confirmation or rediscovery in eastern Texas: *Platanthera conspicua*, *Cleistes bifaria*, and *Habenaria quinqueseta*. All of these are not difficult to spot, and identification of the species themselves is not a problem. After that, literature reports of *Platytheles querceticola* and, although not as likely, *Liparis loeselii* and *Microthelys minutiflora* might be confirmed. Northeastern Texas, on the Oklahoma-Louisiana-Arkansas border, offers the possibility of several species not yet known from Texas but occurring in one or more of those three states within 100 miles of Texas, and several of them much closer than that! This list includes *Calopogon barbatus*, the bearded grass-pink; *Epidendrum magnoliae*, the green-fly orchid; *Pteroglossaspis ecristata*, the crestless plume orchid; *Aplectrum hyemale*, the putty-root; *Galearis spectabilis*, the showy orchis; *Goodyera pubescens*, the downy rattlesnake orchis; and *Liparis liliifolia*, the lily-leaved twayblade.

In the southwestern portion of the state, primarily the Trans-Pecos region, watchful eyes may someday find *Platanthera limosa*, Thurber's rein orchis, and/or *Platanthera brevifolia*, the short-leaved rein orchis—both known from nearby New Mexico and Arizona. Although ideal habitat may not appear to exist in the mountains of the Trans-Pecos similar to that of the sky islands of Arizona and New Mexico, it is always prudent to watch for a trio of adder's-mouths—*Malaxis corymbosa*, the flat-topped adder's-mouths; *M. abieticola*, the fir-loving adder's-mouth; and *Malaxis porphyrea*, the purple adder's-mouth—to fill out the complement of that genus in the Trans-Pecos. Areas with *Malaxis soulei* would be the most promising as that species grows readily with the other three when they are found in Arizona or New Mexico. The final coup would be to locate living plants of the large yellow lady's-slipper, *Cypripedium parviflorum* var. *pubescens*, in the documented region of the western panhandle, although no complaints would be registered if it were found elsewhere!

Appendix 1. Understanding *Platanthera chapmanii*

Its Origins and Hybrids

One of the showiest native orchids of eastern Texas is the brilliantly colored **Chapman's fringed orchis**, *Platanthera chapmanii* (Small) Luer *emend.* Folsom. Although geographically restricted to the southern portion of the southeastern United States, **Chapman's fringed orchis** is an important component of the summer-flowering orchid flora of this area. No other complex within the Orchidaceae in the southeastern United States is in the unique position of including both a species with an ancestral hybrid origin, *P. chapmanii*, and a current or contemporary hybrid, *P. ×channellii*, with the same parentage. Known from the Big Thicket in East Texas as well as from much of northern Florida and (historically) two sites in southeastern Georgia, plants are now best found in a few of the Texas locations and in the central panhandle of Florida. Although Correll cited the range for *Platanthera chapmanii* (as *Habenaria × Chapmanii*) as New Jersey to Georgia and Florida and west to Texas, he based this on his knowledge of specimens of both *P. chapmanii* and *P. ×channellii*. True *P. chapmanii* has always been, and continues to be, one of the rarest orchids found in North America and is endemic to this lower portion of the southeastern Coastal Plain (Brown and Folsom, 2002; Brown, 2004).

    Chapman's fringed orchis was originally described by Small in 1903 as *Blephariglottis chapmanii*. Ames (1910), noting its intermediacy between *Habenaria ciliaris* and *H. cristata*, made a new combination as *Habenaria × Chapmanii*. This hybrid status remained for many years, including the new combination of *Platanthera ×chapmanii* (Small) Luer made by Dr. Luer in 1972. It was not until Jim Folsom's work in 1984 that the taxon was restored to its rightful status of full species and a new, contemporary hybrid, *P. ×channellii*, was described (Folsom, 1984).

    Understanding *Platanthera chapmanii* and its relationships to the closely related **orange fringed orchis**, *P. ciliaris*, and **orange crested orchis**, *P. cristata*, is greatly simplified if the observer can see all three taxa in one field session. This can be accomplished only in the Osceola National Forest of Florida, because *P. ciliaris* is historically and apparently currently absent from any of the other known localities. The Liggios (1999) clearly state that *P. ciliaris* has never been found in any of the Texas locales for *P. chapmanii*. Conversely, *P. cristata* is often found growing in or near many of the *P. chapmanii* sites, especially in eastern Florida.

Folsom (1984) convincingly demonstrated that the origins of *Platanthera chapmanii* were most likely an ancient hybridization of *P. ciliaris* and *P. cristata*. Therefore *P. chapmanii* is intermediate in size and characters between the two ancestors. Over the years it has evolved into a stable, reproducing species with a very distinctive bent column. This evolution of the column shape is critical in the pollination of the species. At the same time the contemporary hybrid of *P. ciliaris* and *P. cristata*, **Channell's hybrid fringed orchis**, *P.* ×*channellii*, occurs in rare situations when both parents are present. It, too, is intermediate between the parents, but the column is unlike that of *P. chapmanii*. Folsom (1984) illustrates all of these characters in great detail. Because Folsom's original publication in *Orquidea* was not readily available to many interested orchidists, the article, with minor revisions, was reprinted in the *North American Native Orchid Journal* in 1995, including all of Folsom's graphics (Folsom, 1995).

One of the best aids in the initial determination of plants in the field is an observation of what species predominate in the area. If both *Platanthera ciliaris* and *P. cristata* are present and only a few intermediates can be found, then they are probably the hybrid *P.* ×*channellii*. If the majority of plants appear intermediate between *P. ciliaris* and *P. cristata* and only a few or neither of the latter species is present, then the observer needs to look carefully at the shape of the column; the majority of plants are most likely *P. chapmanii*. The rostellum lobes of the column in *P. chapmanii* have a characteristic prominent hook that is clearly visible, whereas the rostellum lobes of the columns of *P. ciliaris* are triangular with tips pointing straight forward, and those of *P. cristata* are much shorter, nearly truncated, and with a very slight hook.

In addition, characters that help in determining which species are present may also include geographic location, diameter of raceme, size of flower, length and position of spur, and shape of orifice (Folsom, 1985; 1995). Stating simply that *Platanthera ciliaris* is larger, *P. chapmanii* is intermediate, and *P. cristata* is smaller has led to much confusion. For many orchid enthusiasts this rule of thumb, although not explicitly stated, seemed to refer to overall size, especially height. That is not accurate and height should never be taken into account. All three species can grow from 10 or 15 cm to, in the case of *P. chapmanii* and *P. ciliaris*, more than a meter in height! When size comparisons are made, they refer to the diameter of the raceme and the measurements of the individual flowers. Even the overall height of the flowering raceme is not a good criterion for identification. Because of the ancestral parentage of *P. chapmanii*, plants can easily favor the overall raceme shape of either parent, but the raceme diameter appears to remain constant. Spur length in the three species is helpful as well. Typically in *P. ciliaris* the spur is

20–25 mm long, in *P. chapmanii* 10–14 mm long, and in *P. cristata* 5–8 mm long. Illustrations on p. 000 show the relationships among *P. cristata, P. chapmanii,* and *P. ciliaris* and will assist in understanding this comparison.

In addition to understanding the species, orchid observers need to be aware that the hybrids involved in this complex include:

Platanthera ×*apalachicola* P.M. Brown & S. Stewart

(*P. chapmanii* × *P. cristata)*

Platanthera ×*channellii* Folsom

(*P. ciliaris* × *P. cristata)*

Platanthera ×*osceola* P.M. Brown & S. Stewart

(*P. chapmanii* × *P. ciliaris)*

Relationships among this group are best summed up in the accompanying diagram. *Platanthera blephariglottis, P. conspicua,* and *P. integrilabia* are included in this diagram for completeness of the group (Brown, 2003; Brown and Folsom, 2004). These relationships and putative parentages are based upon morphological criteria. Artificially created hybrids, cytological studies, and molecular work have yet to be done on this entire complex.

Because hybrid swarms of some or all three species occur, it may be difficult to determine individual plants. *Platanthera* ×*apalachicola* is locally common where both parents frequently grow together. They usually occur as individuals and may appear within stands of *P. chapmanii* as smaller flowered, more slender plants or within stands of *P. cristata* as larger flowered, more robust individuals.

Relationships in the orange and white fringed orchis complex.

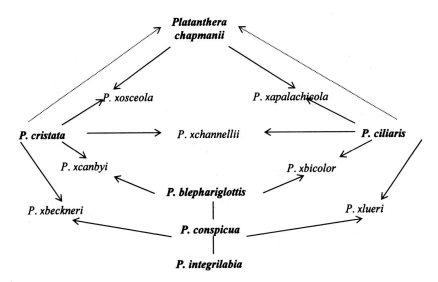

The hooked column of *P. chapmanii* is usually dominant, but the spur length and position is intermediate (Brown and Stewart, 2003).

Platanthera ×channellii and *P. chapmanii* can be difficult to tell apart. In the field one of the best ways is to look about and see which other species are growing nearby. If all the plants observed are the same and within the range of *P. chapmanii*, it is most likely *P. chapmanii*, whereas if it is a colony of mixed species and only a few intermediate plants are present, it is more likely to be *P. ×channellii*. Unless extant stands of *P. ciliaris* are found near *P. chapmanii,* it remains unlikely that confusion between the hybrid and the species would exist.

Platanthera ×osceola is known originally from the Osceola National Forest of northern Florida, the only place documented where both parents are found growing together. Plants of the hybrid usually occur as individuals and may appear within stands of *P. chapmanii* as larger flowered, more robust plants with decidedly longer spurs or within stands of *P. ciliaris* as smaller, more compactly flowered individuals. The hooked column of *P. chapmanii* is not as dominant as that of *P. ×apalachicola* (Brown and Stewart, 2003).

Understanding both the history of *Platanthera chapmanii* and the hybrid swarms that may accompany plants in the wild hopefully will help in clarifying some of the mystery around this rare and spectacular orchid. All orange-flowered plants throughout the overlapping ranges of *P. ciliaris*, *P. cristata*, and *P. chapmanii* should be carefully examined for the possibility of additional sites for **Chapman's fringed orchis**. While many of these hybrids may have been found previously in Texas, watchful eyes should be kept for them, remembering that individual hybrids often persist much longer than either parent and therefore may occur as isolated individuals.

P. chapmanii

P. cristata   *P. ciliaris*

P. cristata   *P. chapmanii*   *P. ciliaris*

Note: This essay appeared in slightly different versions in *Wild Orchids of the Southeastern United States* (2004) and in *Sida* (2004) 21: 853–59.

Appendix 2. Distribution of the Wild Orchids of Texas

1=Pineywoods, 2=Gulf Prairies and Marshes, 3=Post Oak Savannah,
4=Blackland Prairies, 5=Cross Timbers and Prairies, 6=South Texas Plains,
7=Edwards Plateau, 8=Rolling Plains, 9=High Plains, 10=Trans-Pecos
R = report ; ? assumed region

	1	2	3	4	5	6	7	8	9	10
Calopogon oklahomensis Oklahoma grass-pink	X	X	X							
Calopogon tuberosus common grass-pink	X	X	X							
Cleistes bifaria upland spreading pogonia	X?									
Corallorhiza maculata var. *occidentalis* western spotted coralroot							R			X
Corallorhiza odontorhiza autumn coralroot	X	X								
Corallorhiza striata striped coralroot										X
Corallorhiza wisteriana Wister's coralroot	X	X	X	X			X			
Cypripedium kentuckiense ivory-lipped lady's-slippe	X		X							
Cypripedium parviflorum var. *pubescens* large yellow lady's-slipper									X	
Deiregyne confusa rimrock ladies'-tresses										X
Dichromanthus cinnabarinus cinnabar ladies'-tresses										X
Dichromanthus michuacanus Michoacan ladies'-tresses										X
Epipactis gigantea stream orchid				X	X		X	X	X	X
Gymnadeniopsis clavellata little club-spur orchis	X									
Gymnadeniopsis integra yellow fringeless orchis	X									
Gymnadeniopsis nivea snowy orchis	X	X		X						
Habenaria quinqueseta Michaux's orchid	X?									
Habenaria repens water spider orchid	X	X	X	X		X				
Hexalectris grandiflora Greenman's crested coralroot				X						X
	1	2	3	4	5	6	7	8	9	10

1=Pineywoods 2=Gulf Prairies and Marshes 3=Post Oak Savannah
4=Blackland Prairies 5=Cross Timbers and Prairies 6=South Texas Plains
7=Edwards Plateau 8=Rolling Plains 9=High Plains 10=Trans-Pecos Texas
R = report ; ? assumed region

	1	2	3	4	5	6	7	8	9	10
Hexalectris nitida										
shining crested coralroot				X	X		X			X
Hexalectris revoluta										
recurved crested coralroot										X
Hexalectris spicata var. *spicata*										
crested coralroot	X	X	X	X	X		X			X
Hexalectris spicata var. *arizonica*										
Arizona crested coralroot	X			X	X		X			X
Hexalectris warnockii										
Texas purple-spike					X		X			X
Isotria verticillata										
large whorled pogonia	X									
Listera australis										
southern twayblade	X									
Malaxis soulei										
rat-tailed adder's-mouth									X	
Malaxis unifolia										
green adder's-mouth	X	R								
Malaxis wendtii										
Wendt's adder's-mouth										X
Platanthera chapmanii										
Chapman's fringed orchis	X									
Platanthera ciliaris										
orange fringed orchis	X	X	X	X	X					
Platanthera conspicua										
southern white fringed orchis		X								
Platanthera cristata										
orange crested orchis	X	X	X	X	X					
Platanthera flava var. *flava*										
southern tubercled orchis	X	X								
Platanthera flava var. *herbiola*										
northern tubercled orchis	X									
Platanthera lacera										
green fringed orchis	X									
Pogonia ophioglossoides										
rose pogonia	X			X						
Ponthieva racemosa										
shadow-witch	X									
Schiedeella arizonica										
Indian braids									X	
	1	2	3	4	5	6	7	8	9	10

	1	2	3	4	5	6	7	8	9	10
Spiranthes brevilabris Texas ladies'-tresses	X	X								
Spiranthes cernua nodding ladies'-tresses	X	X	X	X	X	X	X			
Spiranthes eatonii Eaton's ladies'-tresses	X	X								
Spiranthes floridana Florida ladies'-tresses	X	X	X							
Spiranthes lacera var. *gracilis* southern slender ladies'-tresses			X	X	X	X	X	X	X	
Spiranthes laciniata lace-lipped ladies'-tresses	X	X								
Spiranthes longilabris long-lipped ladies'-tresses	X	X								
Spiranthes magnicamporum Great Plains ladies'-tresses		X	X	X		X				
Spiranthes odorata fragrant ladies'-tresses	X	X	X	X						
Spiranthes ovalis southern oval ladies'-tresses	X	X	X							
Spiranthes parksii Navasota ladies'-tresses	X		X							
Spiranthes praecox giant ladies'-tresses	X	X	X							
Spiranthes sylvatica woodland ladies'-tresses	X	X								
Spiranthes tuberosa little ladies'-tresses	X	X	X	X						
Spiranthes vernalis grass-leaved ladies'-tresses	X	X	X	X				X		
Tipularia discolor crane-fly orchis	X									
Triphora trianthophora var. *trianthophora* three-birds orchis; nodding pogonia	X									
Triphora trianthophora var. *texensis* Texas three-birds orchis; Pike's three birds	X									
Zeuxine strateumatica lawn orchid*	X	X								
	1	2	3	4	5	6	7	8	9	10

Appendix 3. Flowering Times for the Wild Orchids of Texas

Jan. Feb. Mar. Apr. May Jun. Jul. Aug. Sept. Oct. Nov. Dec.

Calopogon oklahomensis
Oklahoma grass-pink

Calopogon tuberosus
common grass-pink

Cleistes bifaria
upland spreading pogonia

Corallorhiza maculata var. *occidentalis*
western spotted coralroot

Corallorhiza odontorhiza
autumn coralroot

Corallorhiza striata
striped coralroot

Corallorhiza wisteriana
Wister's coralroot

Cypripedium kentuckiense
ivory-lipped lady's-slipper

Cypripedium parviflorum var. *pubescens*
large yellow lady's-slipper

Deiregyne confusa
rimrock ladies'-tresses

Dichromanthus cinnabarinus
cinnabar ladies'-tresses

Dichromanthus michuacanus
Michoacan ladies'-tresses

Epipactis gigantea
stream orchid

Gymnadeniopsis clavellata
little club-spur orchis

Gymnadeniopsis integra
yellow fringeless orchis

Gymnadeniopsis nivea
snowy orchis

Habenaria quinqueseta
Michaux's orchid

Habenaria repens
water spider orchid

Hexalectris grandiflora
Greenman's crested coralroot

Hexalectris nitida
shining crested coralroot

Hexalectris revoluta
recurved crested coralroot

Hexalectris spicata var. *spicata*
crested coralroot

Hexalectris spicata var. *arizonica*
Arizona crested coralroot

Hexalectris warnockii
Texas purple-spike

Isotria verticillata
large whorled pogonia

Listera australis
southern twayblade

Malaxis soulei
rat-tailed adder's-mouth

Malaxis unifolia
green adder's-mouth

Malaxis wendtii
Wendt's adder's-mouth

Platanthera chapmanii
Chapman's fringed orchis

Platanthera ciliaris
orange fringed orchis

Platanthera conspicua
southern white fringed orchis

Platanthera cristata
orange crested orchis

Platanthera flava var. *flava*
southern tubercled orchis

Platanthera flava var. *herbiola*
northern tubercled orchis

Platanthera lacera
green fringed orchis

Pogonia ophioglossoides
rose pogonia

Ponthieva racemosa
shadow-witch

Schiedeella arizonica
Indian braids

Spiranthes brevilabris
Texas ladies'-tresses

Spiranthes cernua
nodding ladies'-tresses

Spiranthes eatonii
Eaton's ladies'-tresses

Spiranthes floridana
Florida ladies'-tresses

Spiranthes lacera var. *gracilis*
southern slender ladies'-tresses

Spiranthes laciniata
lace-lipped ladies'-tresses

Spiranthes longilabris
long-lipped ladies'-tresses

Spiranthes magnicamporum
Great Plains ladies'-tresses

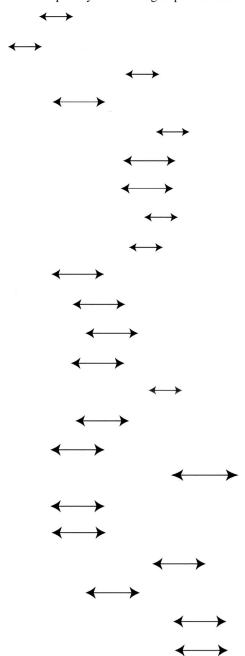

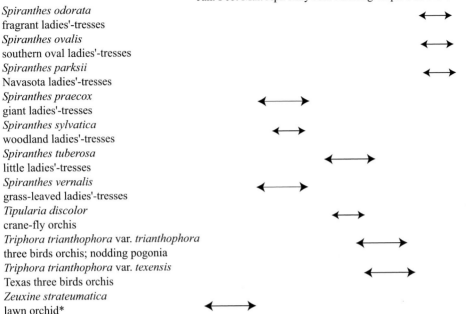

Jan. Feb. Mar. Apr. May Jun. Jul. Aug. Sept. Oct. Nov. Dec.

Spiranthes odorata
fragrant ladies'-tresses

Spiranthes ovalis
southern oval ladies'-tresses

Spiranthes parksii
Navasota ladies'-tresses

Spiranthes praecox
giant ladies'-tresses

Spiranthes sylvatica
woodland ladies'-tresses

Spiranthes tuberosa
little ladies'-tresses

Spiranthes vernalis
grass-leaved ladies'-tresses

Tipularia discolor
crane-fly orchis

Triphora trianthophora var. *trianthophora*
three birds orchis; nodding pogonia

Triphora trianthophora var. *texensis*
Texas three birds orchis

Zeuxine strateumatica
lawn orchid*

Glossary

adventive: non-native to a specific region

anterior: front or upper

anthesis: time of flowering

apomictic: fertilized within the embryo without pollination; an asexual means of reproduction

appressed: placed tightly against; opposite of divergent

approximate: the (flowers) lying close by, but not overlapping

articulate: jointed, pertaining to leaves or other organs having a clear abscission layer or joint, usually at the base

autogamous: one of several means of self-pollination

axillary: on the side

basal rosette: a cluster of leaves all arising at the base of the plant

bog: a low-lying area fed by water runoff from surrounding forested areas; coniferous forests tend to produce bogs with an acidic or low pH.

bract: a modified leaf

calcareous: limy

calciphile: a lime lover

callus: a thickened area, usually at the base of the lip

capitate: like a head; "with capitate hairs" refers to hairs with ball-like tips

cauline: on the stem

chasmogamous: with fully opened, usually sexual, flowers

chlorophyll: a green pigment manufactured by the plant and essential for photosynthesis

ciliate: with short, slender hairs

circumneutral: a pH of about 6.5

clavate: club-shaped

cleistogamous: with closed flowers that are usually self-pollinating

column: the structure in an orchid that has both the anthers and the pistil

conduplicate: longitudinally folded upward or downward along the central axis so that the ventral and/or dorsal sides face each other

confluent: the merging or blending of one part with another.

coralloid: coral-like

cordate: heart-shaped

coriaceous: leathery

corymb: a determinate inflorescence where all of the branches are the same length and with the outer flowers opening first crenulate: with a short, wavy margin; minutely scalloped

crest: a series of ridges or a group of hairs; usually yellow or a color contrasting with the lip

cuneate: wedge-shaped; triangular, with the narrow part at the point of attachment

cyme: a determinate inflorescence with the central flowers opening first

dentate: toothed

determinate: with a specific ending, not continuing to grow indefinitely

dilated: broadened

disjunct: occurring apart from the normal range of the species

distal: away from the center or main body, or pertaining to the underside

divergent: spreading or widely separated

dorsal sepal: the sepal opposite the lip; usually uppermost in most orchids

emarginate: notched at the tip

endemic: native to a specific area

ephemeral: appearing for a brief time; often a few weeks each season

epiphyte, epiphytic: living in the air

erose: with an irregular margin

extant: still in existence

extirpated: no longer in existence

extralimital: occurring on the very edge of the species' normal range

falcate: sickle-shaped

fen: a low-lying area fed by groundwater upwelling and seepage with neutral or slightly higher pH levels

filiform: slender and thread-like

foliaceous: leaf-like, as in foliaceous bracts, which have the appearance of leaves

glabrous: smooth

glaucous: with a whitish cast

habit: form or mode of growth; e.g., upright, or sprawling

habitat: the particular environment of a plant

hemi-epiphyte: usually growing on the base of trees or on logs

hydric: a perennially wet habitat

isthmus: a narrowed portion, often at the base of the lip

keel: a ridge

lacerate: slashed

lateral sepals: the sepals positioned on the side of the flower

lax: (flowers) loosely arranged

lip: the modified third petal of an orchid

lithophytic: growing on rocks

madder: dusky-purple in color

marcescent: withering but not falling off

marl: a calcareous or limy wetland

mentum: a short, rounded, thickened projection formed by the base of the petals; similar to a spur but not tapered to a point

mesic: of medium conditions

monotypic (genus): a genus having only one species

mucronate: a short, sharp point

mycotrophic: obtaining food through mycorrhizal fungi

naturalized: a non-native species that is reproducing in its adopted habitat

Neotropical: new world tropics

nominate, nominate variety: the pure species, exclusive of subspecies, variety, or form

non-resupinate: with only a single twist so the lip is at the top

oblanceolate: narrowly oblong

obovate: broadly oblong

orbicular: rounded

orifice: opening

ovary: the female structure that produces the seed

panicle: a branching inflorescence similar to a raceme, the flowers stalked

pedicellate flowers: those flowers held on pedicels or stalks

pedicellate ovary: typically the ovary of an orchid flower, where the ovary and the flower stalk merge into one structure

peduncle: the stalk of a flower

peloric: an abnormality of the lip like the other petals, or vice versa; a radially symmetrical mutant of a species normally having bilaterally symmetrical flowers

perianth: the combined petals and sepals of the flower

petiole: the stem portion of the leaf

plicate: soft and with many longitudinal ribs, often folded

pollinia: the structure in orchids that contains the pollen

posterior: lower or rear

pseudobulb: a swollen storage organ that is prominent in many epiphytic orchids and occasionally in a few genera of terrestrial orchids

puberulent: with a fine dusting of very short, soft hairs

pubescent, pubescence: downy with short, soft hairs

putative: assumed, but not scientifically proven; refers to hybrid parentage

raceme: an unbranched, indeterminate inflorescence with stalked flowers; branched racemes are technically panicles

rank: the arrangement of flowers in lines or vertical rows, especially in *Spiranthes*

reflexed: bent backwards

reniform: kidney-shaped

resupinate: twisted around so that the lip is lowermost

rhizome: an elongated basal stem; typically underground in terrestrials and along the strata (tree trunks, branches, rocks, etc.) in epiphytes

rhombic: with parallel sides but then tapered on both ends

rostellum: the part of the column, usually beak-shaped, that contains the stigmatic surface and to which the pollen adheres

saccate: sack-shaped

saprophytic, saprophyte: living off decaying vegetable matter

scape: a leafless stem that arises from the base of the plant

secund: all to one side

segregate genus (species): a genus or species that has been separated from another larger genus or from a species

senesces: withers

sepals: the outer floral envelope

sessile: without a stem or stalk

spatulate: oblong with a narrowed base

sphagnous: an area with sphagnum moss

spike: an unbranched inflorescence with sessile or unstalked flowers

spiranthoid: a *Spiranthes* or member of a genus closely allied to *Spiranthes*

spur: a slender, tubular, or sac-like structure usually formed at the base of the lip, and often containing nectar

striated, striations: with stripes

subtend: beneath the flower at the point of attachment to the stem

sympatric: growing together in the same habitat

taxa (sing., taxon): subspecies, variety, species, form

tepal: sepals and petals of similar morphology

terete: rounded

terminal: at the end

transverse: growing across; perpendicular to an axis or stem

tubercle: a thickened projection

tuberoid: a tuber-like organ; the term is often used to describe thickened roots as, strictly speaking, a tuber is a thickened stem

ultramafic; ultramific: soils and substrates found in serpentine areas with very high minerals such as nickel, magnesium, and asbestos

umbel: an inflorescence where the flower stems all arise from the same point like the spokes of an umbrella

undulate: wavy

waif: applied to a random individual occurrence

whorl: all coming from around the same point on an axis, like spokes

xeric: a perennially dry habitat

Bibliography

Ajilvsgi, G. 1979. *Wildflowers of the Big Thicket: East Texas and Western Louisiana*. College Station: Texas A&M University Press.

Amerson, P. A., A. Lodwick, L. N. Lodwick, and D.H. Riskind. 1975. The incredible orchid family. *Texas Parks & Wildlife* 25 (October): 16–20.

Ambs, S. 2006. The elusive *Deiregyne confusa*. *Native Orchid Conference Journal* 3(2): 1–5.

Ames, O. 1910. *Orchidaceae*. Vol. 4, *The Genus* Habenaria *in North America*. North Easton, Mass.: Ames Botanical Laboratory.

———. 1924. *An Enumeration of the Orchids of the United States and Canada*. Boston: The American Orchid Society.

Ames, O., and D. S. Correll. 1943. Notes on American Orchids. *Botanical Museum Leaflets* [Harvard University] 11: 1–28.

Amos, B. B., and F. R. Gehlbach, eds. 1988. *Edwards Plateau vegetation*. Waco, Tex.: Baylor University Press.

Atwood, J. T. 1985. The range of *Cypripedium kentuckiense*. *American Orchid Society Bulletin* 54: 1197–99.

Bridges, E. L., and S. L. Orzell. 1989. Additions and noteworthy vascular plant collections from Texas and Louisiana, with historical, ecological and geographical notes. *Phytologia* 66(1): 12–69.

———. 1989b. Longleaf pine communities of the west Gulf Coastal Plain. *Natural Areas Journal* 9(4): 246–63.

Brown, P. M. 1993. *A Field and Study Guide to the Orchids of New England and New York*. Jamaica Plain, Mass.: Orchis Press.

———. 1996. *Schieedella fauci-sanguinea*: a new name for an old plant. *North American Native Orchid Journal* 2(1): 66–68.

———. 1999. Recent taxonomic and distributional notes from Florida 1: *Spiranthes eatonii*. *North American Native Orchid Journal* 5(1): 3–15.

———. 2001. Recent taxonomic and distributional notes from Florida 11: *Spiranthes sylvatica*. *North American Native Orchid Journal* 7(3): 193–205.

———. 2002a. Revalidation of *Platanthera conspicua*. *North American Native Orchid Journal* 8: 3–14.

———. 2002b. Resurrection of the genus *Gymnadeniopsis* Rydberg. *North American Native Orchid Journal* 8: 32–40.

———. 2004. Understanding *Platanthera chapmanii*. *Sida* 21: 853–59.

———. 2005. Additions and emendations to *The Wild Orchids of North America, North of Mexico*. *Sida* 21(4): 2297–319.

———. 2006. Four new color forms from the Southwestern United States. *McAllen International Orchid Society Journal* 7(12): 4–11.

———. 2007. Notes on Texas orchids. *Journal of the Botanical Institute of Texas* 1(2): forthcoming.

Brown, P. M., and R. A. Coleman. 2000. *Schiedeella arizonica. North American Native Orchid Journal* 6(3): 3–17.

Brown, P. M., and S. N. Folsom. 1997. *Wild Orchids of the Northeastern United States.* Ithaca, N.Y.: Cornell University Press.

———. 2002. *Wild Orchids of Florida.* Gainesville: University Press of Florida.

———. 2003. *The Wild Orchids of North America, North of Mexico.* Gainesville: University Press of Florida.

———. 2004. *Wild Orchids of the Southeastern United States, North of Peninsular Florida.* Gainesville: University Press of Florida.

———. 2006. *Wild Orchids of the Canadian Maritimes and Northern Great Lakes Region.* Gainesville: University Press of Florida.

———. 2006b. *Wild Orchids of the Pacific Northwest and Canadian Rockies.* Gainesville: University Press of Florida.

———. 2006c. *Wild Orchids of the Prairies and Great Plains Region of North America.* Gainesville: University Press of Florida.

———. 2007. *Wild Orchids of the Northeast: New England, New York, Pennsylvania, and New Jersey.* Gainesville: University Press of Florida.

Brown, P. M., and R. Pike. 2006. *Triphora trianthophora* var. *texensis* (Orchidaceae), a new variety endemic to Texas. *North American Native Orchid Journal* 12: 4–10.

Brown-Marsden, M., and A. B. Collins. 2006. Range expansion of *Hexalectris grandiflora* (Orchidaceae) in Texas. *Sida* 22(2): 1239–44.

Carr, W. J. 2005. *An Annotated List of the G3/T3 and Rarer Plant Taxa of Texas.* Austin: Texas Conservation Data Center, The Nature Conservancy of Texas.

Catling, P. M. 1983. *Spiranthes ovalis* var. *erostellata* (Orchidaceae), a new autogamous variety from the eastern United States *Brittonia* 35: 120–25.

———. 1989. Biology of North American representatives of the subfamily Spiranthoideae, in *North American Native Terrestrial Orchid Propagation and Production.* Chadds Ford, Pa.: Brandywine Conservancy.

———. 2004. A synopsis of the genus *Hexalectris* in the United States and a new variety of *Hexalectris revoluta. Native Orchid Conference Journal* 1(2): 5–25.

Catling, P. M., and V. R. Catling. 1991. A synopsis of breeding systems and pollination in North American orchids. *Lindleyana* 6(4): 187–210.

Catling, P. M., and V. S. Engel. 1993. Systematics and distribution of *Hexalectris spicata* var. *arizonica* (Orchidaceae). *Lindleyana* 8(3): 119–25.

Catling, P. M., and K. B. Gregg. 1992. Systematics of the genus *Cleistes* in North America. *Lindleyana* 7(2): 57–73.

Catling, P. M., and K. L. McIntosh. 1979. Rediscovery of *Spiranthes parksii* Correll. *Sida* 8: 188–93.

Coleman, R. A. 1995. *The Wild Orchids of California*. Ithaca: Cornell University Press.

———. 1996. *Stenorrhynchos michuacana*. *Orchids* 65(12): 1284–87.

2002. *The Wild Orchids of Arizona and New Mexico*. Ithaca: Cornell University Press.

Coleman, R. A., and M. Baker. 2006. *Microthelys rubrocallosa*. *Orchids* 75(1): 56–57.

Coleman, R. A., J. Sirotnak, and A. Leavitt. 2006. The hunt for *Deiregyne confusa*. *Native Orchid Conference Journal* 3(3): 7–8,13.

Collins, A., J. Varnum, and M. Brown-Marsden. 2005. Soil and ecological features of *Hexalectris* (Orchidaceae) sites. *Sida* 21: 1879–91.

Correll, D. S. 1938. *Cypripedium calceolus* var. *pubescens*. *Botanical Museum Leaflets* [Harvard University] 7: 1–18.

———. 1944. Orchidaceae. Vol. 3, pt. 3, in Lundell, *Flora of Texas*. Renner, Tex.: Texas Research Foundation.

———. 1947a. Additions to the orchids of Texas. *Wrightia* 1(3): 166–82.

———. 1947b. A new *Spiranthes* from Texas. *American Orchid Society Bulletin* 16: 400–401.

———. 1950. *Native Orchids of North America*. Waltham, Mass.: Chronica Botanica.

———. 1962. Orchidaceae. In: F. W. Gould, *Texas Plants—A Checklist and Ecological Summary*. College Station: Texas Agricultural Experimental Station.

———. 1969. Orchidaceae. In: F. W. Gould, *Texas Plants—A Checklist and Ecological Summary* with supplement. College Station: Texas Agricultural Experimental Station.

———. 1975. Orchidaceae. In: F. W. Gould, *Texas Plants—A Checklist and Ecological Summary*. College Station: Texas Agricultural Experimental Station.

Correll, D. S., and M. C. Johnston. 1979. *Manual of vascular flora of Texas*. Richardson: University of Texas at Dallas.

Cory, V. L., and H. B. Parks. 1937. Catalogue of the flora of the state of Texas. *Texas Agricultural Experiment Station Bulletin* 550: 34–35.

Coulter, J. M. 1890. Upon a collection of plants made by Mr. G. C. Nealley in the region of the Rio Grande, in Texas, from Brazos Santiago to El Paso county. *Contributions from the United States National Herbarium* 1: 25–65.

———. 1894. Botany of Western Texas. *Contributions from the United States National Herbarium* 2: 422–25.

Cribb, P. 1997. *The Genus* Cypripedium. Portland, Ore.: Timber Press.

Diggs, G. M., Jr., B. Lipscomb, and R. J. O'Kennon. 1999. *Shinner's and Mahler's Illustrated Flora of North Central Texas*. Ft. Worth: Botanical Research Institute of Texas.

Diggs, G. M., Jr., B. Lipscomb, M. D. Reed, and R. J. O'Kennon. 2006. *Illustrated Flora of East Texas*. Ft. Worth: Botanical Research Institute of Texas.

Engel, V. 1987. Saprophytic orchids of Dallas. *American Orchid Society Bulletin* 56(8): 831–35.

———. 1997. Saprophytic orchids of Dallas. *North American Native Orchid Journal* 2(10): 156–67.

[*FNA*] Flora of North America Editorial Committee, eds. 2002. *Flora of North America North of Mexico*. Vol. 26. New York and Oxford: Oxford University Press.

Folsom, J. P. 1984. Reinterpretation of the status and relationships of the yellow-fringed orchid complex. *Orquidea* (Mexico) 9(2): 337–45.

Freudenstein, J. V. 1997. A monograph of *Corallorhiza* (Orchidaceae). *Harvard Papers in Botany* 10: 5–51.

Garay, L. A. 1980 [1982]. A generic revision of the Spiranthinae. *Botanical Museum Leaflets* [Harvard University] 28(4): 277–426.

Gehlbach, F. R. 1988. Forests and woodlands of the northeastern Balcones Escarpment. In: B. B. Amos and F. R. Gehlbach, eds., *Edwards Plateau Vegetation*, 57–77. Waco, Tex.: Baylor University Press.

Goldman, D. H. 1995. A new species of *Calopogon* from the midwestern United States. *Lindleyana* 10(1): 37–42.

Goldman, D. H. 2000. Systematics of *Calopogon* and the tribe Arethuseae (Orchidaceae). Ph.D. diss., University of Texas.

Goldman, D. H., R. K. Jansen, C. van den Berg, I. J. Leitch, M. F. Fay, and M. W. Chase. 2004. Molecular and cytological examination of *Calopogon* (Orchidaceae, Epidendroideae): circumscription, phylogeny, polyploidy, and possible hybrid speciation. *American Journal of Botany* 91: 707–23.

Gould, F. W. 1969. *Texas Plants: A Checklist and Ecological Summary* with supplement. College Station: Texas Agricultural Experimental Station.

———. 1975. *Texas Plants: A Checklist and Ecological Summary*. College Station: Texas Agricultural Experimental Station.

Gould, F. W., G. O. Hoffman, and C. A. Rechenthin. 1960. *Vegetational Areas of Texas*. Agricultural Extension Service L-492.

Greuter, W. et al., eds. 2000. *International Code of Botanical Nomenclature* (St. Louis Code): *Regnum Vegetabile*. 138. http://www.bgbm.fu-berlin.de/iapt/nomenclature/code/st. louis.htm.

Gunter, A. Y. 1972. *The Big Thicket*. Austin, Tex.: Jenkins.

Hágsater, E., M. Á. Soto Arenas, G. A. Salazar Chávez, R. Jiménez Machorro, M. A. López Rosas, and R. L. Dressler. 2005. *Orchids of Mexico*. Mexico City: Instituto Chinoin, A.C.

Hall, E. 1873. *Plantae Texanae*: A list of the plants collected in eastern Texas in 1872, and distributed to subscribers, Published by the author, Salem, Mass.

Hatch, S. L. 1991. *Texas Vascular Plant Checklist*. Texas A&M University (TAMU). http://www.csdl.tamu.edu.FLORA/ftc/dft/ftc_orc.htm.

———. ca. 2000. *Digital Flora of Texas* and the *Texas Vascular Plant Checklist*. Texas A&M University (TAMU). http://www.csdl.tamu.edu.FLORA/ftc/dft/ftc_orc.htm.

Hatch, S. L., K. N. Gandhi, and L. E. Brown. 1990. Checklist of the vascular plants of Texas. Mp-1655. College Station: Texas Agricultural Experiment Station.

Havard, V. 1885. Report on the flora of western and southern Texas. *Proceedings of the United States National Museum* 8: 449–533.

Heller, A. A. 1895. Botanical explorations in southern Texas during the season of 1894. *Contributions from the Herbarium*. Franklin and Marshall College, Lancaster, Pa.

Holmes, W. C. 1983. The distribution of *Habenaria integra* (Nutt.) Spreng. (Orchidaceae) in Mississippi, Louisiana, and Texas. *The Southwestern Naturalist* 28(4): 451–56.

Hooker, V. T. 1835. Notice concerning Mr. Drummond's collections made chiefly in the southern and western parts of the United States. *Hooker's Companion to the Botanical Magazine* 1: 30–49.

International Plant Names Index. http://www.ipni.org/index.html.

Johnston, M. C. 1990. *The vascular plants of Texas*, 2nd ed.: A list, updating the *Manual of the Vascular Plants of Texas*. Austin: Marshall C. Johnston. Self-published.

Jones, S. D., J. K. Wipff, and P. Montgomery. 1997. *Vascular plants of Texas: A comprehensive checklist including synonymy, bibliography, and index*. Austin: University of Texas Press.

Kartesz, J. T. 1994. *A synonymized checklist of the vascular plants of United States, Canada and Greenland*, 2nd ed. Portland, Ore.: Timber Press. 2 vols.

Kartesz, J. T., and C. A. Meacham. 1999. *Synthesis of the North American Flora*, ver. 1.0. Chapel Hill, N.C.

Keenan, P. E. 1999. *Wild Orchids Across North America*. Portland, Ore.: Timber Press.

Kaul, R. B. 1986. In: R. L. McGregor et al., *Flora of the Great Plains*, 1268–84. Lawrence: University Press of Kansas.

Liggio, J. 2000. The genus *Hexalectris* in the United States. *North American Native Orchid Journal* 6(4): 262–67.

Liggio, J., and A. O. Liggio. 1999. *Wild Orchids of Texas*. Austin: University of Texas Press.

Luer, C. A. 1972. *The native orchids of Florida*. Bronx: New York Botanical Garden.

———. 1975. *The native orchids of the United States and Canada excluding Florida*. Bronx: New York Botanical Garden.

Lundell, C. L. 1944. *Flora of Texas*. Renner, Tex.: Texas Research Foundation.

MacRoberts, B. R., and M. H. MacRoberts. 1997. Floristics of beech-hardwood forests in East Texas. *Phytologia* 82(1): 20–29.

MacRoberts, M. H., and B. R. MacRoberts. 1995. Noteworthy vascular plant collections on the Kisachie National Forest, Louisiana. *Phytologia* 78(4): 291–313.

Magrath, L. K. 1971. Native orchids of Kansas. *Transactions of the Kansas Academy of Science* 74: 287–309.

———. 1973. *Orchids of the Prairies and Plains Regions of North America*. Ph.D. diss. University of Kansas, Lawrence.

———. 1989. Nomenclatural notes on *Calopogon, Corallorhiza*, and *Cypripedium* (Orchidaceae) in the Great Plains region. *Sida* 13(3): 371.

———. 2001. Native orchids of Oklahoma. *Crosstimbers* (Spring): 18–25.

Marks, P. H., and P. A. Harcombe. 1975. Community diversity of coastal plain forests in southeast Texas. *Ecology* 56: 1004–8.

———. 1981. Forest vegetation of the Big Thicket, southeast Texas. *Ecological Monographs* 51: 287–303.

Montgomery, J. A. 1993. The nature and origin of the blackland prairies of Texas. In: M. R. Sharpless and J. C. Yelderman, eds. *The Texas Blackland Prairie: land, history, and culture* pp. 24–40. Waco, Tex.: Baylor University

Nature Conservancy. 2004. G3 Taxa Abstracts. http://www.nature.org/wherewework/northamerica/states/texas/files/g3taxaabstracts720044.pdf.

Orzell, S. L. 1990. *Inventory of National Forests and National Grasslands in Texas.* Austin: Texas Natural Heritage Program.

Orzell, S. L., and E. L. Bridges. 1987. Further additions and noteworthy collections in the flora of Arkansas, with historical, ecological, and phytogeographic notes. *Phytologia* 64(2): 81–144.

Palmer, E. 1880. List of plants collected in S.W. Texas and N. Mexico. Unpublished papers. Library of the Gray Herbarium.

Pelchat, C. 2000. *Spiranthes parksii. North American Native Orchid Journal* 6(4): 268–79.

———. 2005. *Spiranthes parksii. McAllen International Orchid Society Journal* 6(3): 9–15.

———. 2005. *Spiranthes parksii*—additions to last issue's article. *McAllen International Orchid Society Journal* 6(4): 9.

Petrie, W. 1981. *Guide to the Orchids of North America.* Blaine, Wash.: Hancock House.

Poole, J. M., W. R. Carr, D. M. Price, and J. R. Singhurst. 2007. *Rare Plants of Texas: A Field Guide.* College Station: Texas A&M University Press.

Poole, J. M., and D. H. Riskind. 1987. *Endangered, Threatened, or Protected Native Plants of Texas.* Austin: Texas Parks and Wildlife Department.

Pridgeon, A. M., P. J. Cribb, M. W. Chase, and F. Rasmussen, eds. 1999. *Genera Orchidacearum.* Vol. 1, *General Introduction, Apostasioideae, Cypripedioideae.* 1999. New York: Oxford University Press.

———. 2001. *Genera Orchidacearum.* Vol. 2, *Orchidoideae,*(Part I). New York: Oxford University Press.

———. 2003. *Genera Orchidacearum.* Vol. 3, *Orchidoideae,* (Part II), *Vanilloideae.* New York: Oxford University Press.

———. 2005. *Genera Orchidacearum.* Vol. 4, *Epidendroideae,* Part I. New York: Oxford University Press.

Reed, C. F. 1981. *Cypripedium kentuckiense* Reed, a new species of orchid in Kentucky. *Phytologia* 48: 426–28.

Riskind, D. H., and D. D. Diamond. 1988. An introduction to environments and vegetation. In: B. B. Amos and F. R. Gehlbach, *Edwards Plateau Vegetation,* 1–15. Waco, Tex.: Baylor University Press.

Rydberg, P. A. 1901. *Gymnadeniopsis* Rydberg. In: Britton, *Manual of the Flora of the Northeastern United States,* 293.

———. 1965. *Flora of the Prairies and Plains of Central North America.* New York: Hafner.

Salazar, G. A. 1993. *Malaxis wendtii,* a new orchid species from Coahuila and Nuevo Leon, Mexico. *Orquidea* (Mexico) 13(1–2): 281–84.

Salazar, G. A., M. W. Chase, and M. A. Soto Arenas. 2002. Galleotillinae, a new subtribe and other nomenclatural changes in the Spiranthinae. *Lindleyana* 17(3): 172–76.

Sanders, R. W. 1997. Vegetation of Lennox Woods Preserve, Red River County, Texas. Texas Society of Ecological Restoration, *Texas Restoration Notes* 2(1).

Sheviak, C. J. 1973. A new *Spiranthes* from the grasslands of central North America. *Botanical Museum Leaflets* [Harvard University] 23(7).

———. 1974. *An Introduction to the Ecology of the Illinois Orchidaceae.* Springfield: Illinois State Museum.

———. 1982. Biosystematic study of the *Spiranthes cernua* complex. *Bulletin* 448. Albany: New York State Museum.

———. 1983. United States terrestrial orchids: patterns and problems. In E. H. Plaxton, ed., *Proceedings from Symposium II & Lectures: North American Terrestrial Orchids,* 49–60. Livonia, Mich.: Michigan Orchid Society.

———. 1991. Morphological variation in the compilospecies *Spiranthes cernua* (L.) L.C. Rich.: Ecologically-limited effects on gene flow. *Lindleyana* 6(4): 228–34.

———. 1994. *Cypripedium parviflorum* Salisbury I: The small-flowered varieties. *American Orchid Society Bulletin* 63: 664–69.

———. 1995. *Cypripedium parviflorum* Salisbury II: The large-flowered plants and patterns of variation. *American Orchid Society Bulletin* 64: 606–12.

Singhurst, J. R. 1996. The status of nine endangered plants of East Texas: historical, ecological, and phytogeographic notes. Master's thesis, Stephen F. Austin State University.

Small, J. K. 1901. *Flora of the Southeastern United States.* New York: Science Press.

Sorrie, B. A. 1998. Noteworthy records of Mississippi vascular plants. *Sida* 18(3): 904.

Stones, M., and L. Urbatsch. 1991. *Flora of Louisiana.* Baton Rouge: Louisiana State University Press.

Szlachetko, D. L. 1995. Systema Orchidalium. *Fragmenta Floristica Geobotanica* Supplement 3: 121–22.

Szlachetko, D. L., P. Rutkowski, and J. Mytnik. 2004. New taxa and new combinations in Mesoamerican Spiranthinae (Orchidaceae). *Annales Botanici Fennici* 41(6): 471–77.

———. 2005. Contributions to the taxonomic revision of the subtribes Spiranthinae, Stenorrhynchidinae, and Cyclopogoninae (Orchidaceae) in Mesoamerica and the Antilles. *Polish Botanical Studies* 20.

Tamayo, R. G., and D. L. Szlachetko. 1998. A new definition of the genus *Tamayorkis*. *Annales Botanici Fennici* 35(1): 21–27.

Todsen, T. K. 1995. *Malaxis wendtii* (Orchidaceae) in the United States. *Sida* 16(3): 591.

———. 1997. Naming a southwestern *Malaxis* (Orchidaceae). *Sida* 17(3): 637–38.

Todzia, C. A. 1994. *Galeottiella hintoniorum*, a new epiphytic species of Spiranthinae (Orchidaceae) from Nuevo Leon, Mexico. *Brittonia* 46(4): 331–34.

Turner, B. L., H. Nichols, G. Denny, and O. Doron. 2003. *Atlas of the vascular plants of Texas.* Sida Botanical Miscellany. Fort Worth: Botanical Research Institute of Texas.

USGS Biological Informatics Office. 2004. Big Bend Sensitive Plant Project-2004 Field Season Discoveries. http://cswgcin.nbii.org/ecoregion/trans-pecos/field/index.html.

Ward, L. R., and E. R. Nixon. 1992. Woody vegetation of the dry sandy uplands of eastern Texas. *Texas Journal of Science* 44: 283–94.

Warnock, B. H. 1970. *Wildflowers of the Big Bend Country, Texas.* Alpine, Tex.: Sul Ross State University Press.

———. 1974. *Wildflowers of the Guadalupe Mountains and the Sand Dune Country, Texas.* Alpine, Tex.: Sul Ross State University Press.

———. 1977. *Wildflowers of the Davis Mountains and the Marathon Basin, Texas.* Alpine, Tex.: Sul Ross State University Press.

Watson, G. 1979. *Big Thicket Plant Ecology: An introduction*, 2nd ed. Saratoga, Tex.: Big Thicket Museum.

Watson, S. 1882. List of plants from southwestern Texas and northern Mexico, collected chiefly by Dr. E. Palmer in 1879–80. *Proceedings of the American Academy.* 17: 316–61.

———. 1883. List of plants from southwestern Texas and northern Mexico, collected chiefly by Dr. E. Palmer in 1879–80. *Proceedings of the American Academy.* 18: 96–191.

Wildlife Diversity Program. 2004. *A List of the Rare Plants of Texas.* Texas Parks and Wildlife Department and Texas Conservation Data Center of The Nature Conservancy of Texas. http://www.nature.org/wherewework/northamerica/states/texas/files/listofrareplants.pdf.

Williams, J. G., A. E. Williams, and N. Arlott. 1983. *A Field Guide to the Orchids of North America.* New York: Universe Books.

Williams, L. O. 1965. *The Orchidaceae of Mexico.* Tegucigalpa, Honduras: Escuela Agricola Panamericana.

Photo and Map Credits

All photographs were taken by Paul Martin Brown, except for the following, which were generously loaned by those credited.
r = right, c = center, l = left, t = top, b = bottom

Betty Alex (BBNP): *Deiregyne confusa* p. 47 bc; *Dichromanthus cinnabarinus* tc; *D. michuacanus* p. 49 tl, tr, br; *Malaxis wendtii* p. 101 l, r

Margaret Brown-Waite: *Hexalectris nitida* whitish-yellow form; *Hexalectris warnockii* forma *lutea*

Curtis Hawthorne: *Hexalectris grandiflora*: Dallas County

Bill Jennings: *Hexalectris spicata* var. *arizonica*, open flower form

Aaron Kennedy: *Hexalectris nitida* p. 77 bl, tl, p. 247; *H. revoluta*; *H. spicata* var. *arizonica* p. 83 tl, tc, br; *H. warnockii* p. 85

Allison Leavitt (BBNP): *Dichromanthus cinnabarinus* p. 77 br; *Hexalectris grandiflora* p. 75 bc, br; *H. nitida* p. 77 tc, tr; *Malaxis wendtii* p. 101 c

Cliff Pelchat: *Deiregyne confusa*, p. 47 tl, tr, br; *Platanthera flava* var. *herbiola*; *Spiranthes parksii* p. 155 tl, tc

Dick Pike: *Triphora trianthophora* var. *texensis*

Gerardo Salazar: *Microthelys minutiflora*

Myron D. Shufelt: *Hexalectris spicata* forma *wilderi*

Jim Smith: *Dichromanthus cinnabarinus* forma *aureus*; *Hexalectris grandiflora* forma *albolutea*

Wally Wilder: *Ponthieva racemosa* p. 127 tl

Richard Worthington (UTEP): *Schiedeella arizonica* p. 131 tc

Map 1.1 of the geophysical regions of Texas is based upon and reproduced by permission from *Preserving Texas' Natural Heritage*, Policy Research Project Report No. 31 (Austin: Lyndon B. Johnson School of Public Affairs, University of Texas at Austin, 1978), p. 18.

Index

Primary entries for taxa are in **bold** and photographs are in *italics*

Fragrant ladies'-tresses, 126, 133, 136, 146, 148,
  150, *151*, 164–65, 195–96, 198–200, 208–9,
  212, 218, 234, 237–38, 240, 243, 249–50,
  256, 258, 262, 275, 286
Fragrant tresses, 240
Fringed orchis
  Apalachicola hybrid, 104, ***118***–19, 194,
    281–82
  Beckner's hybrid, **118**, 246, 281
  Bicolor hybrid, 119, 246, 281
  Canby's hybrid fringed, 118, 206, 246, 281
  Channell's hybrid, 104, 106, 110, ***119***, 194,
    279–82
  Chapman's, 103, **104**, *105*, 106, 118–19, 186,
    194, 197, 208–9, 212, 224, 232, 235–36,
    238, 239, 246, 248, 256, 258, 275, 279–83,
    286, 288, 295
  crested, 103, **110**, 111, 194, 197, 208–9, 212,
    232, 235–36, 241, 248, 256, 275, 286, 288
  pale-flowered form, **110**, 111, 194
  green, 103, **116**, *117*, 194, 198, 208–9, 211–
    12, 217, 225, 233, 236, 240–41, 256, 2458,
    275, 286, 288
  Luer's hybrid, 106, ***118***–19, 246, 281
  orange, 14, 103, 104, 105, **106**, *107*, 110,
    119, 193–94, 197–98, 208–9, 212, 217,
    232, 235–36, 240–41, 243, 248, 256, 258,
    279–83, 286, 288
  Osceola hybrid, 104, ***119***, 194, 279, 281–82
  Southern white, 103, 106, 107, **108**, *109*,
    110, 118, 119, 198, 207–9, 211, 212, 215,
    217, 220, 225, 232, 235–37, 240–43, 246,
    261–62, 275, 277, 281, 286, 288, 295
Frog-arrow, 240
Frog spear, 240
Frog-spike, 240

Galearis spectabilis*, *183, 227, 278
Giant coralroot, **74**, *75*
Giant helleborine, 240
Giant ladies'-tresses, 133, **156**, *157*, 158, 165,
  195–96, 198–99, 200, 206, 212, 214, 218,
  234, 240–1, 251, 256–57, 262, 275, 286
  white-lipped form, **156**, *157*, 196
Giant rattlesnake orchis, 187
Giant spiral ladies'-tresses, 240
Giant spiral orchid, 240
Glandular *Neottia*, 240

Glass Mountain coralroot, 224, 240, 272
Glass Mountain crested coralroot, 240
Glass Mountain State Park, 271
Glass Mountains, 5, 76, 271–72
Golden fret-lip, 240
Golden fringe orchid, 240
Golden frog-arrow, 240
Golden slipper, 240
Goodyera, 177
  oblongifolia, 187
  pubescens*, *183, 278
  repens, 187
Grass-pink, bearded, 20, 32, **180**, 205–6, 209,
  214, 229, 237, 239, 257, 278
  common, 19, 20, **22**, *23*, 191, 197–99, 208–9,
    212, 217, 227, 229, 235, 237, 243, 256,
    271, 271, 284, 287
    white-flowered form, **22**, *23*, 191
  Oklahoma, 3, 15, 19, **20**, *21*, 32, 180, 191,
    197–99, 205, 208–9, 212, 214, 217, 246,
    256–57, 262, 284, 287
    white-flowered form, **20**, *21*
Gray's ladies'-tresses, 240
Grass-leaved ladies'-tresses, 133, 134, 140, 156,
  162, *163*, 165, 196, 198–201, 204, 215, 234,
  237, 239, 240, 243, 256–57, 262, 268–69,
  275, 286
Great Plains ladies'-tresses, 132–33, 136, **148**,
  149, 195, 199, 200–201, 204, 208–9, 221,
  240–41, 249–50, 265–66, 268, 286
Green adder's-mouth, 95, **98**, *99*, 193, 197, 203,
  212, 232, 235, 237, 240, 246, 257, 286, 288
  two-leaved form, **98**, *99*, 193
  variegated-leaf form, **98**, *99*, 193
Green-fly orchid, 7, **180**, 204, 240, 278
Green fringed orchis, 103, **116**, *117*, 194, 198,
  208–9, 211–12, 217, 225, 233, 236, 240–41,
  256, 258, 275, 286, 288
Greenman's cock's-comb, **74**, *75*
Greenman's crested coralroot, 73, **74**, *75*, 192,
  199, 201, 208–9, 211, 213, 217, 220, 225,
  231, 235, 237, 240, 267–68, 272, 276, 284,
  287, 287, 296, 303
  whitish-yellow flowering form, **74**, *75*, 192
Green rein orchid, 240
Green-veined ladies'-tresses, 240
Green woodland orchid, 240
Green wood orchid, 240

Paul Martin Brown is a research associate with the Botanical Research Institute of Texas, Fort Worth, and University of Florida Herbarium at the Florida Museum of Natural History in Gainesville. He is the founder of the North American Native Orchid Alliance and the editor of the *North American Native Orchid Journal*. Brown and his partner Stan Folsom have published *Wild Orchids of the Northeastern United States* (1997), *Wild Orchids of Florida* (UPF, 2002), *The Wild Orchids of North America, North of Mexico* (UPF, 2003), *Wild Orchids of the Southeastern United States, North of Peninsula Florida* (UPF, 2004), *Wild Orchids of Florida, updated and expanded edition* (UPF, 2005), *Wild Orchids of the Canadian Maritimes and Northern Great Lakes Region, Wild Orchids of the Pacific Northwest and Canadian Rockies*, and *Wild Orchids of the Prairies and Great Plains Region of North America* (all UPF, 2006), and *Wild Orchids of the Northeast: New England, New York, Pennsylvania, and New Jersey* (UPF, 2007).

Stan Folsom is a retired art teacher and botanical illustrator. His primary medium is watercolor. His work is represented in several permanent collections including the Federal Reserve Bank of Boston.

Related-interest titles from University Press of Florida

Wild Orchids of the Canadian Maritimes and Northern Great Lakes Region
Paul Martin Brown with drawings by Stan Folsom

Wild Orchids of Florida, Updated and Expanded Edition: With References to the Atlantic and Gulf Coastal Plains
Paul Martin Brown with drawings by Stan Folsom

The Wild Orchids of North America, North of Mexico
Paul Martin Brown with drawings by Stan Folsom

Wild Orchids of the Northeast: New England, New York, Pennsylvania, and New Jersey
Paul Martin Brown with original artwork by Stan Folsom

Wild Orchids of the Pacific Northwest and Canadian Rockies
Paul Martin Brown with drawings by Stan Folsom

Wild Orchids of the Prairies and Great Plains Region of North America
Paul Martin Brown with original artwork by Stan Folsom

Wild Orchids of the Southeastern United States, North of Peninsular Florida
Paul Martin Brown with drawings by Stan Folsom

For more information on these and other books, visit our website at www.upf.com.

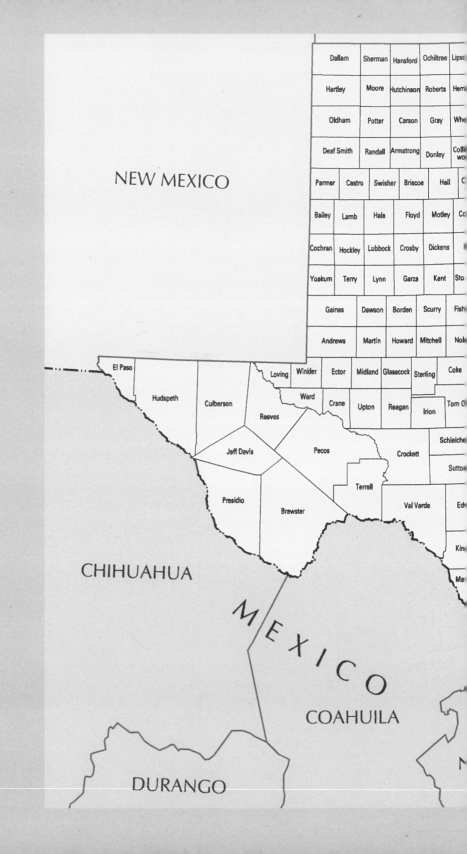